Publications in the Inner Cities Research Programme Series

SUNBELT CITY?

A Study of Economic Change in Britain's M4 Growth Corridor

MARTIN BODDY,
JOHN LOVERING,
and
KEITH BASSETT

CLARENDON PRESS · OXFORD
1986

Oxford University Press, Walton Street, Oxford OX2 6DP
Oxford New York Toronto
Delhi Bombay Calcutta Madras Karachi
Kuala Lumpur Singapore Hong Kong Tokyo
Nairobi Dar es Salaam Cape Town
Melbourne Auckland
and associated companies in
Beirut Berlin Ibadan Nicosia

Oxford is a trade mark of Oxford University Press

Published in the United States
by Oxford University Press, New York

© ESRC 1986

British Library Cataloguing in Publication Data
Boddy, Martin
Sunbelt city?: a study of economic change
in Britain's M4 growth corridor.—(Inner cities in context)
1. Bristol (Avon)—Economic condition
I. Title   II. Lovering, John   III. Bassett, Keith   IV. Series
330.9423'93   HC258.B/
ISBN 0-19-823265-9

Set by Promenade Graphics Ltd., Cheltenham
Printed in Great Britain
at the University Printing House, Oxford
by David Stanford
Printer to the University

FOREWORD

In 1982 the Environment and Planning Committee of the Economic and Social Research Council (SSRC at the time) initiated a three year comparative research programme to examine inner city problems within the broad context of major structural and spatial changes occurring in Great Britain. The programme was developed by the then SSRC Inner Cities Working Party, chaired by Professor Peter Hall, and subsequently the Executive Panel on the Inner Cities, chaired by Professor Gordon Cameron. The proposal for the research was originally described in 'A Research Agenda' (chapter 8) of *The Inner City in Context* (ed. Peter Hall, Heinemann, 1981). The purpose of the programme was to examine the processes of urban change, the effects on urban socio-economic welfare, and the prospects, constraints, and requirements for more successful urban adjustment to structural change. The programme arose from concerns with the urban problems of economic decline, labour market imbalances, social distress, and the effectiveness of public policies in addressing these problems. It was hoped that the programme's findings would be useful for the improvement of public policies to strengthen urban economies (that is, foster growth, employment, and competitiveness), alleviate the distress caused by change and improve the conditions of distressed inner city areas and deprived urban residents.

In practice, the overall programme focused on the economic aspects of urban change. Specifically, the programme sought to identify the key factors affecting urban economic change and to describe and explain the processes of local economic change. Secondly, it aimed to describe the consequences of change for the urban economy and the employment of its residents. Finally, the programme attempted to assess the effects of public policies on the process of change.

The programme was based on the idea that there is diversity in the economic performance of different urban and inner city areas in the UK and in their adjustment to external forces of change; for example, changes in business competition, technology, and residential patterns. A comparative examination of the nature, processes, and effects of economic change on different urban centres should help to clarify and explain the differences in the experiences of economic change among and within urban areas and to identify those factors (including public policies) which impede or facilitate urban and inner city adjustment to change: that is, economic growth, increased business competitiveness, employment generation, employment for the disadvantaged in urban labour markets, and the effectiveness of urban economic policies. The ESRC programme utilized a general framework of topics to assist

individual urban studies and the comparative examination of urban economic change. The topics were: the changing nature or urban economic problems; the nature and causes of imbalances in urban labour markets; the
unintended effects of central and local government policies on urban economic change, and the effectiveness of national and local urban economic policies; and the capabilities of local authorities to design and implement more
effective economic development policies.

The Inner Cities Research Programme addressed these concerns through
two avenues of work. The core of the programme was independent studies of
four major urban centres of Great Britian which were selected by the SSRC
as examples of the diversity of urban economic adjustment experiences: Glasgow and the Clydeside conurbation as an example of 'persistent economic
decline'; Birmingham and the West Midlands conurbation as one of 'falter-
ing growth'; the Bristol region as one of 'successful adaptation'; and two
areas in London, one (Greenwich, Southwark, and Lewisham) exhibiting
'severe problems', the other (Brent, Ealing, and Hounslow) exemplifying
more 'successful adaptation'. These were largely secondary research studies
using existing data and analysing existing research. The studies were conducted by independent research teams with distinctive approaches and concerns, but linked by the overall programme's objectives and general
framework of topical concerns, dialogue, information exchange, and some
common data and analysis. The different research teams decided on the particular approach, subjects, and hypotheses which they considered most relevant to an understanding of economic change in their study areas; and
critically examined the characterizations of those areas.

To these four initial studies a fifth study of the Newcastle metropolitan
region was added, funded by the Department of the Environment, in order to
broaden the sample of urban areas and focus particularly on an assessment of
the relationship, impacts, and effectiveness of central and local government
urban and regional economic development policies on an economically distressed city region that was a long-term recipient of government assistance.

In addition to these five core studies a number of smaller 'cross-cutting'
studies were conducted by various researchers in order to provide a national
statistical framework for the five city studies and uniform comparative data
on the five city study areas, to examine in greater detail important aspects of
urban economic change in a broader sample of urban areas, to explore the
effects on change of important public policies, to provide a comparative
international perspective, and to increase the general relevance of a case-
study-based research programme. A list of the publications and their
authors, resulting from all of these elements of the programme, appears at
the beginning of this book.

In order to enhance the relevance of the research programme to public
policy issues and communication with central government policy-makers'
discussions were held with officials of three government agencies: the Depart-

ment of the Environment, the Department of Trade and Industry, and the Manpower Services Commission. These agencies also assisted the programme through the provision of data, special analyses, and the co-operation of their regional offices. The individual city and cross-cutting studies involved extensive local contacts with government officials, representatives of business, labour and voluntary organizations, and other researchers and analysts.

The five city studies were conducted by members of research teams at the following institutions: the Department of Social and Economic Research at the University of Glasgow; the Institute of Local Government Studies and the Centre for Urban and Regional Studies at the University of Birmingham; the School for Advanced Urban Studies and the Department of Geography at the University of Bristol; the Policy Studies Institute in London and the Urban and Regional Studies Unit at the University of Kent; and the Centre for Urban and Regional Development Studies at the University of Newcastle upon Tyne.

Professor Brian Robson, chairman of the ESRC Environment and Planning Committee, and Professor Noel Boaden and Paul McQuail, both members of the Committee, advised on the implementation of the programme. They were assisted by Dr Angela Williams, Senior Scientific Officer to the Committee. Members of the former SSRC Executive Panel discussed, reviewed papers, and advised on the research during the course of the programme. The programme also benefited from the advice and comments of other urban analysts.

London 1985 Victor A. Hausner
Director, ESRC Inner Cities Research Programme

PREFACE

The work on which this book is based relied in part on extensive interview-based information gathering. We would like to thank the many individuals in the companies, local authorities, employment and training agencies, and other organizations in the locality who contributed to this. Frankie Ashton and Tom Davies at the School for Advanced Urban Studies were involved in earlier stages of the research and we would like to acknowledge their contributions. The book itself was in many ways a collective effort. However, Keith Bassett was largely responsible for Chapters 2 and 6, John Lovering for Chapters 4 and 5, and Martin Boddy for 1, 3, and 7. The work was funded by the Economic and Social Research Council, grant number DO 320005, as part of the Inner Cities Research Programme.

CONTENTS

LIST OF TABLES

LIST OF FIGURES

1

Introduction

A decade of decline since the early 1970s has cast long shadows across Britain's economic landscape. It has brought deepening gloom to the peripheral problem regions, economic and social malaise to the inner cities, deindustrialization and spiralling unemployment to formerly prosperous manufacturing areas like the West Midlands. Superimposed on this, new patterns of economic and employment change have emerged. Manufacturing employment has fallen fastest in the conurbations and larger urban areas and has actually increased to some extent in small towns and rural locations. There has been a major shift from manufacturing to service employment. Related to this, a decline in male manufacturing employment has been juxtaposed with increasing female service employment, much of it part-time.

National hopes of an economic renaissance have above all been pinned on the broad swathe of country from Cambridge through to London, Berkshire, and Hampshire and on to Swindon and Bristol—Britain's 'Sunbelt'. This has generally escaped the worst of the recession and rising unemployment and has raised hopes of future growth based, above all, around a new wave of electronics and high-technology activities and advanced services. Particularly central to such hopes is the M4 corridor, 'Britain's sunrise strip . . . California in the Home Counties', according to *The Economist*,[1] which runs west past Heathrow, Reading, and Newbury, to Swindon, Bristol, and on to South Wales. Property agents Knight, Frank, and Rutley (1983) described it as 'the country's breeding ground where new types of industry are being developed, innovative forms of business accommodation are taking shape, and new patterns of industrial relations are being established. . . . When looking back at development in the Western Corridor we may recognize that the base is being laid here for a new industrial revolution with a comparable impact to the one that took place some 200 years ago.' With companies like ICL established at Maidenhead, Digital at Reading, Intel and Logica at Swindon, and Hewlett Packard and Inmos at Bristol, optimistic parallels have been drawn with California's Silicon Valley.

This study focuses in detail on one particular locality within the M4 growth corridor, Bristol, which has been seen as integral to the sunbelt phenomenon. It is in fact a major urban area in its own right. With over half a million people in the continuous built-up area, it is the sixth largest city in the country and by far the largest M4 population and employment centre. The easy image is that of a city successfully adapting in the face of national recession and rising unemployment: 'Bristol is a city that has rarely fallen on hard times and in the current recession it is once again demonstrating its economic resilience.' [2] By 1981 it was, according to the *Sunday Times*, 'well on the way to becoming the high-technology centre of Britain . . . set to become Britain's Silicon Valley of the 1980s.'[3]

Unemployment has of course risen in Bristol, as elsewhere; it was up to 11.6 per cent by January 1985. This was however significantly down on the national figure of 13.7 per cent, and compared very favourably with places like Glasgow (17.7 per cent), Newcastle (18.5 per cent), or Birmingham (16.4 per cent). Indices of 'urban deprivation' suggest that the city as a whole shares little of the problems of London's inner boroughs, or cities of the Midlands and North. Reinforcing this image, 'high-tech' firms including Hewlett Packard, Digital, and Inmos have set up in the city, and major insurance companies have relocated their headquarters operations to its expanding office-based service sector. There has been marked employment decline in the locality's traditional manufacturing sectors including tobacco, and paper, printing, and packaging. However, this has been largely offset, numerically at least, by the growth of service employment; and technologically advanced manufacturing, mainly in the aerospace sector, has continued to prosper.

Bristol was one of only a handful of the country's main urban areas which was larger in employment terms in 1981 than in 1951 (Begg *et al.* 1985). This has, moreover, been achieved without the range of explicit urban and regional policy measures directed to selected regions and inner-city areas. Nor has the city experienced the proliferation of economic development agencies typical of these areas. Local authority economic development policies have been established but, apart from that, the area is very much an example of 'hands off' development so far as explicit policy measures are concerned. Other government programmes, in particular defence spending, support for aerospace, and transport infrastructure, are however, as we demonstrate later, heavily implicated in the locality's economic fortunes.

As this account suggests, relative success has been underlain by major shifts in economic structure. This in turn has had an impact on the labour market and on the fortunes of different groups in the local population, both in and out of formal employment. As elsewhere, male manufacturing employment has been replaced by female service employment, much of it part-time, with 'high tech', sunrise industries doing little to compensate for the collapse of manufacturing employment. While unemployment rates generally compare favourably with the national picture, youth and long-term unemployment rates have risen towards national levels. There are also pockets of high unemployment and multiple deprivation, both in the inner area and in outlying council estates, that are as severe as in the conurbations of the Midlands and North. And, underlining some of the contradictions in Bristol's 'sunbelt city' image, it was in Bristol, not Brixton, that the urban violence of the early 1980s first erupted. While not denying the contrasts with these other localities, it is clearly necessary to look a little more closely at the image of success and effective 'adaptation'.

The city is thus at one level a specific case study of a relatively prosperous sub-region to set alongside the experience of localities such as Glasgow, Newcastle, or Birmingham. Urban and regional analysis and policy considerations have been preoccupied with economic decline and with the 'problem areas' themselves. The processes of change in relatively prosperous localities, intimately related to the same pattern of restructuring affecting the regions and inner cities, have until recently been relatively neglected. Massey and Meegan's (1982) study of industrial restructuring, for example, set out to dissect the anatomy of job loss, while a recent collection of essays on 'British cities and regions during periods of crisis' focused almost exclusively on the traditional 'problem' regions and inner cities (Anderson *et al.* 1983).

The Bristol case also exemplifies, however, in a specific urban context, more general changes in national and indeed international economic structures. In many ways it appears to be at the forefront of emerging trends in terms of economic restructuring and labour market change, including the growth of high-technology industry, 'deindustrialization', the expansion of the service sector, and the rise in female employment.

The study itself was a component of the Economic and Social Research Council's 'Inner City in Context' research programme. Within this programme, Bristol was specifically intended to represent an example of a relatively prosperous locality, 'successfully adapting' in the face of the recession. The programme included comparable studies focused on Clydeside as a locality which had experienced severe long-term decline, on the West Midlands, which had only recently started to experience the impacts of recession, and on two contrasting areas of Greater London—Greenwich, Lewisham, and Southwark in inner London, and Brent, Ealing, and Hounslow in more buoyant outer west London. A fifth study, funded by the Department of the Environment, was subsequently linked to the programme, looking at Newcastle-upon-Tyne, representing an English, as opposed to Scottish, Assisted Region.

The Bristol study had three specific aims, reflecting the agenda of the programme as a whole. The first was to put together a case study of a more resilient locality which could tell us something about the anatomy of success and the processes of economic and labour market change underlying its apparently successful adaptation. The second was to look more closely at the extent to which the impacts of 'success' reverberate through the structure of the economy and the local labour market, to look at who shares in the benefits of success and at the extent of spatial inequalities and inner-city issues specifically in a more prosperous locality. Is 'The Good City' the good city for everyone, as Donnison and Soto (1980) concluded?[4] The final objective was to assess the extent to which public policy, central or local, has been

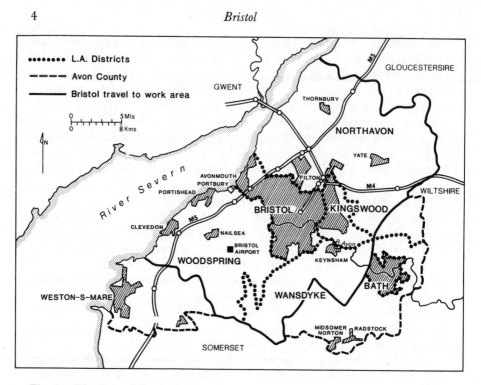

Fig. 1.1 The Bristol Study Area

implicated in the particular patterns of economic and employment change. Related to this was the question of what conclusions if any can be drawn which may be relevant to the problems of places like Glasgow, the North-East, the West Midlands, and elsewhere.

The study focuses mainly on the period since 1971. In practical terms, this allows comparison between 1971 and 1981 population census data. It coincides, in turn, with the most recent Annual Census of Employment conducted in 1981. Substantively, this period includes the phase of deepening recession and rapid increase in unemployment since the early 1970s.

While focusing primarily on the period since the early 1970s, however, the legacy of previous rounds of economic activity is central to any understanding of the present. Chapter 2 therefore includes a brief historical sketch, while subsequent studies of individual sectors of economic activity and of the policy dimension take a longer-term perspective. The study area, illustrated in Fig. 1.1, was for most purposes the Bristol 'travel-to-work area' as defined by the Department of Employment. With an employment total of around 300,000 in 1981, this includes the contiguous built-up area, plus parts of the rural fringe and commuter belt. It covers roughly the same area as Avon County with the exception of Bath to the east and Weston-super-Mare to the west. In local authority terms, it includes Bristol, Northavon, Kingswood, and much of Wansdyke and Woodspring Districts.

The analysis drew on a wide range of sources, including official statistics, documentary sources, semi-structured interviews, and many less formal discussions with representatives of local authorities, labour market agencies, and other bodies. This was supplemented by an extensive programme of interviews with thirty employers in key sectors in the locality. These included Tobacco, Paper and Packaging, Aerospace, Electronics, and Insurance. The aim of the survey was to focus in greater detail on key dimensions and processes of economic structure, employment change, and the labour market. It also provided a more up-to-date picture of change since the last Census of Employment in 1981, since when economic restructuring and job loss has, of course, been particularly marked. The study itself was carried out from November 1982 to January 1985, this particular account being completed in June 1985.

Chapters 2 and 3 present much of the material on economic and labour market change. Chapter 2 relates change in the Bristol economy to a longer-term view of economic change in the UK, then draws on a wide range of statistical and other sources to provide a detailed picture of economic and labour market change, and social and spatial structure in the locality. Chapter 3 focuses in more detail on five key employment sectors which have been central to processes of change in the locality. Chapters 4 and 5 discuss in more general terms a range of issues relating to economic restructuring and the labour market, drawing out in particular the underlying processes. Chapter 6 then concentrates on public policy issues. Finally Chapter 7 draws together some of the main conclusions of the study as a whole and considers a number of the wider implications.

Notes

1. *The Economist*, 30 January 1982, p. 78.
2. *Financial Times*, 15 September 1980.
3. *Sunday Times*, 26 August 1981.
4. Donnison and Soto (1980, pp. 175–6) suggested that: 'All social groups and classes tend to benefit from the prosperity of the growing towns which depend more heavily on service industries, public and private, and the newer forms of manufacturing. . . . The growing, prosperous city, the city which is kindest to its more vulnerable citizens, and the city which distributes its opportunities more equally than most can all be the same place.'

2

Economic Restructuring and Social Change in the Bristol Region

This chapter presents a detailed picture of economic restructuring and changes in the labour market in the Bristol locality. While focusing primarily on the period since the early 1970s, it begins with a brief overview of economic and social change since the eighteenth century in order to set more recent developments in context. This is followed by an analysis of economic changes in the decade 1971–81. The chapter concludes by looking at the social and spatial impacts of these changes, including the patterns of unemployment and associated indicators of economic and social disadvantage.

Historical Background: The Economic Development of the Bristol Region from the Eighteenth Century to the End of the 1960s.

The history of British capitalism since the eighteenth century has been marked by successive waves of development and decline. Each wave has had specific and uneven sectoral and spatial impacts, and each has been associated with a distinctive pattern of change in urban and regional systems. This first section begins by relating the major characteristics of Bristol's longer-term development to these broader patterns of change.

Bristol in the eighteenth century: the 'Mercantile City'

Although Bristol was one of the most important urban centres in the medieval period, the eighteenth century was something of a 'golden age' in terms of prosperity. Until the end of the eighteenth century Bristol was the third largest city in England, a city 'grown fat on the proceeds of slaves and sugar' (Fraser 1979, p. 112). Its prosperity in this period was founded upon export trade to the Empire and the related local processing of imported goods such as sugar, tobacco, and cocoa. A local commercial élite built impressive fortunes from the 'triangular' trade in manufactured goods, slaves, and raw materials between Britain, West Africa, and the Americas. This pattern of economic growth helped to shape a distinctive political structure, based on the dominance of a conservative local oligarchy, and a distinctive urban structure, marked by extremes of inequality between the slums of the central areas and the palatial elegance of Clifton.

From the 1790s to the late 1840s: Bristol in the first wave of the industrial revolution

The first wave of British industrial growth, led by industries such as textiles, was concentrated in a number of 'islands of industrialization' where local resources could be exploited (Dunford and Perrons 1984). Bristol was not one of these major 'islands', however, and did not experience a dramatic change based on the emergence of new staple industries. The city was somewhat peripheral to the main core of growth running from London through the Midlands to the North-West, and it lost something of its central role in the British economy. As a result, Bristol's transition to an industrial capitalist city in the nineteenth century was in many ways more gradual than that experienced by cities in the Midlands and the North and was based more on the gradual modification of older established industries. Foreign trade was disrupted in the early part of the century by the Napoleonic Wars, and, in spite of major dock improvements, the trade of the port declined relative to that of its chief rivals, in particular Liverpool (Walker 1972). The conservatively minded merchant oligarchy that ran the city was locked into traditional trading patterns and was ill adapted to respond to the new challenge of industrial entrepreneurship. Nevertheless, the traditional tobacco, cocoa, and chocolate industries survived and developed, and a range of engineering, paper, and leatherworking industries were added to provide a varied industrial base for future growth.

From the 1840s to the 1890s: Bristol in the golden age of industrial capitalism

This second wave of capitalist industrial growth was led by staple industries such as coal, iron and steel, railway engineering, and shipbuilding and was associated with marked regional specialization and uneven development. In this period Bristol began to 'catch up' with industrial growth, and from the 1860s onwards there was something of a renaissance in local manufacturing development (Alford 1976). Although industries such as coal mining and shipbuilding played their part, growth was more associated with the transformation of traditional industries, such as tobacco and chocolate, and the rapid expansion of newer industries such as metal-working, engineering, printing and packaging, and boot and shoe manufacture. Overall, 'variety was . . . the keynote of engineering and of industry as a whole in the city and its immediate neighbourhood' (Walker 1972, p. 277). Certain key sectors were already becoming dominated by large firms by the 1880s, signalling the transition from competitive to monopoly capitalism. In the tobacco industry, for example, the leading Bristol firm, W. D. and H. O. Wills, had a national market by 1860, and by 1886 the firm's products were being sold through agencies in Europe, Egypt, South Africa, and Australia (Alford 1973).

From the 1890s to 1939

This period witnessed something of a second industrial revolution based on the emergence of new industrial sectors. On the one hand, technological developments underlay the expansion of production of electrical goods, vehicles, aircraft, and precision instruments. On the other hand, the emergence of mass consumer markets facilitated the growth of consumer goods industries. The staple industries of the previous wave began to decline rapidly, particularly from the 1920s onwards. Growth and decline was associated with merger booms at the turn of the century and in the 1920s which took the share of output of the 100 largest firms from 10 per cent in 1880 to 26 per cent in 1930 (Hannah 1976). Finally, the decline of the old staple industries and the rapid growth of new industrial sectors was associated with a significant shift of production away from the traditional industrial regions of the North towards the Midlands and the South-East.

The Bristol area was well placed to take advantage of these emerging patterns of growth and change. The tobacco, chocolate, boot and shoe, and paper, printing, and packaging industries expanded to meet growing mass consumer markets. Their expansion encouraged further diversified engineering growth. The decade before the First World War saw the foundation of the city's aircraft industry. The growing dominance of large firms was also evident in the local economy. The Wills tobacco company had already dominated the tobacco industry in the city by the 1880s, and with its merger into the Imperial Tobacco Company in 1901 Bristol became the headquarters of the largest company in Britain at that date (Alford 1973). Similarly, Frys came to dominate the chocolate industry and Mardons and Robinsons the paper and packaging industry. The aircraft industry was dominated from the beginning by the Bristol Aeroplane Company.

The survival and long-term growth of firms like Wills, Frys, and Robinsons maintained a considerable continuity in industrial development, and their readiness to pay high wages and provide non-work benefits consolidated a paternalistic tradition of labour relations in key sectors of the local economy. Nevertheless, the period from the 1880s saw the gradual extension of trade union organization in the city, and in the decade before the First World War there was an upsurge of militancy by dock and transport workers under the leadership of Ernest Bevin and Ben Tillet.

Bristol was less affected by the interwar depression than were the heavy industrial cities of the Midlands and the North, dependent on a narrow range of staple industries. Unemployment was generally lower, and a 1937 survey confirmed that the proportion of the working class 'in poverty' (6.9 per cent) was below that of London (9.8 per cent) and probably of most other large cities (Tout 1938). This differential seems to have reflected not only Bristol's industrial structure, but also the fact that Bristol industries performed better than their counterparts elsewhere. Major Bristol manufacturers, such as the

Imperial Tobacco Company, consolidated a monopolistic grip on national and interational markets, aided by national policies of imperial preference. Government aid during and after the war led to the establishment of a large lead and zinc smelter at Avonmouth which came under the control of the Imperial Smelting Company in 1929. Collaboration between Imperial and Fisons led in turn to the establishment of an adjacent fertilizer plant. Finally, and most importantly, from about 1935 onwards, the rearmament pro-gramme stimulated a massive expansion of Bristol's aircraft industry. Male employment in this industry jumped from 4,350 in 1935 to 14,068 in 1938 (Shannon and Grebenik 1944). These developments were accelerated during the war period.

The interwar period also witnessed a marked increase in the involvement of local government, particularly in the field of housing policy. Conservative councils came under increasing pressure from a growing Labour opposition, and although Bristol built fewer houses than the national average under the 1919 Addison Act, the city's rate of 23.1 houses per 1,000 population under the Chamberlain and Wheatley Acts exceeded that of cities such as Leeds and Manchester. Much of this housing was built on new green-field sites on the edge of the city, some of the estates serving growing industrial areas such as Avonmouth (docks-related industry) and Filton (the aircraft industry). Finally, in the 1930s, as a private building boom got under way, local hous-ing policy switched to slum clearance and the relocation of inner-city dwellers to large estates to the south of the city.

From the 1940s to the 1960s: the postwar 'long boom'

The ending of the Second World War was followed by two decades of unpre-cedented growth in most industrial countries. This 'long boom' was charac-terized by historically high growth rates, low unemployment, and relatively stable prices. Britain rode on the back of this boom, although the country's growth rates were lower than elsewhere and concealed deeper structural weaknesses in the British economy (Pollard 1983). The period was also marked by the emergence of a new form of global capitalism, in which trans-national conglomerates played a dominant role in a new international div-ision of labour. The long boom clearly had different impacts on different regions and cities depending upon factors such as the local industrial base and relative location, but on the whole Bristol again found itself well situated to take advantage of growth.

Initially, in the immediate postwar period, women were rapidly expelled from the manufacturing industries in Bristol, although they had provided a major source of labour during the war. The male bias of employment in the 1950s was so marked that one analyst commented that 'attitudes to female employment [in Bristol] have apparently not simulated those of the nation'

(Britton 1967, p. 90). Generally, however, the major manufacturing sectors could response to expanding markets, and manufacturing employment in the wider Bristol region expanded at twice the national average in the 1950s, although the growth rate in Bristol itself was somewhat lower (Britton 1967). In 1961 the manufacturing sector in Bristol accounted for 44 per cent of total employment, with 64 per cent of this employment concentrated in three major sectors: there were 29,580 workers in the Vehicles sector (mainly aircraft); 24,400 in Food, Drink, and Tobacco; and 17,790 in Paper, Printing, and Publishing. The aircraft industry benefited from government contracts, both civil and defence, while the other two major sectors benefited from the expansion of mass consumer markets. Growth in output did not necessarily imply growth in employment, but the total number of manufacturing jobs remained approximately stable throughout the 1960s. Employment in Food, Drink, and Tobacco was about the same in 1969 as 1961, but the Vehicles sector declined by 7.1 per cent and the Paper, Printing, and Publishing sector by 9.0 per cent. To compensate, there were employment increases in the Chemical and Engineering industries.

By the late 1960s Bristol was widely regarded as a 'boom town'. An enthusiastic *Daily Mirror* special feature in 1967 described a city brimming with 'Power, Energy, Wealth, Style', where prosperity had brought about a social revolution manifested in nightclubs, arts centres, the biggest entertainment centre in Europe, and the expectation that the population would double by the end of the century (*Daily Mirror* 1967). The leading manufacturing sectors were at a peak: Wills Woodbine cigarettes remained large sellers, while the newer Embassy tipped cigarette took a quarter of the market. G. B. Britton manufactured the 'Tuf' shoe range, yet to be threatened by more stylish imports. Cadburys and Robertsons remained unchallenged in their consumer food markets, as did Harveys in the sherry trade. The major printing and packaging companies, including E. S. and A. Robinson and Mardon Son and Hall, were among the largest of their kind, and Bristol contained the biggest carton and paper bag factories in the country. The major packaging manufacturers, moreover, retained important links with the local engineering industry, which provided them with packaging machinery. Key firms had secured niches in various other intermediate and consumer goods markets, notably Kleen-e-ze, which manufactured brushes; Trist Draper, which supplied brake shoes and allied products to the railway and motor vehicle industries; and Parnells, which supplied shop fittings. In the heavy industrial sector, ICI were completing a major new project on Severnside. Most conspicuous of all was the aircraft industry, partly because of its size, but also because of its heavy involvement in the much publicized Concorde project, at that time the biggest single industrial project in the world outside the US space programme.

Although journalists traced the cause of Bristol's prosperity to the city's 'three hundred different industries', the greater part of the increase in employment was nevertheless provided by the service sector. Between 1961 and 1969 total service employment grew by 22 per cent, from 46 per cent of total employment to 52 per cent. Much of this was associated with the expansion of education, health services, and local government services. Professional and Scientific Services and Public Administration expanded by nearly 19,000 between 1961 and 1969, an increase of 66 per cent. This accounted for three-quarters of the total increase in employment in the city region.

One effect of this expansion was an official optimism, tempered only by fears of possible eventual shortage of labour and accommodation. The opening of the Severn Bridge in 1966 was expected to precipitate further rapid growth on both sides of the Bristol Channel (Manners 1966, p. 8). Bristol was also about to acquire a new locational significance in the national motorway network, with the M4 and M5 meeting in the biggest motorway interchange in Europe. It was against this background that the Port of Bristol Authority advocated investment in a new dock on Severnside to raise Bristol to the status of the third international port in Britain (Bassett and Hoare 1984, p. 255). One of the reasons why this plan was rejected at government level was that it was felt that Bristol was already growing well enough and did not need a new dock as much as the Port of Bristol Authority and local politicians claimed.

This optimism was also embodied in the regional planning of the period. The 1967 plan for the South-West, symptomatically entitled 'A Region with a Future', confidently advocated a *laissez-faire* approach, in sharp contrast to the parallel plan for Wales ('Wales, the Way Ahead') which called for wide new powers of intervention to promote industry in that region.

This aura of optimism was reflected in the workplace. The long history of relative prosperity in Bristol, together with the welfare paternalism of some of the traditional employers, helped to sustain a tradition of 'cordial' labour relations. In the 1960s Bristol was, in the words of a national union officer, a 'dozy part of the world' (Nichols and Beynon 1979, p. 3), while some observers considered that the aura of boom had 'put the stamp of complacency on the local working class' (Pollert, 1981). But the view that Bristol could remain a 'boom town' rested on the illusion that the growth of the 1950s and early 1960s would continue. The fortunes of British firms in that era had, however, been based on a transient set of circumstances, and this became all too clear in the following decade. A turning point for the British economy occurred around 1966. Employment reached a peak in that year and fell thereafter (Blackaby 1978) as prosperity gave way to long-term de-industrialization and decline, but as late as 1967 Bristol planners were predicting 9,000 more manufacturing jobs by 1981 if existing growth trends in the region continued, while warning that such an assumption might be 'very dangerous' if economic conditions changed rapidly (Bristol City Council 1967). This was to prove very much the case.

Transition and Crisis: Economic Change since the Early 1970s

National change and its regional impacts

National economic change since the early 1970s can be divided into two phases. The first covers the transitional period of hesitant growth and increasing instability from about 1971 to 1979, and the second covers the onset of economic crisis from 1979 onwards. The pattern of economic change differed in these two phases in important ways, and this was particularly so in the Bristol region.

Nationally, manufacturing *output* barely rose between 1971 and 1979, recovering only slightly from recessions in 1971 and 1975 (Pollard 1983). Manufacturing *employment*, however, declined by 9.7 per cent between 1971 and 1978, a loss of 766,000 jobs. This was offset by service sector growth of 12.6 per cent, a gain of 1,479,000 jobs. Although almost all manufacturing sectors lost jobs, service growth was concentrated in three main sectors; Professional and Scientific Services, Miscellaneous Services, and Insurance, Banking, and Finance. Much of this service growth was associated with the expansion of part-time female employment, and the largest increases were registered in the early 1970s. Service employment growth slowed considerably in the late 1970s, an important component being the slowdown in the growth of public sector employment following the cutbacks in public expenditure by the Labour government after 1975. Unemployment rose to over 3 per cent in 1972 before declining briefly, but oscillated sharply upwards following the 1975 recession to a plateau of 5–6 per cent in the late 1970s (see Figure 2.1).

The impacts of these trends showed important regional and urban variations (e.g. Frost and Spence, 1984). In the conurbations and larger industrial cities manufacturing decline tended to be higher and service growth lower, and core areas declined as peripheries grew. Some of the older industrial regions with large conurbations lost employment, while regions such as the South-West, East Anglia, and the East Midlands registered substantial gains. In the South-West there were some manufacturing gains in sectors such as Instrument Engineering and Chemicals and Allied Industries, and although other sectors declined, they declined at rates below the national average and their losses were more than offset by service employment growth. In summary, this period witnessed a significant recomposition of the national workforce accompanied by important urban and regional shifts in growth and decline.

From 1979 onwards, the UK economy slumped into an economic crisis from which it has yet to recover. A distinct break in government economic policy coincided with the onset of an international recession. Cuts in public expenditure, high interest rates, and high exchange rates reinforced the effects of international recession to cause a slump in output and a rapid rise

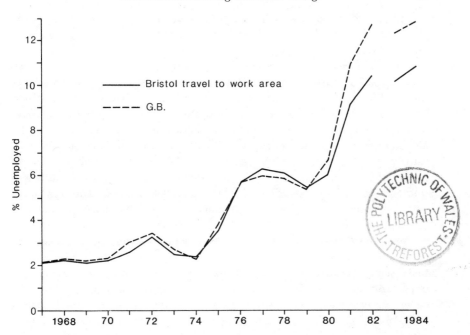

Fig. 2.1. Unemployment rates in the UK and the Bristol travel-to-work area
Source: Monthly unemployment figures, Manpower Services Commission, and Department of the Environment.

in unemployment on a scale unprecedented since the 1930s. Between mid-1979 and mid-1981, national income fell $7\frac{1}{2}$ per cent and manufacturing output fell by 18 per cent. Between June 1978 and September 1981, manufacturing employment fell by 16.8 per cent while service sector employment grew by just 1.7 per cent.

The collapse of the manufacturing sector hit most industries, although some, such as metal manufacture, textiles, clothing and footwear, were hit harder than others (Townsend, 1982). The uneven geographical distribution of these industries meant that some regions were also hit harder than others. Maps of employment change, redundancies, and unemployment all point to a deepening 'two-nation' division between the relative prosperity of the South-East, East Anglia, and South-West regions, and the decline of the West Midlands, northern, and peripheral regions. In the South-West region the 13.1 per cent decline of manufacturing employment between 1978 and 1981 was below the national average of 16.8 per cent, and the 1.7 per cent growth of service employment was equal to the national average.

The changing structure of employment in the Bristol travel-to-work area, 1971–1981

The structure of employment in 1971   The structure of employment in the Bristol travel-to-work area in 1971 (shown in Table 2.1 and Figure 2.2) provides a useful base for an analysis of comparative change.[1] By 1971 the Bristol area already had a slightly lower proportion of total employment in manufacturing (35.7 per cent) than the country as a whole (36.4 per cent) and a higher proportion of service employment (57.3 per cent compared to 54.2 per cent). Within manufacturing, employment was concentrated in three major sectors: Vehicles (mainly aerospace); Food, Drink, and Tobacco; and Paper, Printing, and Publishing. Between them these three sectors employed over 68,000 people, 64 per cent of total manufacturing employment. Each had a location quotient greater than 2.0 (quotients greater than 1.0 signifying specialization relative to the national average). Within services, 80 per cent of employment was concentrated in four major sectors: Professional and Scientific Services; Distributive Trades; Miscellaneous Services; and Transport and Communications. All but Miscellaneous Services had location quotients greater than 1.0.

The importance of the service sectors is brought out clearly when the employment categories are ranked by size (see Table 2.2). Disaggregating these sectors into more detailed Minimum List Headings brings out the importance of medical and dental services in the Professional and Scientific category, aerospace in the Vehicles category, tobacco in the Food, Drink, and Tobacco category, and packaging in the Paper, Printing, and Publishing category.

The distribution of male and female workers between sectors was significantly different. Overall, female workers formed only 36.2 per cent of the total workforce compared with a national figure of 38 per cent. However, over 73 per cent of these female workers were in the service sector (well above the national average of 69 per cent). Within the manufacturing sector, over 58 per cent of the female employment was in Food, Drink, and Tobacco and Paper, Printing, and Publishing. The large Vehicles sector was notably male-dominated. Overall, then, there were proportionately fewer female workers in the local economy, and these were disproportionately concentrated in the service sectors.

Changes in the structure of employment, 1971–1978 It was noted above that during this period there was a major shift in national employment structure. Manufacturing employment declined by 9.7 per cent but service employment grew by 12.6 per cent. In the Bristol area the shift was even greater (Table 2.3). Manufacturing employment in the Bristol area fell by 14.3 per cent (a loss of 15,326 jobs) while service employment grew by 14.3 per cent (a gain of 24,612 jobs). It is also important to note that, although female employment in the manufactured sector in Bristol fell by a faster rate than male employment (−19.3 per cent compared with −11.8 per cent), more than 82 per cent of the increase in service employment was for female workers. The loss of 9,403 jobs for male workers in the manufacturing sector was offset by an increase of only 4,118 in the service sector, compared with an increase of over

Table 2.1. *Employment by sector, Bristol and Great Britain, 1971*

SIC 1968		Bristol				Great Britain %	Location quotient[a]
		Male	Female	Total	Total %		
I	Agriculture, Forestry, Fishing	1 982	891	2 873	0.96	1.94	0.49
II	Mining and Quarrying	530	54	584	0.19	1.82	0.11
I–II	All primary	2 512	945	3 457	1.15	3.76	0.31
III	Food, Drink, and Tobacco	14 254	10 417	24 671	8.21	3.44	2.39
IV	Coal and Petroleum Products	31	12	33	0.01	0.20	0.05
V	Chemicals and Allied Industries	3 158	591	3 749	1.25	2.01	0.62
VI	Metal Manufacture	3 124	302	3 426	1.14	2.57	0.44
VII	Mechanical Engineering	8 527	1 332	9 859	3.28	4.80	0.69
VIII	Instrument Engineering	329	135	464	0.15	0.76	0.20
IX	Electrical Engineering	3 444	1 223	4 667	1.55	3.69	0.42
X	Shipbuilding and Marine Engineering	601	39	640	0.21	0.85	0.25
XI	Vehicles	24 899	2 640	27 539	9.16	3.73	2.46
XII	Metal Goods n.e.s.	3 952	1 195	5 147	1.71	2.64	0.65
XIII	Textiles	753	375	1 128	0.38	2.68	0.14
XIV	Leather, Leather Goods, and Fur	112	37	149	0.05	0.21	0.22
XV	Clothing and Footwear	1 120	2 197	3 317	1.10	1.98	0.56
XVI	Bricks, Pottery, Glass, Cement, etc.	998	176	1 174	0.39	1.39	0.28
XVII	Timber, Furniture, etc.	2 480	422	2 902	0.97	1.22	0.79
XVIII	Paper, Printing, and Publishing	10 888	5 450	16 338	5.44	2.72	2.00
XIX	Other Manufacturing Industries	1 485	735	2 220	0.74	1.53	0.49
III–XIX	All manufacturing	80 155	27 278	107 423	35.74	36.42	0.98
XX	Construction	16 407	1 106	17 513	5.83	5.65	1.03
XXI	Gas, Electricity, and Water	5 410	1 170	6 580	2.19	1.70	1.29
XXII	Transport and Communications	20 185	3 811	23 996	7.98	7.14	1.12
XXIII	Distributive Trades	21 754	20 811	42 565	14.16	11.80	1.20
XXIV	Insurance, Banking, Finance, etc.	5 964	6 970	12 934	4.30	4.45	0.97
XXV	Professional and Scientific Services	16 229	30 001	46 230	15.38	13.47	1.14
XXVI	Miscellaneous Services	11 684	12 911	24 595	8.18	8.81	0.93
XXVII	Public Administration and Defence	11 320	3 987	15 307	5.09	6.80	0.76
XXI–XXVII	All services	92 546	79 661	172 207	57.29	55.88	1.03
I–XXVII	All industries	191 620	108 980	300 600	100.00	100.00	

a = Percentage share Bristol/percentage share GB.
Source: Annual Census of Employment, Department of Employment.

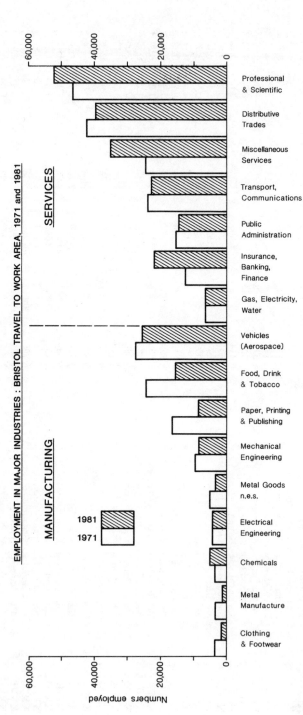

EMPLOYMENT IN MAJOR INDUSTRIES : BRISTOL TRAVEL TO WORK AREA, 1971 and 1981

Fig. 2.2. Employment change in Bristol, 1971 to 1981
Source: Annual Census of Employment, Department of Employment.

Table 2.2. The largest SIC categories in Bristol in rank order, 1971

Rank	SIC	No.	% total
1	Professional and Scientific Services	46 230	15.38
2	Distributive Trades	42 565	14.16
3	Vehicles	27 539	9.16
4	Food, Drink, and Tobacco	24 671	8.21
5	Miscellaneous Services	24 595	8.18
6	Transport and Communications	23 996	7.98
7	Construction	17 513	5.83
8	Paper, Printing, and Publishing	16 338	5.44
	Total	223 447	74.34

20,515 jobs for females. Overall, therefore, female employment grew during this period from 36.2 per cent of total employment to 40.3 per cent in 1978, converging on the national figure of 40.3 per cent.

The pattern of employment changes in Bristol was, not surprisingly, very uneven between sectors. More than 78 per cent of the job losses in manufacturing came from the three largest sectors. The Food, Drink, and Tobacco sector lost 5,165 jobs (a decline of 20 per cent), spread across firms in animal and poultry foods, bread and flour, and tobacco. The Vehicles sector lost 3,691 jobs (a decline of 13.4 per cent), almost all of these losses coming from the aerospace industry which dominated the sector. Finally, the Paper, Printing, and Publishing sector lost another 3,252 jobs (a 19.3 per cent decline) with most of these losses in paper and board and related packaging products. Although there were losses recorded in most other industrial sectors, more than 2,200 new jobs were created in the Chemicals industry; however, most of this growth was associated with the opening of one large new plant near Avonmouth.

Not all of the service sectors grew during this period. Employment in utilities, transport and communications, and distributive trades declined or at best grew slightly. Public Administration grew at a faster rate, but the real growth sectors were Miscellaneous Services, Insurance, Banking, and Finance, and Professional and Scientific Services, which between them generated over 22,300 new jobs. The growth in Miscellaneous Services was an impressive 33 per cent, but the increase in Insurance, Banking, and Finance was a dramatic 61 per cent. Most of the growth in this latter case was in insurance and business services. Most of the growth in Professional and Scientific Services was in education and health care.

In summary, this period witnessed a major structural transformation of the local economy, with rapid employment decline (mainly of male workers) in traditional manufacturing sectors and rapid employment growth (mainly for female workers) in key service sectors. In some respects what happened in

Table 2.3. Employment change by sector, Bristol, 1971–1981

SIC 1968		1971–8 %	1978–81 %	1971–8 Total	1971–8 Total per annum	1978–81 Total	1978–81 Total per annum
I	Agriculture, Forestry, Fishing	+12.7	+8.0	366	52	260	86
II	Mining and Quarrying	−25.0	+30.8	−146	−21	135	45
I–II	Total Extractive Industries	+6.4	+10.7	+220	31	395	132
III	Food, Drink, Tobacco	−20.1	−19.7	−5 165	−788	3 835	−1 878
IV	Coal and Petroleum Products	−84.8	+740.0	−28	−4	37	5
V	Chemicals and Allied Industries	+59.5	−14.7	2 231	319	−878	−293
VI	Metal Manufacture	−50.1	−21.1	−1 717	−245	−361	−120
VII	Mechanical Engineering	−17.1	+3.2	−1 689	−241	264	88
VIII	Instrument Engineering	+83.6	+3.9	388	53	33	11
IX	Electrical Engineering	−14.6	+10.3	−682	−97	409	128
X	Shipbuilding and Marine Engineering	−34.8	−27.3	−223	−32	−114	−38
XI	Vehicles	−13.4	+6.7	−3 691	−527	1 592	+531
XII	Metal Goods n.e.s.	−28.2	−0.7	−1 453	−207	−26	−9
XIII	Textiles	+3.0	−60.9	34	5	−708	−236
XIV	Leather, Leather Goods, and Fur	+38.9	−16.4	58	8	−34	−11
XV	Clothing and Footwear	−16.6	−37.6	−550	−78	−1 041	−347
XVI	Bricks, Pottery, Glass, Cement, etc.	−26.1	+47.3	−306	−44	411	137
XVII	Timber, Furniture, etc.	+16.7	−3.2	485	89	−107	−36
XVIII	Paper, Printing, and Publishing	−19.3	−31.2	−3 152	−450	−4 190	−1 396
XIX	Other Manufacturing Industry	+6.0	+8.9	134	−19	211	70
III–XIX	Total manufacturing industries	−14.3	−9.0	−15 326	−2 189	−8 337	−2 779
XX	Construction	−2.4	−4.6	−427	−61	−788	−263
XXI	Gas, Electricity, Water	+4.7	−3.0	312	44	−207	−69
XXII	Transport and Communication	−3.7	−0.5	−893	−127	−112	−37
XXIII	Distributive Trades	+2.0	−8.0	859	123	−3 484	−1 161
XXIV	Insurance, Banking, and Finance	+61.2	+6.8	8 017	1 145	1 423	474
XXV	Professional and Scientific Services	+13.4	−0.5	6 192	884	−288	−96
XXVI	Miscellaneous Services	+33.0	+7.3	8 129	1 161	2 395	798
XXVII	Public Administration and Defence	+13.0	−14.7	1 996	285	−2 540	−846
XXI–XXVII	Total service industries	+14.3	−1.4	24 612	3 516	−2 813	−938
	Total all industries	+3.0	−3.7	9 506	1 358	−11 543	−3 847

Bristol was an exaggerated version of national trends, with faster manufacturing employment decline and faster service employment growth.

Changes in the structure of employment, 1978–1981   Whereas total employment grew in the 1971–8 period, from 1978 to 1981 it declined by an average of 3,847 jobs per annum. A further 8,337 manufacturing jobs were lost, the rate of job loss increasing to 2,779 jobs per annum compared with 2,189 per annum in the 1971–8 period. The loss of 8,337 jobs represented a 9.0 per cent decline in three years, a substantial figure but nevertheless well below the national average of 16.8 per cent. At the same time service employment, which had shown massive increases in the early 1970s, now began to decline as well. The loss of 2,813 jobs represented a decline of 1.4 per cent compared with the national increase of 1.7 per cent.

As in the previous period, there were important variations between sectors. Within manufacturing, annual job losses in two of the three key industrial sectors increased substantially. Food, Drink, and Tobacco lost over 19 per cent of its total employment, and Paper, Printing, and Publishing over 31 per cent. Of great significance, however, was the fact that the largest industrial sector, Vehicles, reversed its decline in this period against the general trend and gained 1,592 jobs. Within services, in spite of the small overall decline, there were substantial losses in Distributive Trades and Public Administration and smaller losses in all the other sectors except two: Miscellaneous Services (+7.3 per cent) and Insurance, Banking, and Finance (+6.8 per cent) continued to show significant growth.

Female employment continued to decline in the manufacturing sector at a percentage rate almost double that for male manufacturing workers, with losses particularly high in the Food, Drink, and Tobacco sector. At the same time, female employment continued to grow in the service sector, but the growth rate here dropped to an average of just 134 jobs per annum, compared to the gain of 2,879 in the previous period. Overall, then, total female employment declined slightly as more jobs for women were lost in manufacturing than were gained in services. However, female employment still rose slightly as a percentage of total employment, reaching 41 per cent in 1981, with 82 per cent of female workers in the service sector. In summary, this period also witnessed important shifts in employment structure, but the patterns of change both between and within the major sectors were significantly different from the previous period.

The Bristol economy in 1981   Looking back over the past decade of change, it is evident that a substantial restructuring of the local economy has occurred, although the combination of forces at work has varied over time. Between 1971 and 1978 Bristol experienced something of a mini manufacturing crisis and a massive service sector growth. Although manufacturing employment declined at an increasing rate after 1978, the rate of decline was significantly below the national average. On the other hand, service growth came to a halt and went into decline against the national trend. Overall, between 1971 and 1981 Bristol lost 23,663 manufacturing jobs (−22.0 per cent) but gained 21,799 service sector jobs (+12.6 per cent). As a result, by 1981 manufacturing employment had dropped to 28.1 per cent of the total (close to the national average) while service employment had risen to 65 per cent (above the national average). There had been a major decline in male employment (−14,079) and a major increase in female employment (+12,800). As a proportion, female employment had risen from 36 to 41 per cent of total employment.

Within manufacturing, major job losses had been experienced in the Food, Drink, and Tobacco and Paper, Printing, and Packaging sectors, which between them shed 16,342 jobs (Tables 2.3 and 2.4). The Vehicle (aerospace) sector, on the other hand, declined more slowly up to 1978 and staged a recovery after that date. Overall, the proportion of manufacturing employment accounted for by the 'big three' dropped from 64 to 59 per cent, but the proportion accounted for by aerospace increased to 30 per cent. Bristol became more dependent on its key manufacturing sector.

Within the service sector, the most dramatic increases were registered in Miscellaneous Services, which grew by 43 per cent (10,500 jobs), and Insurance, Banking, and Finance, which grew by a remarkable 73 per cent (9,440 jobs). There were also big increases in medical and dental service employment within the Professional and Scientific Services category. The largest SIC categories in 1981 are shown in Table 2.5. The table confirms that Bristol had become even more an economy based upon services, aerospace, and consumer-oriented industries.

Disaggregating employment change: a shift-share analysis[2]

It is possible to gain further insights into the performance of the local economy relative to the national economy by disaggregating employment change into different elements. The *national* change may be defined as that change in employment which would have occurred in a region if employment had changed at the same rate as total employment in the nation as a whole. The *structural* change may be defined as that change in employment that would have occurred in a region if each industry had changed its employment at the same rate as that industry nationally, minus the national component. The structural component thus measures the favourability of a region's employment structure, a positive structural component signifying a favourable mix of industries. The national and structural components sum to the 'expected' employment change. The third, *differential*, change represents the difference between the expected employment change and the actual change. Differential components reflect a variety of influences peculiar to the industry or the region. The full expression for employment change in a region thus becomes:

Table 2.4. Employment by sector, Bristol and Great Britain, 1981

SIC 1968		Bristol Male	Female	Total	Total %	Great Britain %	Location quotient[a]
I	Agriculture, Forestry, Fishing	2 027	1 472	3 499	1.17	1.75	0.67
II	Mining and Quarrying	495	78	573	0.19	1.58	0.12
I–II	All primary	2 522	1 550	4 072	1.36	3.33	0.41
III	Food, Drink, and Tobacco	9 309	6 362	15 671	5.26	3.00	1.75
IV	Coal and Petroleum Products	24	18	42	0.01	0.13	0.08
V	Chemicals and Allied Industries	4 398	704	5 102	1.71	1.90	0.90
VI	Metal Manufacture	1 135	213	1 348	0.45	1.49	0.30
VII	Mechanical Engineering	7 323	1 111	8 484	2.83	3.63	0.78
VIII	Instrument Engineering	593	292	885	0.04	0.63	0.06
IX	Electrical Engineering	3 334	1 060	4 394	1.47	3.18	0.46
X	Shipbuilding and Marine Engineering	284	19	303	0.10	0.68	0.15
XI	Vehicles	22 768	2 672	25 440	8.53	2.79	3.06
XII	Metal Goods n.e.s.	2 932	736	3 668	1.23	2.10	0.59
XIII	Textiles	278	176	454	0.15	1.49	0.10
XIV	Leather, Leather Goods, and Fur	143	30	173	0.06	0.14	0.43
XV	Clothing and Footwear	604	1 122	1 726	0.58	1.25	0.46
XVI	Bricks, Pottery, Glass, Cement, etc.	1 092	187	1 279	0.43	1.01	0.43
XVII	Timber, Furniture, etc.	2 752	528	3 280	1.10	1.02	1.08
XVIII	Paper, Printing, and Publishing	6 345	2 651	8 996	3.02	2.40	1.23
XIX	Other Manufacturing Industries	1 879	686	2 565	0.86	1.18	0.73
III–XIX	All manufacturing	65 193	18 567	83 760	28.10	28.01	1.00
XX	Construction	14 650	1 648	16 298	5.42	5.15	1.05
XXI	Gas, Electricity, and Water	5 118	1 567	6 685	2.24	1.60	1.40
XXII	Transport and Communications	18 495	4 496	22 991	7.71	6.71	1.15
XXIII	Distributive Trades	19 411	20 529	39 940	13.40	12.85	1.05
XXIV	Insurance, Banking, Finance, etc.	10 528	11 846	22 374	7.30	6.19	1.18
XXV	Professional and Scientific Services	16 701	35 433	52 134	17.49	12.85	1.36
XXVI	Miscellaneous Services	13 684	21 435	35 119	11.78	11.96	0.99
XXVII	Public Administration and Defence	9 492	5 271	14 763	4.95	7.17	0.69
XXII–XXVII	All services	93 429	100 577	194 006	65.07	59.33	1.10
I–XXVII	All industries	175 794	122 342	298 136	100.00	100.00	

[a] = Percentage share Bristol/percentage share GB.

Source: Annual Census of Employment, Department of Employment.

Table 2.5. The largest SIC categories in Bristol in rank order, 1981

Rank	SIC	No.	%	1971 rank
1	Professional and Scientific Services	52 134	17.49	1
2	Distributive Trades	39 940	13.40	2
3	Miscellaneous Services	35 119	11.78	5
4	Vehicles	25 440	8.53	3
5	Transport and Communications	22 991	7.71	6
6	Insurance, Banking, and Finance	22 374	7.50	
7	Construction	16 298	5.47	7
8	Food, Drink, and Tobacco	15 671	5.26	4
	Total	229 967	74.14	

Actual change = national component + structural component + differential component.

The results for total employment are shown in Table 2.6 for the two periods 1971–8 and 1978–81. In the 1971–8 period the national component of change was the dominant factor in overall employment change in Bristol, although there was also a small positive structural effect. The negative differential effect, however, indicates that overall employment growth in Bristol was less than expected. An examination of the results for the manufacturing and service sectors reveals why. For the manufacturing sector as a whole, the large negative national component (−1,526 jobs p.a.) was partly offset by a positive structural effect (+212) reflecting Bristol's advantageous industrial mix. However, there was overall a negative differential component (−865), largely because of the worse-than-expected performance of the Food, Drink, and Tobacco, Vehicle, and Paper, Printing, and Publishing sectors. These three key sectors all had large negative differentials. For the service sector as a whole, the large positive national component (+2,937 jobs p.a.) was slightly reinforced by a positive structural effect (+56). There was, however, a sizeable positive differential effect (+552), indicating that the service sector performed even better than expected. This was largely due to the exceptional performances of Insurance, Banking, and Finance and Miscellaneous Services.

Turning to the 1978–81 period, the overall employment decline of 3,838 jobs per annum is disaggregated into a national component of decline of 5,122 jobs per annum, a positive structural component of 1,469 new jobs per annum, and a residual, negative differential component of 185 jobs lost per annum. For manufacturing employment as a whole there were also important changes over the previous period. The large, negative national component (−5,148) was again partly offset by a positive structural component (+1,092). However, there was a significant positive differential component of 1,551 jobs per annum, in sharp contrast to the previous period, when the dif-

Table 2.6. Categories of employment change, Bristol, based on 'shift-share' analysis, 1971–1981 (absolute change in numbers employed, per annum)

SIC 1968		National 1971–8	National 1978–81	Structural 1971–8	Structural 1978–81	Differential 1971–8	Differential 1978–81
I	Agriculture, Forestry, Fishing	−107	25	60	−27	99	91
II	Mining and Quarrying	−104	−3	94	−2	−12	52
I–II	Total Extractive Industries	−211	22	154	−29	87	143
III	Food, Drink, Tobacco	−65	−411	−227	−93	−445	−775
IV	Coal and Petroleum Products	−11	−45	11	45	−3	12
V	Chemicals and Allied Industries	−4	−160	7	1	315	−133
VI	Metal Manufacture	−211	−592	125	412	−159	59
VII	Mechanical Engineering	−247	−646	90	186	−85	549
VIII	Instrument Engineering	−37	−53	31	23	61	41
IX	Electrical Engineering	−126	−244	84	110	−55	271
X	Shipbuilding and Marine Engineering	−28	−100	23	77	−26	−15
XI	Vehicles	−59	−938	−247	−708	−220	2 177
XII	Metal Goods n.e.s.	−76	−372	34	158	−165	206
XIII	Textiles	−269	−582	236	461	39	−114
XIV	Leather, Leather Goods, and Fur	−19	−31	15	17	12	3
XV	Clothing and Footwear	−147	−403	71	160	−2	−104
XVI	Bricks, Pottery, Glass, Cement, etc.	−95	−169	72	118	−20	189
XVII	Timber, Furniture, etc.	−28	−162	8	3	89	123
XVIII	Paper, Printing, and Publishing	−75	−216	−141	2	−233	−1 182
XIX	Other Manufacturing Industry	−29	−294	20	120	29	244
III–XIX	Total manufacturing industries	−1 526	−5 418	+212	+1 092	−865	+1 551
XX	Construction	9	−627	−2	−1	−68	365
XXI	Gas, Electricity, Water	−70	−1	−28	57	143	−125
XXII	Transport and Communications	−154	−243	−30	19	57	187
XXIII	Distributive Trades	363	−118	38	88	−279	−1 130
XXIV	Insurance, Banking, and Finance	433	516	−12	236	724	279
XXV	Professional and Scientific Services	1 335	62	163	49	−614	−207
XXVI	Miscellaneous Services	892	786	−56	−5	325	17
XXVII	Public Administration and Defence	138	−102	−19	−37	166	−707
XXI–XXVII	Total service industries	+2 937	+901	+56	+407	+522	−2 244
	Total all industries	+1 209	−5 122	+420	+1 469	−324	−185

Source: calculated from Annual Census of Employment.

ferential component was negative. Unlike the previous period, the manufacturing sector in Bristol performed better than expected in employment terms, in the sense that, although jobs were lost, they were lost at a rate considerably below what was expected on the basis of national trends and industrial mix. A glance down the column of differential components for individual industries reveals that a major factor was the large positive component for the Vehicles Sector (a reversal over the previous period). The other two major industrial sectors—Food, Drink, and Tobacco and Paper, Printing, and Publishing—continued to decline faster than expected, with negative differential components being larger than in the previous period.

For the service sector as a whole, there were also significant changes from the previous period. The small decline in employment was not expected on the basis of the national and structural components, both of which were positive. The resulting negative differential effect of 2,244 fewer jobs per annum again contrasts sharply with the positive figure of 522 new jobs for the previous period. Whereas in the previous period there were more service sector jobs than expected, in this period there were substantially fewer. A glance down the column of differential components reveals that an important factor was the poorer-than-expected performance of Distributive Trades and Public Administration.

In summary, the shift-share figures suggest that the Bristol region performed better than expected in terms of manufacturing employment after 1978, in spite of accelerating losses, and performed worse than expected in the service sector, in spite of continuing small gains overall. However, although shift-share analysis can highlight distinctive elements of local employment change in this way, it mainly serves to raise questions for more detailed enquiry.

The manufacturing sector: processes behind employment change

The nature of the decline in manufacturing employment can be explored further by examining employment changes by plant size, calculating 'components of change', and identifying the corporate structures that lie behind these components of change. The levels are interrelated in the way shown in Figure 2.3.

Changes by plant size   It is well established that the bulk of manufacturing employment in postwar Britain has been concentrated in large plants. Evidence suggests that this is also the case in most large urban areas. Table 2.7 shows that Bristol was no exception in this period. Employment change by plant size for Bristol and selected urban areas is shown in Table 2.8. Between 1975 and 1978 Bristol's decline in manufacturing employment (−8.8 per cent) was higher than the rate for West Central Scotland and the West Midlands, but lower than the rate for Inner or Outer London. The employment

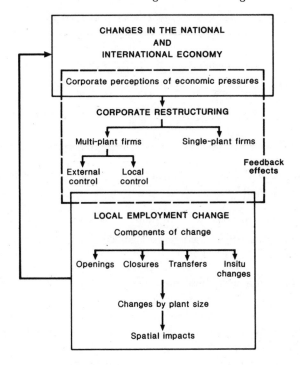

Fig. 2.3. Corporate restructuring and local economic change: a framework for analysis

decline in Bristol plants employing more than 500 workers was 9.1 per cent, but this was low compared with most other areas. In fact, the highest rate of employment loss was in the size range 201–500, and here Bristol exceeded most other areas. However, the most striking differences between Bristol and the other areas concerned the employment change in smaller size plants (below 50). In this size range Bristol's growth rate of 6.3 per cent far exceeded all other areas, suggesting a distinctive pattern of small firm growth, although this was nowhere near enough to offset the employment losses in large plants.

The table also shows that employment decline in Bristol increased to −12.3 per cent between 1978 and 1981. However, this figure was substantially below the figures for other areas. Bristol also had the lowest rates of decline in all the plant size categories above 51 employees; and, even more significantly, Bristol was the only area to show employment growth in the smaller plant size bands. The 16.5 per cent increase in employment in plants employing 11–50 people contrasted sharply with, for example, the 20.5 per cent decline in the same size range in Inner London. This evidence identifies

Table 2.7. Employment changes in Bristol by plant size, 1975–1978

	% of total employment	
Plant size	1975	1978
11–20	1.6	0.3
21–50	3.9	1.9
51–200	11.7	10.3
201–500	13.8	15.1
500+	68.9	72.3

further aspects of Bristol's *relative* improvement in terms of manufacturing employment after 1978.

Components of change analysis Components of change analysis provides a means of isolating some of the key processes at work behind employment change. Using this approach, aggregate employment change can be disaggregated into the effects of plant openings, closures, expansions, and contractions. The data used here have been extracted by the Department of Trade and Industry from their Regional Data System and cover manufacturing employment changes by plant size for the period 1975–1981. There are limitations to these data, particularly with regard to the under-recording of openings, but the figures are accurate enough to identify broad trends, and comparisons can be made with other areas on a common basis. Manufacturing change between 1975 and 1978 can be broken down into the following components:

$$
\begin{array}{l}
\text{Total mfg} \\
\text{employment} \\
\text{(in plants} \\
\text{of 11+) in} \\
\text{1978}
\end{array}
=
\begin{array}{l}
\text{Total mfg} \\
\text{employment} \\
\text{(in plants} \\
\text{of 11+) in} \\
\text{1975}
\end{array}
+ \text{openings} + \text{entries} +
\overbrace{
\begin{array}{l}
\text{expan-} \\
\text{sions}
\end{array}
-
\begin{array}{l}
\text{contract-} \\
\text{sions}
\end{array}
}^{\text{(surviving plants)}}
- \text{closures} - \text{exits}
$$

$$
88{,}692 \quad = 96{,}883 \quad + 206 \quad + 130 \quad + 5{,}048 \quad - 12{,}178 \quad - 1\,210 \quad - 187
$$

Net change = −8,191

where 'openings' refer to new plants, 'entries' to plants that grew from less than 11 employees in the period, and 'exits' to plants that declined to less than 11 employees.

It is evident that the overall net losses in employment were largely due to contraction of employment in existing plants rather than to closures, although the impacts of closure were not negligible. In this respect Bristol differed from the other selected areas, where job losses from closures were generally much higher. Such growth as did occur was largely due to expansion in existing plants rather than to new plants. (Remember, however, that the figures exclude small plants employing fewer than 11 people). It is also possible to calculate components of change for different plant size-bands. Not

Table 2.8. *Employment change by size of workplace in Bristol and selected areas, 1975–1981*[a] (*percentages*)

	Bristol		Inner London		Outer London		Scotland		West Midlands	
	1975–8	1978–81	1975–8	1978–81	1975–8	1978–81	1975–8	1978–81	1975–8	1978–81
11–50	6.3	16.5	−6.0	−14.9	−6.3	−20.5	0.8	−22.6	1.2	−16.0
51–200	−8.0	−12.1	−10.9	−38.4	−9.9	−23.0	−0.6	−26.0	−0.4	−19.5
201–500	−13.9	−12.8	−8.2	−41.9	−8.5	−26.3	−13.9	−32.8	−4.2	−25.0
500+	−9.1	−13.1	−19.3	−34.0	−11.6	−24.1	−11.1	−29.3	−9.1	−32.9
All	−8.8	−12.3	−13.2	−35.4	−10.4	−24.2	−8.7	−29.0	−5.7	−28.4

[a] Shows net employment change as a percentage of employment at the start of the period, in workplaces categorized by initial number employed. Bristol refers to the travel-to-work area. Inner and outer London and the West Midlands are the study areas as defined by the ESRC Inner City in Context Research Programme.

Source: Department of Industry and Trade, special tabulation.

surprisingly, the bulk of the losses from 'contractions' came from plants employing more than 500 workers and all the growth from 'openings' and 'entries' was in smaller plants. In summary, the above figures give us a picture of an area experiencing substantial employment decline, mainly through large plant contractions rather than closures, at a rate higher than, for example, the West Midlands, and in spite of a comparatively high rate of small-firm growth.

For the 1978–81 period the components of change appear as follows:

				(surviving plants)			
Employment, 1981	= Employment, 1978	+ openings	+ entries	+ expansions	− contractions	− closures	− exits
79,039	= 88,692	+ 0	+ 0	+ 4,003	− 9,421	− 3,738	− 497.

The combined figure for contractions and closures was almost the same as in the previous period, but the closure figure had tripled in size and accounted for a larger proportion of this total. Nevertheless, the major source of job loss remained contractions in surviving plants. The major difference over the previous period was the decline in the rate of job growth through expansions, openings, and entries, rather than an acceleration in job losses. In this respect Bristol contrasted with the other project areas, where employment growth declined *and* job losses increased sharply through both closures and contractions. Again, the bulk of the jobs lost through closures and contractions (over 77 per cent) came from the larger plants employing over 500.

Corporate structure and corporate change   Corporate restructuring provides the intermediary links between the components of local employment change and broader changes in the national and international economy. At the national level it is well known that manufacturing employment is dominated by a decreasing number of very large multinational corporations, and evidence suggests that this is also the case in most large urban economies. The restructuring decisions of a small number of major local employers, usually multinational corporations, thus account for the bulk of local employment change. The evidence suggests that this is the case in the Bristol economy. We have already noted that by 1978 over 72 per cent of manufacturing employment in Bristol (in plants employing more than 11 workers) was in plants employing more than 500 people. From the pattern of corporate ownership of these plants, shown in Figure 2.4, it is evident that the bulk of manufacturing employment in the city in 1978/9 was controlled by twenty major corporations occupying leading positions in all the major industries in the area[3] (Bassett, 1984).

Recent research has suggested that, compared with local independent firms, externally owned plants tend to have a smaller proportion of white-collar jobs, more routinized production-line jobs, and higher plant closure rates.

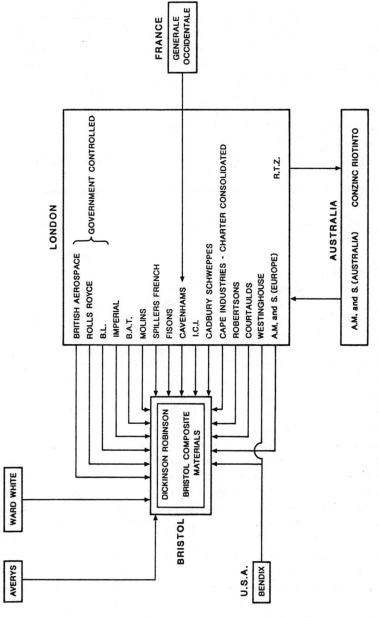

Fig. 2.4. Corporate structure in the Bristol economy, 1979
Source: Bassett (1984).

It has also been suggested that many have fewer linkages to the local economy, have a lower rate of innovation, and offer little stimulation to local entrepreneurship. Although there is conflicting evidence on some of these issues (see Watts 1981), the distinction between independent and externally owned firms does seem to be important, and the degree of external ownership has an important bearing on the nature of local economic growth. With respect to the Bristol data, only two of the twenty companies had their headquarters in the city in 1978–9, of which DRG (the Dickinson-Robinson Group, a printing, packaging, and engineering multinational formed through the merger of Robinsons and John Dickinsons) was the more important. It is evident that the bulk of employment was ultimately controlled from the London headquarters of well-known major British multinationals. Among these companies, the Imperial Group and BAT Industries were particularly important in the tobacco, printing, and packaging sectors, and the government-backed firms, British Aerospace and Rolls Royce, dominated the aerospace sector. Direct foreign ownership was evident in just three cases, although in each case the element of foreign ownership was complex and partial. This comparatively low level of foreign ownership contrasts with the higher levels found in some parts of the country favoured in the past by foreign investment.

These twenty corporations also accounted for the great bulk of the manufacturing jobs lost from 1978 onwards. Their decisions to contract or close branch plants were responses to economic pressures that affected different sectors and companies in different ways. Employment decline in aerospace was accounted for almost entirely by the activities of just two companies, British Aerospace and Rolls Royce. The decline of employment in tobacco was almost entirely the result of rationalization policies adopted by the Imperial Group. Employment declines in paper and board and packaging products were largely the results of decisions made by DRG, BAT, and Imperial. Other major job losses in key sectors resulted from closure decisions by Molins (a packaging machinery plant) and Robertsons (a jam factory). Even when closure or contraction did not occur, there were often important changes in ownership and control that 'relocated' local branch plants in different corporate hierarchies. These and other related changes will be discussed in more detail in the later chapter on sector studies, which also extends the time period of analysis beyond 1981.

The emergence of a 'high-technology' industrial sector ?   By the early 1980s the Bristol area had acquired the image of a 'high-technology' growth area at the western end of the M4 'corridor'. How far is this borne out by the statistics available? An immediate problem is the definition of high-technology industry (Langridge *et al.* 1984). The term may refer to *products*, to *production processes*, or to *occupations*. For present purposes, the high-technology sector is defined in Minimum List Heading (MLH) terms, reflecting product type and, to some extent, occupational structure. The following MLHs are included:

272   Pharmaceutical Chemicals and Preparations
354   Scientific and Industrial Instruments and Systems
363   Telegraph and Telephone Apparatus
363   Radio and Electronic Components
365   Broadcasting Equipment
366   Electronic Computers
367   Radio, Radar, and Electronic Capital Goods
383   Aerospace Equipment

On this basis, the high-technology sector accounted for 24 per cent of total manufacturing employment in Bristol in 1978, and 7.1 per cent of total employment, although 20,396 of the 22,157 jobs involved were in the aerospace sector (and not all of these could be strictly defined as high-technology jobs). By 1981, however, the high-technology sector accounted for 29 per cent of manufacturing employment and 8.2 per cent of total employment. The increase between 1978 and 1981 was accounted for by a 6.1 per cent increase in aerospace jobs and a 60 per cent increase in non-aerospace jobs. Nevertheless, the aerospace sector still accounted for the vast majority of the jobs in the sector as a whole—21,652 jobs out of 24,466. As a result, although Bristol's high-technology industries employed 8.2 per cent of total employment in 1981, compared with the national average of 2.87 per cent, the non-aerospace sector accounted for only 0.77 per cent compared with 1.99 per cent.

The figures thus emphasize both the importance of high-technology employment in the area and the dominance of the aerospace industry within this sector. Although non-aerospace industries grew rapidly, particularly from 1978 onwards, the 1981 total of 2,814 jobs needs to be compared with the loss of over 8,300 jobs in the manufacturing sector as a whole between 1978 and 1981. As we shall see, there have been a number of significant developments in non-aerospace, high-technology employment since 1981, but not on a sufficient scale to modify the picture seriously. Whether the high-technology sector will form the basis for substantial future growth in manufacturing is an issue which will be discussed later in the book.

The service sector: processes behind employment change

The decline of manufacturing employment in Bristol was paralleled by a massive increase in service employment in the 1970s. Given its importance, the service sector therefore merits more detailed discussion and analysis. However, in spite of their dominance in terms of national employment, the service industries have until recently been a neglected area of study, and there is much less understanding of their structure and development compared with manufacturing industries. This partly reflects certain assumptions that are often made concerning the relative 'importance' of manufacturing and services to the economy as a whole. The manufacturing sector has often been regarded as the wealth-creating sector, with service sector growth regarded at best as derivative and capable of looking after itself, and at worst as an unproductive burden on the economy. An extreme version of this latter argument is found in the work of Bacon and Eltis (1976), who have argued that the growth of non-tradable public services in the 1960s and 1970s 'crowded out' productive investment and retarded growth.

However, there have now begun to emerge more detailed analyses and discussions that recognize more fully the complex structure of the service sector and its interrelations with the economy as a whole (e.g. Stanback 1979; Robertson *et al.* 1982; Marquand 1983). Robertson *et al.* (1982), for example, have rejected simple 'crowding-out' theories and demonstrated the interdependencies between services and manufacturing using input–output models of the national economy. According to their estimates, in 1977 12.2 per cent of total service sector employment was related to the demands of the manufacturing sector and 79.8 per cent was geared to final (mainly consumer) demand. There were important variations between services, with Transport and Communications being more dependent on manufacturing demand than, for example, Distribution. The main point of the analysis, however, is to underline the role of a wide range of services in enabling manufacturing industries to produce their output. The input–output framework also enables interdependencies *within* the service sector to be identified, although these are not so strongly developed as those interdependencies within the manufacturing sector.

The recognition of the complex ways in which different services relate to the economy as a whole has led to various attempts to construct more theoretically meaningful classifications. A series of cross-cutting classifications has sought to distinguish public and private, basic and non-basic, and producer and consumer services. Producer services are services purchased by firms to sustain their business operations; consumer services are provided directly to consumers and sustain personal consumption. The basic–non-basic distinction emphasizes that some cities may specialize in the 'export' of services rather than goods to surrounding areas (Fothergill and Gudgin 1982).

The important point, however, is that different categories of services relate to the economy in different ways, responding to different forces over time and showing different spatial patterns of change. The growth of public services, for example, is related to economic pressures on public expenditure and changes in government policy. Producer services are related to the rate of growth of the manufacturing sector and the relative costs of purchasing specialized services rather than providing them 'in house'. The rapid growth of such services over the past few decades seems strongly related to the complex demands of larger and increasingly diversified multinational corporations (Stanback 1979). These services tend to be concentrated in the larger cities and financial centres, with a distinct bias towards south-east England (Massey 1984). Finally, consumer services are related more directly to variations in the level of consumers' disposable income. Such services tend to be more dispersed and more closely related to the distribution of population and income (Marquand 1983).

For purpose of analysis in this study, an initial distinction has been made between *public* and *private* services, and private services have been further subdivided into *producer-oriented* and *consumer-oriented* services. These in turn have been grouped into appropriate sub-categories. The details are as follows (the numbers refer to Minimum List Headings):

Predominantly public   National and local government (901, 906)
Transport and communications (701, 702, 706, 707, 708)
Education (872)
Medical and dental (874)

Predominantly private
Producer-oriented   Transport (703, 704, 705, 709)
Distribution (810, 811, 812, 831, 832)
Business services (861, 862, 863, 864, 865, 866, 871, 873, 876, 879)
Consumer-oriented   Insurance (860)
Retailing (820, 821)
Miscellaneous personal services (875, 881, 882, 883, 884, 885, 886, 887, 888, 889, 892, 893, 894, 895, 899)

Such a classification can only be approximate. Some Minimum List Headings straddle several categories of employment. Where this occurs, local knowledge has been used to allocate employment to the most appropriate category.

The results of the analysis are shown in Table 2.9. The period 1971–8 was clearly a period of massive growth in service employment as a whole (over 24,000 new jobs). The growth was primarily in private consumer-oriented services (13,387 jobs), followed by public services (5,470) and private producer-oriented services (5,443). These overall totals conceal wide variations in growth and decline within categories. Thus, the growth in public service employment was associated mainly with the expansion in education and medical and dental services. The growth of private producer-oriented employment was due almost entirely to the growth of business services (6,265 new jobs); employment in distribution actually declined. All the consumer-oriented categories grew, but the largest growth was in miscellaneous personal services. The increase of 6,265 jobs in this last category was spread across a wide range of activities, with public houses, catering, and 'other' miscellaneous services being particularly important.

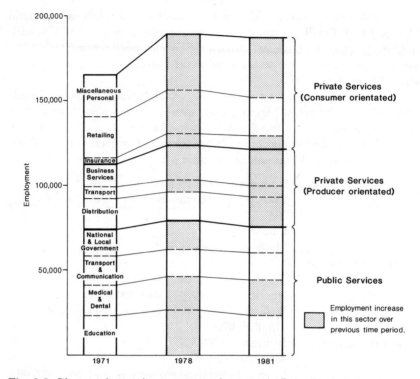

Fig. 2.5. Changes in service sector employment in Bristol, 1971–1981
Source: Annual Census of Employment, Department of Employment.

It seems clear that these variations in rates of growth and decline reflected different combinations of forces at work. The expansion in public service employment probably reflected increased expenditure on the welfare state and the impacts of local government reorganization, which brought a new tier of local government into being in the area in 1974. Within the private producer-oriented category, the slow growth or decline in employment in distribution and transport probably reflected technological improvements. The rapid (45 per cent) expansion in business services, on the other hand, probably reflected the agglomerative growth of Bristol as a centre for financial and specialist services. Within the private consumer-oriented category, the growth of employment in insurance stemmed from the relocation of major companies from London, while the growth of employment in miscellaneous personal services was probably related to growth in consumer incomes, the multiplier effects of central area office development, and increased demand for leisure facilities.

In addition to the categories of jobs created, it is also important to analyse the way these jobs were distributed between male and female workers. As Table 2.10 shows, female service employment rose by over 20,000 between

Table 2.9. *Employment change in the service sector, Bristol, 1971–1981*

	1971	1978	1981	1971–8		1978–81	
				Total	%	Total	%
Total services	165 627	189 927	187 511	+24 300	+14.7	−2 416	−1.4
Public services[a]	74 094	79 564	75 867	+5 470	+7.4	−3 707	−4.6
Education	23 226	26 285	23 331	+3 059	+13.2	−2 954	−11.2
Medical and dental	17 922	19 926	21 594	+2 004	+11.2	+1 668	+8.4
Transport/communications	17 639	16 050	15 979	−1 589	−9.0	−71	−0.4
National/local government	15 307	17 303	14 963	+1 996	+13.0	−2 340	−13.5
Private services[a]							
Producer-oriented	38 740	44 183	45 721	+5 443	+14.0	+1 538	+3.5
Distribution	18 554	17 036	17 151	−1 518	−8.2	+115	+0.7
Transport	6 357	7 053	7 012	+696	+10.9	−41	−0.6
Business services	13 829	20 094	21 558	+6 265	+45.3	+1 464	+7.3
Consumer-oriented	52 793	66 180	65 923	+13 387	+20.2	−257	−0.4
Insurance	3 863	6 672	7 707	+2 809	+72.7	+1 035	+15.5
Retailing	24 011	26 388	22 789	+2 377	+9.9	−3 599	−13.6
Miscellaneous peronal services	24 919	33 120	35 427	+8 201	+32.9	+2 307	+7.0

[a] See text for definition of sub-sectors.
Source: Annual Census of Employment.

1971 and 1978, accounting for over 83 per cent of the total increase in this sector. The major categories of increase were miscellaneous personal services, business services, education, medical and dental services, and national and local government. In terms of skill and income level, it has been suggested that, at the national level at least, service sector growth tends to generate a large proportion of relatively low paid and unskilled jobs at the lower end of the job market and a smaller number of higher paid professional and technical jobs at the upper end. The lower paid, less secure, and often non-unionized jobs tend to be occupied by female workers, many part-time. This may certainly be the case in the miscellaneous personal service sector in Bristol, but precise information is lacking.

The growth of service employment came to an end in the late 1970s. Between 1978 and 1981, as Table 2.9 shows, there was a slight decline in the overall number of service sector jobs ($-2,416$); but, whereas employment in both public and private consumer-oriented services declined (by 3,707 and 257 jobs, respectively), employment in private producer-oriented services continued to increase (by 1,538). Again, as in the earlier period, there were important variations within categories. Medical and dental employment continued to grow within the declining public sector total. The slight decline in private consumer-oriented employment was only due to the fact that retailing losses outweighed the continuing gains in insurance and miscellaneous personal services (mainly clubs, restaurants, sports, and 'other' miscellaneous services). Finally, the expansion of private producer-oriented services was again due almost entirely to growth in the business services. Female employment in the service sector grew by just 411 in this period, compared with a growth of 20,108 in the previous period. The dramatic slowdown from an average increase of 2,872 jobs per annum to just 137 resulted largely from heavy losses in public service employment (particularly education and local government) and retailing. Nevertheless, there was continuing and substantial growth in medical and dental services and miscellaneous personal services. Female employment rose as a percentage of total employment in every category, with education, medical and dental services, retailing, business, and miscellaneous services all becoming predominantly female (more than 50 per cent) by 1981.

These differences in growth and decline again reflected different processes at work in different sub-sectors. Thus, the post-1978 decline in public service employment reflected public expenditure cuts and increasing financial pressures on local authorities (although even then employment in medical and dental services continued to grow). The continuing growth in private producer-oriented services probably reflected a mixture of factors relating to the relative prosperity of the local economy and the continuing impacts of previous office expansion. Within private consumer-oriented services, the considerable decline in retailing employment was related to technological changes and the growth of supermarkets and hypermarkets, while the growth

Table 2.10. *Female service employment change, Bristol, 1971–1981*

	Proportion of service category, 1971 %	Change, 1971–8		Change, 1978–81		Proportion of service category, 1981 %
		Total	Per annum	Total	Per annum	
Total services	47.4	+20 108	+2 873	+411	+137	52.8
Public services[a]	46.9	+7 332	+1 047	-1 479	-493	53.5
Education	62.8	+2 866	+409	-2 303	-767	64.9
Medical and dental	73.9	+2 131	+304	+1 664	+555	78.9
Transport/communications	16.6	-21	-3	+232	+77	19.7
National/local government	26.0	+2 356	+336	-1 072	-357	32.2
Private services[a]						
Producer-oriented	35.0	+3 602	+514	+1 168	+389	40.1
Distribution	28.9	-413	-59	+567	+189	32.2
Transport	13.7	+387	+55	+87	+29	19.2
Business services	52.9	+3 628	+518	+514	+171	53.2
Consumer-oriented	57.1	+9 174	+1 310	+722	+241	60.7
Insurance	43.5	+1 271	+181	+524	+175	45.1
Retailing	64.3	+1 318	+188	-1 754	-585	65.8
Miscellaneous personal services	52.3	+6 583	+940	+1 952	+651	60.9

[a] See test for definition of sub-sectors.
Source: Annual Census of Employment.

of miscellaneous service employment reflected rising real incomes for those in
employment and an increased demand for leisure services.

The Social and Spatial Impacts of Economic Change

The two previous sections have outlined some of the basic changes in
employment structure that have taken place in the Bristol region since the
early 1970s. These changes in employment structure are interrelated with
broader changes in socioeconomic and spatial structures. This section
explores some of these broader changes, with particular emphasis upon
changes in the spatial distribution of employment and the workforce,
changes in the relative importance of different socioeconomic groups, and the
impacts of economic change on unemployment, social stress, and intra-urban
inequalities.

The distribution of employment

Figure 2.6 shows the level of employment and the scale of employment
change in Bristol and the surrounding districts over the period 1971–81.
Clearly, Bristol has been the dominant source of employment in the region
over the decade. It has also experienced the most substantial restructuring of
employment, with large losses in manufacturing employment and large gains
in service employment. The bulk of the manufacturing job losses came from
plants in inner and south Bristol, which shed an estimated 17,500 employees
in the decade. Further substantial employment losses have been experienced
since 1981. Most of these job losses resulted from redundancies and closures
in branch plants of major multinational companies in old established Bristol
industries. Losses between 200 and 1,700 were recorded in plants owned by
Imperial (tobacco plants and a board mill), BAT (packaging plants), DRG
(packaging and stationery plants), Molins (packaging machinery plant),
Robertson's (jam factory), Cape Industries (brake shoe plant) and British
Leyland (bus chassis plant). Elsewhere in Bristol significant manufacturing
losses were also experienced in the heavier industries of the Avonmouth area,
again associated with redundancies in branch plants of major multinational
corporations such as Rio Tinto Zinc (RTZ) (lead and zinc smelter) and
Fisons (fertilizers).

At the same time, industrial floor space declined by 14.2 per cent between
1974 and 1982, but the floor space devoted to covered warehousing increased
by 28 per cent. This increase in warehousing, reflecting Bristol's growing role
as a major distribution centre, was partly at the expense of industrial floor
space on existing trading estates and partly the result of major new estate
developments on land owned by the City Council, in the Avonmouth area in
particular. The big increase in service employment in Bristol, which
occurred particularly in the early 1970s, was associated with a massive

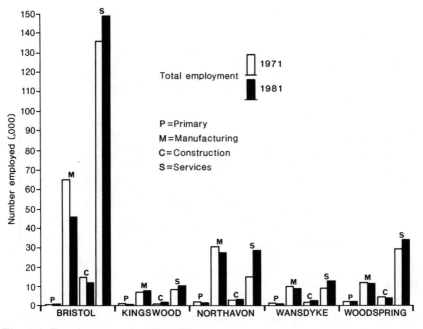

Fig. 2.6. Employment change in Bristol and the surrounding districts, 1971–1981.
Source: Avon County Planning Department.

increase in central area office space. Figure 2.7 shows the scale of the success-ive office building booms in the city. The major boom of the early 1970s cul-minated in over 1 million square feet of major office completions in 1974, transforming large parts of the central area. Following a slump, office devel-opment took off again in the later 1970s, to the extent that since 1975 an esti-mated 7.5 million square feet of new office floor space has been added in developments larger than 10,000 square feet.

Outside of Bristol, employment restructuring was less dramatic. Although manufacturing employment grew slightly in Kingswood District, in the other areas it declined while service employment grew. Some of the most signifi-cant developments in this period occurred in the 'Northern Fringe' or 'Motorway Triangle' area, just outside the Bristol boundary, in the southern part of Northavon between the M4 and M5. Much of the Filton aerospace complex with more than 20,000 workers falls within this zone, and it is here that the newer, 'high-technology' companies have preferred to locate on new 'campus-style' industrial estates. The Aztec West business park has attracted a number of big-name computer firms, and Hewlett Packard have located their new factory nearby, within sight of the M4 and the High Speed Rail link to London and Heathrow. The 'sunbelt' image of this growth zone

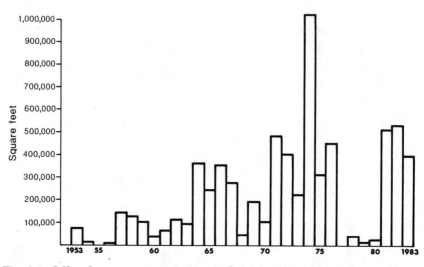

Fig. 2.7. Office floorspace completions in Bristol, 1953–1984
Source: Avon County Planning Department.

contrasts strongly with the recession-struck image of south Bristol on the opposite side of the city. However, new high-technology developments were not confined to the north fringe. Small, computer-related plants have been established in small estates in the semi-rural fringe; and, to the west, the fast growing dormitory town of Nailsea attracted a GEC–Marconi avionics plant in the late 1970s.

In summary, the overall pattern of manufacturing employment decline and service sector growth has been associated with important spatial shifts in employment within the locality, with new zones of growth emerging along-side zones of stagnation and decline. This will become more evident when we examine the distribution of unemployment and social stress within the region.

The distribution of the workforce

Along with changes in the distribution of employment, there have also been shifts in the distribution of the resident workforce. The workforce of Avon County as a whole grew by over 22,000 in the decade between 1971 and 1981. Net migration contributed only about 1,000 workers a year through much of the 1970s, and much of the employment growth, particularly during the early 1970s, resulted from rising female activity rates as an increasing number of women were drawn into service sector employment. Although increases in female activity rates levelled off in the late 1970s, the overall activity rate for the county converged towards the national average during the decade, differ-

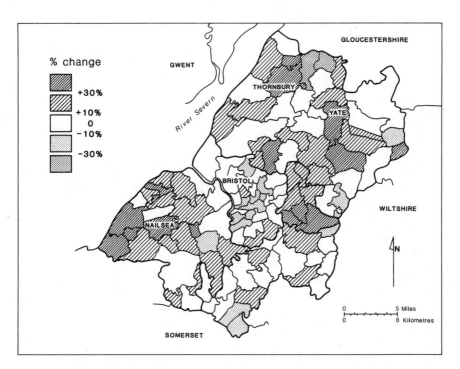

Fig. 2.8. Changes in the distribution of the resident workforce, Bristol travel-to-work area, 1971–1981
Source: Population Censuses, 1971 and 1981, Small Area Statistics.

ing by only −0.7 per cent in 1981 compared with −2.2 per cent in 1971. Within the county, the resident workforce grew in all the districts except Bristol, where it declined by over 8,500 during the decade 1971–81. The detailed pattern of changes is shown in figure 2.8. There were substantial percentage declines in inner and south Bristol, while major increases were registered on the Kingswood fringe to the east, in the north and north-east around the towns of Thornbury and Yate, and along the Nailsea–Clevedon axis to the south-west. Overall, the decade saw the pattern, familiar in most large cities, of decline in the central core and rapid growth on the urban fringe and in outlying towns and dormitory settlements.

Occupational structures, socioeconomic groups, and social classes

The restructuring of industry and employment over the past decade has also generated changes in occupational structures and the relative importance of different socioeconomic groups. The large-scale expansion of the office sector, and the relocation of central office functions from London, generated

Table 2.11. Socioeconomic structure: Avon County and England and Wales

	Avon	England and Wales	Avon	England and Wales
	1971		1981	
	%	%	%	%
Employers and managers (SEGs 1 ,2)	9.4	9.1	11.5	11.4
Professional workers (SEGs 3, 4)	4.3	3.6	4.8	3.7
Clerical and administrative	32.6	28.9	33.5	30.5
Intermediate (SEG 5)	9.0	7.6	11.0	11.1
Junior (SEG 6)	23.6	21.3	22.5	20.4
Skilled manual workers (SEGs 8, 9, 12)	28.5	27.3	23.5	24.2
Unskilled and Semiskilled (SEGs 7, 10, 11)	23.4	24.9	21.2	23.7

Source: Population Censuses, 1971 and 1981.

jobs for managers, professionals, administrative and clerical workers, and associated miscellaneous service workers in fields such as catering. At the same time, manufacturing plant closures and redundancies, corporate centralization and the introduction of new technology reduced the number of jobs for branch plant managers, many categories of skilled workers, and less skilled assembly-line workers. The broad outcome of these and related changes in terms of socioeconomic groups is shown in Table 2.11.

It is clear from the table that, even in 1971, Avon County as a whole had a higher proportion of employers and managers, professional workers, clerical and administrative workers, and skilled manual workers than the average for England and Wales and a lower proportion of semi- and unskilled workers. By 1981 manufacturing job losses had brought the Avon average for skilled manual workers below the national average, as well. However, the area continued to exceed the average for most 'white-collar' groups, and although there was some convergence towards the national average in some sectors, the Avon bias towards professional workers actually increased.

The different socioeconomic groups have been unevenly distributed over space. Figure 2.9 shows the distribution of manual workers and personal service workers within the travel-to-work area. The concentration of manual and personal service workers in central and south Bristol, Avonmouth, and Kingswood is apparent, together with scattered concentrations in more peripheral rural areas. The map also brings out the relatively high proportions of white-collar workers in parts of north Bristol and in peripheral areas extending particularly to the north and south-west. The importance of certain 'élite' areas within these zones is brought out even more clearly in Figure 2.10, which maps the distribution of employers, managers and professional workers. The zone extending south-west from Westbury across the Bristol

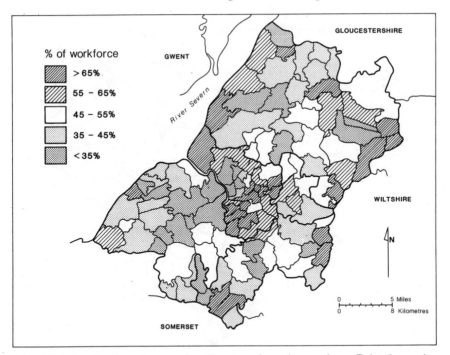

Fig. 2.9. Distribution of manual and personal service workers, Bristol travel-to-work area, 1981
Source: Population Census, 1981, Small Area Statistics.

boundary towards Nailsea stands out, as does the concentration around the country town of Thornbury in the north. Much of the attractiveness of the Bristol area to incoming firms is the ease with which top managers and professionals can live in the lush semi-rural fringe, yet commute daily with relative ease into the central areas of the city and its outer industrial zones.

Changes in occupational and socioeconomic group structures are interrelated with changes in social class structures. The Census groups occupational categories into 'social classes' based upon similar levels of occupational skill. The relative sizes of these different classes is shown in Table 2.12 for Avon, and England and Wales, in 1981. The figures point to the greater dominance in Avon of those social classes covering professional, intermediate, and skilled non-manual occupations. Altogether, 43.9 per cent of workers in Avon were classified in the top three classes in 1981, compared with 38.6 per cent in England and Wales as a whole.

Unemployment, its structure and distribution

Changes in the structure and distribution of unemployment have been amoung the most important changes over the past decade in terms of their

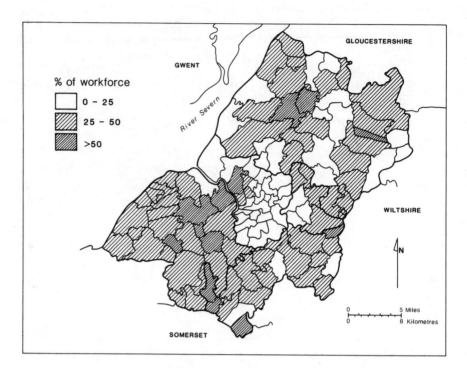

Fig. 2.10. Distribution of employers, managers and professional workers,
Bristol travel-to-work area, 1981
Source: Population Census, 1981, Small Area Statistics.

Table 2.12. Social class in Avon County and England and Wales, 1981

Social classes	Avon %	England and Wales %
I Professional, etc., occupations	7.2	5.5
II Intermediate occupations	22.4	21.7
III Skilled occupations		
(N) non-manual	13.3	11.4
(M) manual	33.8	34.7
IV Partly skilled occupations	14.2	16.1
V Unskilled occupations	5.1	5.9

Source: Population Census, 1981.

social effects. Changes in unemployment rates for the Bristol travel-to-work
area and the country as a whole for the period 1976–84 have already been
illustrated in Figure 2.1. Following a long period of relatively full employment in the 1950s and 1960s, unemployment began to rise in the early 1970s.

Since then the Bristol pattern has tended to echo the national pattern, but with the significant difference that Bristol rates rose *above* the national average between 1977 and 1979 and have remained *below* the national average since 1979. In April 1984, for example, the Bristol rate of 10.8 per cent was two percentage points below the national average of 12.8 per cent. Therefore, although unemployment has risen sharply in the city since 1979, Bristol has not experienced the scale of unemployment of many of the industrial cities of the West Midlands and the North and, indeed, has *improved* its relative position since the late 1970s.

The official unemployment figures underestimate the 'real' unemployment rate in the area. They include only people drawing benefit and exclude many who are ineligible for benefit but are seeking work (mainly women). Avon County planners have estimated that if these were included the 'real' level of unemployment in Avon in October 1984 would have been 7,500 higher, at 53,500 (a rate of 12 per cent). In addition, a figure of around 10,000 could be included for 'marginal' workers discouraged from seeking work by poor employment prospects, and 7,000+ for those engaged on government training schemes, giving a total pool of about 70,000 unemployed (Avon County Council 1985).

A significant feature of the rise in unemployment has also been the increase in the proportion of long-term unemployment. In January 1976 16 per cent of the registered unemployed in the county had been out of work for a year or more; by January 1982 that figure had risen to 30 per cent, and by 1984 to around 36 per cent. This seems to suggest an increasing polarization in the local labour market between those who are moving in and out of the job market through spells of temporary unemployment, and those whose age, sex, or skills condemn them to more permanent unemployment.

Many of the jobs that have been lost over the past decade have been jobs for less skilled manual workers. As a result, the unemployment rates for different occupational groups in 1982 indicated that about two-thirds of unemployed adults in the county belonged to the manual occupational categories even though this group accounted for only about one-third of the workforce (Avon County Council 1985).

Unemployment rates have also varied significantly by age group. By 1983 unemployment rates for the young (16–24) were up to twice the rates for older workers. The rate for 18–19-year-olds, for example, was 22.4 per cent compared with the 6.2 per cent for 35–44-year-olds. Between 1983 and 1984, as overall unemployment rates increased, the rates for the 16–19 age group remained stable or dropped slightly under the impact of YTS schemes, but the rate for the 20–24 group increased sharply. On the other hand, long-term unemployment rates were much higher for older workers, particularly those above the age of 55.

The above figures are all aggregate figures for the whole region. When these figures are disaggregated for sub-areas, important variations emerge which show that the impact of unemployment has been spatially very uneven. Bristol has borne the brunt of the rise in unemployment, with parts of the inner city and south Bristol being particularly hard-hit. In October 1984, for example, when the Avon rate was 10.7 per cent (and the UK rate was 12.0 per cent), there were employment exchange areas on the eastern fringe with rates as low as 6.4 per cent, while the Bristol exchange area (covering inner and south Bristol) had an unemployment rate of 16.9 per cent. The high Bristol rate was particularly associated with the heavy loss of less skilled manufacturing jobs in inner and south Bristol through redundancies and closures.

The detailed pattern of unemployment rates within the Bristol district is shown for 1976 and 1981 in Figures 2.11 and 2.12. In 1976 the average unemployment rate in the district was 6.0 per cent. Figure 2.11 shows that even at this time there was a distinct cluster of areas with unemployment rates of over 20 per cent (the highest being 26.4 per cent) extending in a small arc around the central area of the city and including St Pauls, Montpelier, and Easton. Although high unemployment rates also appeared in areas covering the poorer parts of some of the outer council estates (see Figure 2.13), such as Knowle and Hartcliffe in the south, the bulk of the high-unemployment areas were enclosed within the Bristol Planning Department's 'inner-city' boundary, as defined in 1977.

However, the definition of the inner city used by the planners was a very broad one. Rates of unemployment and a measure of housing quality were used to define a compact inner-city area covering approximately one-third of the city with a population of around 128,000. The designation of such an area was essentially part of Bristol's campaign to obtain government recognition of its urban problems in the late 1970s, a campaign which will be discussed in more detail in a later chapter on politics and policy. The precise boundaries served useful political functions, but they give a false sense of internal homogeneity. Thus, Bassett and Short (1978) used census data to identify seven different neighbourhood types within this zone. These included areas of social stress and overcrowding with a large multi-ethnic population; areas of public housing with an older, largely white, population; areas of private renting; and areas of owner-occupation. Some of the areas dominated by private renting and owner-occupation, such as Clifton and Redland to the northwest of the city centre, were in fact among the most affluent areas in the city on a range of other variables. High unemployment rates were associated only with specific sub-areas within this inner-city zone.

Figure 2.12 shows the distribution of unemployment in 1981 after the recession had deepened and the city-wide unemployment rate had risen to 11.2 per cent. The core of areas with unemployment rates above 20 per cent still centred on St Pauls (where unemployment rates had risen to over 42 per cent), but the areas experiencing unemployment rates of over 10 per cent had spread to cover most of the inner city. At the same time, unemployment on

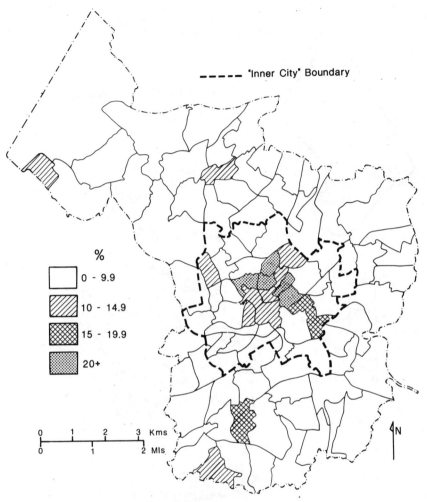

Fig. 2.11. Unemployment rates in Bristol, 1976
Source: Department of Employment and Avon County Planning Department.

some of the outer council estates had risen rapidly to over 15 per cent. This deterioration was particularly strongly marked on the large council estates in south Bristol and on the Southmead estate in the north. As a result, although the highest unemployment rates were still to be found in the inner-city area, only 38.4 per cent of the total *number* unemployed were found within this area. However, if allowance is made for the general rise in unemployment over time, a considerable degree of continuity emerges in the relative impacts of unemployment within the city. The twenty worst ranking areas in terms of unemployment rates for 1971 turn out to be almost identical to the twenty worst ranking areas in 1981. Only three areas appear in 1981 that were not in

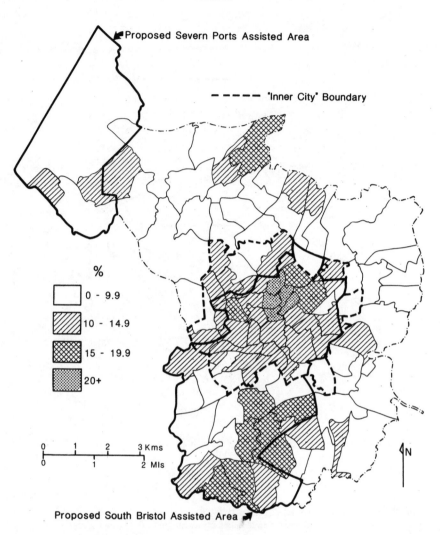

Fig. 2.12. Unemployment rates in Bristol, 1981
Source: Department of Employment and Avon County Planning Department.

the 1971 list. Both lists include the central core centring on St Pauls and the poorer areas of the south Bristol and Southmead council estates.

Social stress and inequality

The association between unemployment and other measures of disadvantage has been explored in some detail by Bristol's Planning Department in a report on poverty and deprivation in the city (Bristol City Council 1984).

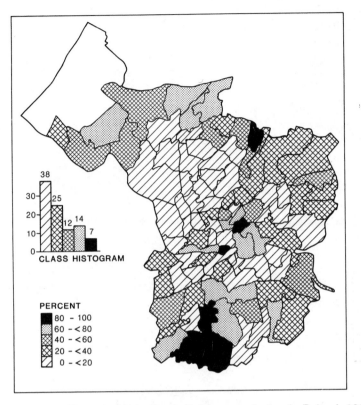

Fig. 2.13. Households in Council Accommodation in Bristol, 1981
Source: Population Census, 1981, Small Area Statistics.

The report examined the distribution of six key indicators for 1981. Two related to income (unemployment and children in receipt of free school meals), one to housing circumstances (overcrowding), one to family circumstances (children subject to supervision orders), one to the incidence of debt (electricity disconnections), and one to the possession of consumer goods (households without a car). Each indicator was mapped separately, and the 'worst fifth' areas (those areas with the highest scores which, when added together, comprised 20 per cent of the population) were identified in each case.

Not surprisingly, there was a considerable degree of overlap between the distribution of these indicators. This led to the identification of areas with 'multiple problems'—i.e., areas which fell in the worst fifth category on at least four of the indicators. The areas are shown in figure 2.14. One-fifth of the population of Bristol was estimated to live in these areas, although many would not be directly affected by any or all of these problems. Although an

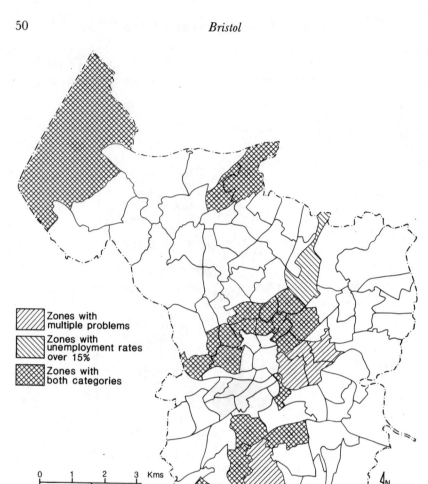

Fig. 2.14. Areas with multiple indicators of disadvantage in Bristol, 1981
Source: Bristol Planning Department.

inner-city block of areas emerged, this was clearly different in its form and extent from the area designated as the 'inner city' by Bristol planners in 1977. This more sophisticated definition identified a 'crescent' extending only partly around the city centre. The analysis also clearly identified three other blocks of areas outside of any definition of the inner city, covering parts of the south Bristol council estates, the Southmead estate, and Avonmouth.

It is evident, therefore, that not all areas close to the central area, or all council estates, were multiple-problem areas. Areas of older terrace housing to the south-west of the city centre, such as Southville and Bedminster, traditionally included as part of the inner city, did not emerge as multiple-problem areas. At the same time, certain council estates did not feature in the list of worst areas on any indicator. For example, although parts of the Southmead estate featured among the worst areas on five indicators, the nearby Henbury estate did not feature at all. Furthermore, there was also considerable diversity within the blocks of multiple-problem areas. Although the four inner-city neighbourhoods of St Pauls, Easton, Barton Hill, and Cotham and Hotwells all stood out as areas with 'multiple problems', there were considerable differences between them. St Pauls, for example, stood out because of its very high unemployment rates and the proportion of households from ethnic minority groups (almost 30 per cent). It was, and still is, an area with a mix of owner-occupation, private renting, and council housing. Barton Hill, on the other hand, is an area with a much higher proportion of council housing, having experienced substantial redevelopment from the late 1950s to the early 1970s. The Cotham and Hotwells area includes a mix of high-status owner-occupation and lower-quality renting.

Some of this diversity is brought out by the variations in unemployment rates within these different multiple-problem areas. As figure 2.14 shows, most of the high-unemployment zones fell within the multiple-problem areas, but there were considerable differences in the levels of unemployment. The multiple-problem areas centred on St Pauls all experienced very high unemployment (over 30 per cent). They also ranked very highly on all the other indicators. Other inner-city areas, such as Cotham and Hotwells, had generally lower unemployment rates (15–20 per cent) and ranked even lower on the other indicators. The Barton Hill area had low unemployment rates (below 15 per cent) but figured within the 'worst fifth' zones more on indicators such as statutory supervisions and free school meals.

Finally, an important question is whether inequalities between areas within the city increased over time as overall economic conditions worsened. One way of approaching this is to compare the same data on multiple problems for 1976 and 1981, looking in particular at the relative concentration of problems in the 'worst fifth' areas. On the basis of such comparisons, the . Bristol Planning Department has concluded that there was considerable continuity in the distribution and relative concentration of social problems in the city, with little evidence of increased polarization. In fact, there was slight evidence that the incidence of problems was spreading out, with faster increases being registered in areas outside the multiple problem zones (Bristol City Council 1984).

In conclusion, it would appear that by 1981 there was only a loose association between concentrations of poverty and deprivation and a geographically defined 'inner-city' area. Multiple problems were found with similar intensity within inner-city areas and on outer council estates. The St Pauls area, however, stood out as something of an exception in terms of the scale of its problems. Finally, there were also important variations in the way the different indicators were associated in different multiple-problem zones.

The Good City? Bristol's Problems in Comparative Perspective

It is clear from what has been said above that Bristol has experienced rapidly rising unemployment and increasing social problems over the past decade. However, this is an experience common to most major urban areas in the country. How do Bristol's problems compare with those of other cities? A recent survey of social problems in the nineteen largest cities in England and Wales outside London provides some useful information (Redfern 1982). Bristol ranked sixth in terms of population in this list. The report used 1981 Census data and distinguished between city-wide and inner-city averages. Inner cities were defined fairly crudely as those wards nearest the city centre containing approximately one-third of the city's population. Cluster analysis was then used to group wards into ten socioeconomic categories with different characteristics and different combinations of problems. Certain of these categories of wards were designated as 'problem' categories, most of them being located in inner-city areas. When the cities were ranked in terms of the numbers and percentages of the population living in problem wards, Bristol came twelfth in population terms, with a problem ward population of 62,000, and joint thirteenth in percentage terms, with 16 per cent of the total population in problem wards. In numbers it ranked just below Newcastle and just above Coventry. In percentage terms it ranked below Coventry and above Derby. The percentage rankings, in particular, brought out a significant break between the top eleven cities, with percentages above 26 per cent, and the bottom group of cities (which included Bristol), which had percentages below 17 per cent. These problem ward percentages were found to be highly correlated with levels of unemployment.

From this analysis, one can conclude that in 1981 Bristol appeared to fare relatively well for its size in comparison with other major cities in the country. Bristol is grouped with cities such as Southampton, Plymouth, Cardiff, Derby, and Sheffield, which are referred to as enjoying 'more favourable conditions' than the rest. Nevertheless, Bristol was one of only eight cities which contained 'Category One' wards with the worst combination of conditions. These were centred on the St Pauls area. In other words, Bristol had inner-city conditions comparable to the worst in the country, but these were concentrated in a relatively small area.

The above analysis is suggestive, although the comparisons are inevitably crude at this scale and the data capture only part of the complexity of social problems. Nevertheless, a similar picture emerges from the Department of the Environment's (DOE's) analysis of the ranking of local authorities in 1981 on various urban deprivation indices. In a list of 150 local authorities, Bristol ranked twenty-sixth in terms of population decline, fifty-fifth in terms of single-parent households, ninetieth in terms of unemployment, and lower still on other variables such as overcrowding and mortality. Bristol did not in fact appear in the list of the fifty worst authorities in the DOE's classification.

In summary, one can conclude that, on the available evidence, although Bristol has substantial problem areas, and conditions within them have got considerably worse over the past decade or so, the city has fared relatively well compared with other major cities in the country. This fact is of course no consolation to those experiencing those problems in the city.

Notes

1. Employment data are drawn from the Census of Employment. Annual Census data were available until 1978, when there was a two-year gap before the 1981 Census, the latest available at the time of the research.
2. Shift-share analysis, although widely used, has been the subject of much discussion and criticism. The view taken here is broadly in line with that of Fothergill and Gudgin (1979), who conclude that the technique is reasonably robust and provides a useful method of standardization that can point to questions for further research. It is important, however, not to harbour unrealistic expectations about what can be explained by the technique. Some of the more detailed technical criticisms of the technique are avoided by adopting the modified formula proposed by Bishop and Simpson (1972), which provides a more accurate measure of the structural affect than alternative methods.
3. The pattern of corporate ownership has been traced through a variety of sources detailed in Bassett (1984). The data relate to the built-up urban area and exclude a handful of plants in the semi-rural periphery.

3

Economic and Employment Change in Five Key Sectors

This chapter focuses in greater detail on a number of sectors which have been central to the processes of change in the locality. The aim is to elaborate on the actual patterns of change and to examine the underlying causal mechanisms in a way that more aggregate analysis is incapable of doing. This sets the scene for the general consideration of the restructuring process, labour market issues, and public policy in the chapters which follow. Five sectors are looked at (summarized in Table 3.1). Two—Tobacco, and Paper, Board, and Packaging—are long established in the locality but have suffered major job losses more recently. Aerospace, despite some employment decline, remains buoyant and has to some extent retarded the more general decline of manufacturing. Electronics, at the heart of the locality's high-technology image, has expanded rapidly but from a very narrow employment base and has in fact had little real impact in terms of job numbers. Finally, Insurance, has been a major growth sector in the locality along with other financial services. With the exception of Electronics, these sectors account for a high proportion of local employment relative to the national picture. They have also experienced particularly rapid restructuring and employment change. The inclusion of Insurance allows specific consideration of at least one important element of the service sector. Tobacco in the manufacturing sector, and Insurance in the service sector, are, moreover, particularly important in relation to female employment.

The aim was, for each sector, to analyse economic restructuring and employment change in the locality, situated in their broader sectoral and corporate context. Local processes and patterns of change in a particular sector reflect competitive pressures, changes in market demand, technological change, changes in the production process, and other factors such as national government policies operating within the sector as a whole at national and international scales. They also reflect the specific corporate make-up of particular sectors in the locality—change in local workplaces reflects processes, including conscious strategy, operating at the level of the overall corporate structures of which they are a part, which may well be national or international and extend across different sectors and markets.

Much of the emphasis is on employment change. It is important, however, to remember that change in employment and change in output are by no means synonymous. Indeed, increased productivity, represented by an increase in output per head, is generally, from a management perspective at

Table 3.1. *Key sectors: summary employment statistics, Bristol, 1981*

Sector[a]	Employment 1981	Proportion of total employment %	Female employment as a proportion of sectoral %	Location[b] quotient	Employment change, 1971–81				
					Total No.	Total %	Male %	Female %	Great Britain %
Tobacco	5,430	1.8	52.4	1.4	−2,373	−30.4	−19.9	−37.8	−17.9
Paper, Printing, and Packaging	9,000	3.0	29.5	1.2	−7,342	−44.9	−41.7	−51.4	−13.6
Paper, Board, and Packaging	5,110	1.7	28.5	2.2	−6,345	−55.4	−52.6	−61.2	−26.1
Aerospace	21,650	7.3	10.4	8.3	−2,146	−9.0	−10.0	1.4	−12.3
Electrical Engineering	4,390	1.5	24.1	0.5	−273	−5.9	−3.2	−13.3	−15.8
Electronics	2,130	0.7	18.4	0.6	1,244	141.0	162.9	76.1	−12.5
Insurance, Banking, and Finance	22,370	7.6	53.0	1.2	9,440	73.0	76.5	70.0	35.9
Insurance	7,610	2.6	45.3	1.8	3,747	97.0	91.0	104.8	10.2
All manufacturing	83,760	28.2	22.2	1.0	−22,990	−21.5	−18.0	−31.8	−24.9
All services	187,320	63.8	52.9	1.0	21,694	13.1	1.4	26.1	15.3
Total employment	298,520	100.0	41.0		−1,411	−0.5	−7.8	12.5	−2.3

[a] Sectors are defined in terms of 1968 SIC and MLH categories as follows: Tobacco, MLH 240; Paper, Printing, and Packaging, SIC XVIII; Paper, Board, and Packaging, MLHs 481–4; Aerospace, MLH 383; Electrical Engineering, SIC IX; Electronics, MLHs 364–7; Insurance, Banking, and Finance, SIC XXIV; Insurance, MLH 860; Manufacturing, SICs III–XIX; Services, SICs XXII–XXVII.

[b] Proportion of total employment in the sector locally, divided by the proportion of total employment in the sector nationally.

Source: Annual Census of Employment, Department of Employment.

Table 3.2. Change in net output and net output per head in key sectors, Great Britain, 1971–1982 (in real terms)[a]

Sector[b]	Change, 1971–9			Change, 1979–82		
	Employ-ment[c] %	Total output %	Output per head %	Employ-ment[c] %	Total output %	Output per head %
Tobacco	−8.1	2.9	12.1	−16.4	20.4	44.4
Paper, Printing, and Packaging	−10.1	22.2	36.0	−14.1	−7.7	7.4
Paper, Board, and Packaging	−14.4	22.4	41.8	−21.9	−23.8	−2.4
Aerospace	−10.3	10.9	23.6	−1.6	20.4	17.9
Electrical Engineering	−11.2	11.6	25.6	−19.6	−5.4	17.7
Electronics	−12.2	17.9	37.7	−9.6	9.3	20.8
All manufacturing	−11.6	16.2	31.4	−22.4	−19.1	−4.3

[a] Original information converted to real terms using GDP deflator at factor cost. (*Source*: *Economic Trends*, HMSO).

[b] Sectors for 1971–9 defined as in Table 3.1. Sectors for 1979–81 are based on equivalent 1980 SIC categories which do not correspond exactly to 1968 SICs. Manufacturing is defined as 1968 SICs III–XIX. Census of Production information is not available for service industries.

[c] Employment figures are derived from the Census of Production and do not correspond exactly with Census of Employment figures.

Source: Annual Census of Production, HMSO.

least, an explicit objective of production change. This is the case whether output is rising or falling. Employment change itself is in a sense the outcome of a combination of change in output and change in productivity. This is clear from Table 3.2, which indicates, at the national level, the relationship between employment change, output, and productivity for four of the five key sectors.[1]

The table shows that from 1971 to 1979, although employment fell in each sector, output actually increased across the board, albeit to varying degrees—the phenomenon of 'job-loss', as opposed to jobless, growth. The pattern after 1979 was more diverse, reflecting the differential impacts of deepening recession. Again, employment in each sector fell. Output however increased strongly in Aerospace and Tobacco, with productivity increasing in Tobacco in particular, contrasting with Paper, Board, and Packaging, where output slumped along with employment.

The study itself was based on an extensive programme of information-gathering, and in particular on semi-structured interviews with a range of general and personnel managers in a panel of thirty local workplaces, primarily the major employers, spread across the five sectors.[2] This was supplemented from a number of secondary sources including company reports and accounts, the trade and general press, and other academic or industry studies relating to the firms themselves and the sectors of which they are a part. This both fleshed out material relating to individual workplaces and helped to establish the sectoral and corporate context.

The five sectors accounted for over 40 per cent of manufacturing employment in the locality in 1981. Coverage of services was however much thinner, with Insurance representing only 4 per cent and Financial Services as a whole, 12 per cent of all service employment. Conventional arguments that much of the service sector is 'dependent' on local economic activity and employment rather than fundamental to it only partly justify this imbalance, particularly given the scale of growth in Miscellaneous Services identified in Chapter 2. It in part reflects the methodology, which of necessity focused primarily on the major employers in order to pick up broad patterns of change in each sector—much of Miscellaneous Services employment, in particular, is in a vast range of smaller workplaces, and smaller workplaces in general are not covered in any detail.

The summaries, focusing in turn on each of the five sectors, follow the same general format, including an outline of the sector locally, the broader corporate and sectoral context, the main dimensions of production change, and, finally, employment change and related labour market issues. The nature of the analysis, however, varies to some extent with the composition of each sector. Tobacco employment, for example, is accounted for by a single major employer, whereas Electronics encompasses many individual workplaces across a variety of different markets. Aerospace and Insurance are both characterized by a small number of major employers, but whereas the Insurance sector is relatively homogeneous in terms of market forces and product, Aerospace employment has been tied to the fortunes of a range of different major projects.

The analysis of production change was informed to some extent by Massey and Meegan's (1982) analysis of job loss, in which they identified three main forms of production reorganization: *intensification*, defined as changes designed to increase labour productivity but without major new investment or reorganization of production techniques; *investment and technical change*, where job loss occurred in the context of significant investment and often related to changes in production techniques; and *rationalization*, defined as simple capacity cuts. All represented different responses to the recession, different attempts to restore profitability. This emphasized the fact that different causal mechanisms and combinations of mechanisms underly job change.

In practice, as Massey and Meegan themselves suggested, it proved necessary in the Bristol study to extend and elaborate on these basic forms of production reorganization. In part this reflected the fact that the study included sectors characterized by employment increase as well as job loss. It also, however, reflected the complexity of the processes of production reorganization on the ground. Broad patterns of sectoral change are difficult to distinguish in locality-based analyses, and at the level of specific workplaces and corporate structures. This made it particularly difficult to separate out the relative importance of different 'pure' forms of production change.

Production change is not, however, simply reflected in job gain or job loss but has specific impacts on different groups in the labour market. The analysis of employment issues looks, therefore, at the impacts of production change in terms of specific processes of employment change and their implications for the composition of the labour force. This involves focusing on the details of job loss and recruitment, and on labour markets internal to particular workplaces. This in turn emphasizes the fact that recruitment processes, employment practices, the operation of internal labour markets, and the organization of the work process are all integral parts of the continuous process of production change.

Tobacco

Tobacco processing, rooted in Bristol's mercantilist past, represents one of the locality's traditionally dominant manufacturing sectors. By the early nineteenth century tobacco was one of the city's largest single sources of employment, and, following the formation of the Imperial Tobacco Company in 1901, was the headquarters of the country's largest company (Alford 1973). Though still important locally, with 1.8 per cent of employment compared with 1.3 per cent nationally, employment in this sector has declined markedly both in the long term and more recently. Employment locally fell by 30 per cent (nearly 2,500) over the decade to 1981 compared with only 19 per cent nationally, and by a further 20 per cent up to 1984. Total employment locally fell from nearly 8,000 in 1971 to 5,500 by 1981 and to just over 4,000 by 1984—almost half the 1971 figure. However, Bristol still accounted for nearly 20 per cent of all UK tobacco employment in 1981.

Two particular aspects of tobacco employment can be noted. First, it has been a major source of female manufacturing employment in the locality. Women represented 59 per cent of total employment in 1971, over 4,500 in absolute terms. Female employment has however declined more rapidly than male, falling by 39 per cent over 1971–81 compared with 20 per cent. It nevertheless employed almost 3,000 women in 1981, 15 per cent of all female manufacturing employment in the locality. Second, employment—and job loss—has been particularly concentrated in south Bristol, an area which, as described in Chapter 2, has experienced high and rising unemployment relative to the rest of the locality as unemployment generally has climbed.

Employment locally is associated almost entirely with the Bristol operations of one company, Imperial Tobacco Limited (ITL). This in turn is the Tobacco Division of the Imperial Group, whose interests include brewing, foods and leisure, and a US hotel chain. The Tobacco Division accounts for just over half of group turnover. It represents Britain's only domestically based tobacco producer, with 45 per cent of the UK cigarette market. Bristol was, historically, the headquarters of Wills, one of the two main branches within the Group's Tobacco Division; the other, Players, was headquartered at Nottingham. A third branch, Ogdens, producing pipe tobacco, was based at Liverpool. These branches were relatively autonomous up to 1973, when a holding company was established, and were subsequently merged in 1983.

Bristol is now the Tobacco Division's largest employment centre with a third of the UK total. It is a major production centre for cigarettes and hand-rolled tobacco. Following recent restructuring, however, it also accounts for the bulk of higher-order functions, including ITL's head office and one of the three regional distribution centres. Bristol thus has around 21 per cent of hourly paid and supervisory production staff, but over half of all salaried staff and two-thirds of management personnel in the company as a whole. The other main production centres include Nottingham (32 per cent of hourly paid and supervisory staff), Glasgow (14 per cent), Ipswich (9 per cent), Newcastle (9 per cent), Liverpool (6 per cent), and Swindon (3 per cent)—see Table 3.3 below. Production capacity at Stirling was closed down in 1983, and the closure of Newcastle was announced in mid-1985. Historically rooted in Bristol, a major part of overall Group functions are still locally based, as are around three-quarters of nearly 400 head office staff, although the Board meets in London.

Employment decline and recomposition in Bristol reflect a major process of restructuring in the early 1970s, involving investment in and relocation to new factory and office premises within Bristol and a more radical reorganization of the Tobacco Division as a whole in the 1980s. This reflected both the market context for tobacco products and, in the later period particularly, a more general attempt to restructure the Group as a whole following a major slump in the late 1970s. In this sense, change in the Tobacco sector reflects both the specific structure, performance, and strategy of a single major employer and the more general sectoral context.

Corporate context

Reorganization at Group level formed the context for change in tobacco production. There has been a common pattern of diversification away from tobacco among all the leading companies, both in the long term and more recently in the face of market decline. This was facilitated by the strong cash flow and considerable profits generated from tobacco products. The Bristol company had historic interests in paper and packaging. From the early 1960s, however, it pursued a vigorous strategy of diversification, mainly into food products and subsequently into additional paper and packaging products, brewing and leisure, and a US hotel chain. Diversification failed, however, to establish a firm alternative base in the face of declining tobacco markets, and the Group ran into serious difficulties by the late 1970s. It was less successful in this sense than its competitors who had followed a similar strategy. Pre-tax profits fell by 25 per cent in 1979–81, having failed to grow in previous years. This reflected, in particular, a slump in tobacco profits, but also the declining performance of other divisions as the recession hit consumer spending. The Group had pulled out of its paper and packaging interests by 1982, including the closure of an unprofitable Bristol board mill in 1980 with the loss of 1,700 jobs. Some food interests had also been disposed of.

A major programme of new investment was initiated in the Tobacco Division in 1980. With the overall slump in group profits, a more general 'recovery programme' was put into action, involving a general productivity drive, corporate restructuring, and the disposal of less profitable or less strategically appropriate businesses; job losses were 'unfortunately a necessary feature of the process of ensuring a prosperous future for the Group as a whole' (1981 Company Report). A broader strategic framework was also developed within which divisional profitability was to be pursued. In the case of tobacco, this essentially involved an attempt to secure the company's market share and, by maximizing cost efficiency and productivity, to generate acceptable rates of profit albeit from a mature market in which long-term secular decline was likely to continue, strongly dependent on future levels of taxation.

Sectoral context

The sector is characterized by a strongly competitive UK market based on branding and heavy expenditure on the marketing of virtually standard products. The overall UK market has been shrinking since the early 1970s— cigarettes by 2–3 per cent per annum—reflecting the decreasing popularity of smoking in general, the health issue in particular, and price increases arising mainly from taxation. Sharp increases in taxation in 1981, superimposed on the long-term decline, were reflected in a 15 per cent drop in cigarette sales over the year. European markets have also been shrinking. There has however been some growth in Third World markets and other opportunities for market penetration beyond Europe.

Six major multinationals account for around 40 per cent of cigarette production worldwide, the rest largely being produced in the communist countries or by state monopolies, as in France. Although it has 45 per cent of the domestic cigarette market—which constitutes the major part of overall tobacco products—the Bristol-based company is unique among the major producers in that non-UK sales or production are minimal. The US-based BAT, for example, generated 46 per cent of its 1981 profits from the expanding Latin American, Asian, and African markets; Philip Morris (Marlboro) produce in the USSR and Eastern Europe; and RJ Reynolds produce in China. In part this reflects an earlier market-sharing agreement with American Tobacco Company which allocated the European market to the US company and the UK market to domestic companies. Wider geographical diversification into growth markets has not however been a subsequent part of company strategy.

Tied to the shrinking UK market, ITL's market share was also falling from the mid-1970s in the face of strong competition from overseas multinationals. Its share of the cigarette market in particular fell, from 66 per cent in 1976 to 45 per cent by 1983. One specific factor was the harmonization of UK and EEC taxation which cheapened king-size brands, leading to a significant shift in demand; the company's existing markets, unlike rivals such as the US-owned Gallahers marketing Benson and Hedges, were mainly in smaller cigarettes, and it failed, initially at least, to break into the king-size market. Its competitors were able to build on their established market presence.

Production change

The development of tobacco products manufacture has turned on successive investments in faster machines for 'making and packing' and the mechanization of preparation, handling, and storage of materials and products. Cigarettes in particular represent a highly standardized product with low costs and few risks related to innovation. With the emphasis on process innovation, this has encouraged capital investment and the replacement of labour by capital equipment. Reflecting this, there was a major investment in Bristol in the early 1970s in a new production unit and a head office building for the Bristol branch of the Tobacco Division. The development also involved major capital investment in the automated preparation, blending, storage, and handling of tobacco, making it the company's most modern productive unit. The aim was to relocate production from an outdated complex of buildings just to the south of the city centre, so as to centralize and reorganize production and facilitate new investment with a view to achieving major increases in efficiency and productivity. Increased output as such was not envisaged, and significant reductions in employment were therefore achieved. Faced with declining market shares, the company in 1980 then initiated a major programme of re-equipment. This however was overaken by more drastic action following the profit slump in 1980 and 1981. Restructuring has involved a combination of re-equipment, management restructuring, and the reorganization of production. Computer modelling of the various options across different production locations was used as part of the decision process.

Investment in process technology. Re-equipment initiated in 1980 aimed to achieve a major increase in productivity in order to retain profitability, price competitiveness and market share against manufacturers who were themselves investing heavily in process technology. 'New generation machines'

(NGMs) can make cigarettes at 7,200 per minute compared with 2,500 for conventional machines and can pack 360 packets compared with 135. NGM production modules allow 6 employees to generate the same output per unit time as 14 with older machines. NGMs were introduced across all production centres, partially replacing older machines. Under this programme, there was major investment in Bristol. Further investment is not anticipated in the short term. The automatic weighing and packing of hand-rolling tobacco, particularly labour-intensive in the past, has similarly dramatic implications for productivity, with a new module allowing 3.3 employees to produce the same as 9.25 on old equipment. With hand-rolling tobacco based solely at Bristol, this has significant, specifically local, employment implications—with further investment to come, employment was expected to fall from 500 to 150–60. Other investment has been mainly in incremental improvement in mechanization and handling. This is likely to be an ongoing process.

Management reorganization   The Tobacco Division holding company established in 1973 was concerned mainly with financial planning and control. The operating units centred on Bristol, Nottingham, and Liverpool retained separate head offices and a considerable degree of autonomy and corporate identity. In 1982–83 the three units were merged into one and virtually all divisional, as opposed to production, management functions were centralized in Bristol. This constituted the head office for the whole Tobacco Division and occupied the head office originally built for the Bristol operating unit. Only the sales forces, tied to separate brand names, retained their identity for marketing purposes, although some traditional Nottingham brands are now produced in Bristol and vice versa.

The aim of this reorganization was to cut overheads and administrative costs, to centralize management, and to increase its efficiency and effectiveness, with significant reductions in managerial and staff grades. Most Bristol branch personnel were transformed into new head office staff, and there were some transfers to Bristol from Nottingham (about 56 in all) and elsewhere. Liverpool and Nottingham in particular, as formerly distinct head office locations suffered considerable reductions in managerial and salaried grades (Table 3.3). Other functions have subsequently been rationalized and centralized on Bristol, including R & D, which was formerly split between Bristol and Nottingham.

Bristol was thus confirmed as the head office for the Division as a whole, with an increase in higher-order functions and an expansion of managerial staff in absolute but especially in relative terms. Salaried and managerial staff fell by 13 per cent in 1980–4 in the Division as a whole and by 25 per cent in Nottingham, but *increased* in Bristol by 14 per cent.

This raises the question of why Bristol was selected as the new divisional base. The obvious main alternative was Nottingham, historically a major

Table 3.3. *Employment change, tobacco case study, 1980–1984*

Production site	October 1980		March 1984		Percentage change		
	Production staff	Salaried & managerial	Production staff	Salaried & managerial	Production staff	Salaried & managerial	Total
Nottingham	4,200	1,392	2,700	1,044	−36	−25	−33
Stirling		24	—	1	—	—	—
Glasgow	2,800	232	1,200	151	−57	−35	−55
Newcastle	1,047	174	720	95	−31	−45	−33
Bristol	**2,880**	**1,528**	**1,810**	**1,742**	**−37**	**+14**	**−19**
Swindon	349	20	244	19	−30	−5	−29
Ipswich	933	52	728	44	−22	−15	−22
Liverpool	828	259	610	110	−26	−58	−34
Total	13,037	3,681	8,012	3,206	−39	−13	−33

operating unit and company in its own right, and comparable in terms of scale of production to Bristol. In fact, the choice was reported to have been fairly close. Bristol was however selected for three main reasons. First, it was the 'seat' of the Group as a whole, which originated in Bristol, the 'natural centre to which other things gravitate', as one manager put it. The majority of group functions are based in Bristol and the divisional holding company was also established here in 1973. Bristol was in a sense more 'central' than Nottingham in corporate terms.

Second, it was estimated that redundancy and transfer costs would be lower than for Nottingham, particularly given the number of holding company and other management staff already established in Bristol. Echoing insurance company relocation, there was also the danger that key staff would refuse to move to Nottingham, or prove costly in the form of inducements. Staff transfer from Nottingham was seen as easier, given Bristol's attractiveness. It seems likely, as well, that Bristol-based managers may also have had more influence and an element of personal interest in the decision-making process. Finally, the new Wills head office at Bristol represented very suitable and prestigious premises for the overall divisional head office compared with Nottingham, where new investment would have been required.

Restructuring production   A programme of rationalization and relocation of production was initiated in 1982 in response to long-term market shrinkage, the financial crises of 1981, and the impact of that year's Budget. By 1980, production overall was down to 60 per cent of design capacity and was carrying the overheads of ten production sites (including two each in Bristol and Glasgow) plus three head offices. Increased productivity through re-equipment was exacerbating the situation. With production expected to be halved over the decade to 1985, the company had reached a point where it could no longer wait for re-equipment to be completed before more fundamental restructuring had to be undertaken.

A strategy was developed based on a computer model of the options in terms of investment, relocation, closure, shift systems, etc., under different market assumptions, taking account of the existing structure of production, distribution, and fixed capital. The company sought 'the most economical solution consistent with social, political, and employee relations factors'. Although not included in the model itself, the company was aware of local unemployment levels. It needed a package that was acceptable to unions nationally. It also saw a risk, in terms of brand image and sales north of the border, attached to a complete withdrawal from Scotland (Glasgow and Stirling). In strictly economic terms, this was marginally more favourable than the strategy adopted and was seriously considered, but it would have increased the risk and aggravation. Political pressures at government level were not apparently implicated in the selected strategy.

The strategy that emerged involved concentrating production on a smaller number of sites in order to save on overheads and non-production staff. A single new green-field site was considered as an option (Cwmbran was mentioned as an example). This option was ruled out, however, by the combined costs of closing existing capacity and of new development.

Under the agreed strategy, the cigarette factory in Stirling was closed. There were major changes at Glasgow, where one of two factories was closed and cigarette manufacture was replaced by increased production of cigars and the addition of hand-rolling tobacco production. New investment was supplemented by £600,000 from the Scottish Department of Industry and attracted a 22 per cent Regional Development Grant—financial assistance was described as an advantage but not crucial, 'something of a bonus', and was not in fact built into the formal modelling exercise. Employment at Glasgow fell from 2,800 in October 1980 to 1,200 by March 1984—proportionately well above losses in the Division as a whole. In Bristol a cigar factory employing 700, mainly women, was closed and cigar production was concentrated at Glasgow. There was some increase of cigarette production in Bristol after production was ended in Glasgow. Hand-rolling tobacco production was transferred from the old factory complex to the new factory, initiating the final vacating of these premises.

Distribution was also reorganized into three regional centres at Bristol, Nottingham, and Glasgow, entailing some new investment in these centres and the closure of distribution centres elsewhere. Finally, reorganization of production was accompanied by continuing intensification through negotiated reductions in staffing involving demanding and productivity agreements in different areas, although, with most of production already very capital-intensive and production tied to continuous machine-based processes, opportunities are limited. Commenting on the overall programme in its 1983 Annual Report, the Group observed that:

the closure during the year of three factories in Bristol, Glasgow, and Stirling and the completion of the major reorganization of the Division's structure have contributed significant cost saving benefits. . . . [The Tobacco Division] has continued to implement a series of major productivity improvement programmes, including substantial investment in new generation production machinery and the initial stages of rationalization of its distribution into three regional distribution centres. In consequence, manufacture has benefited from significant real gains in productivity.

The employment implications of the overall restructuring process are detailed in the following section.

Urban and regional policy as such has been only marginally relevant to the overall process of change. The local authority role in the Bristol area has been primarily through the planning system, in relation to the development of the new site in the 1970s and, more recently, the company's plans to redevelop redundant land and premises. The local Jobcentre did develop a special relationship with the company in relation to employees taking redundancy but seeking new employment. Central government departments have not played any apparent role in Bristol, although, as already noted, the Regional Development Grant plus additional assistance was useful though not essential to the restructuring of production at Glasgow. The major way in which government impinges on this sector as a whole, and specifically on employment, is in fact through the level of taxation. Fiscal policies, parliamentary lobbying, and related representations, and the continuing battles over the smoking-and-health issue, are obviously directly relevant to the future of the sector and of tobacco-related employment nationally and locally.

Employment

As indicated earlier, overall tobacco employment fell by 30 per cent locally over the decade to 1981, compared with only 19 per cent nationally. This relatively rapid fall reflected primarily the process of relocating production to new factory premises, involving heavy investment in new plant and equipment plus the reorganization and intensification of work practices. Employment transfer was accompanied by increased 'natural wastage', mainly among female staff. Company-level information allows a more detailed look at the more recent period.

The impact of restructuring   The corporate context at Group level was itself one of employment decline—total UK employment across all divisions fell by 28 per cent (25,000) between 1980 and 1983, reflecting both closures and disposals as well as job reductions in continuing operations. Sales, on the other hand, rose by 8 per cent in real terms, in part indicating rising productivity. Tobacco Division employment at the national level declined more rapidly— by 33 per cent over roughly the same period (October 1980–March 1984). Locally, however, decline was less severe (Table 3.3). In Bristol, Tobacco Division employment fell by only 19 per cent (860) compared with, for example, 33 per cent in Newcastle and 55 per cent in Glasgow, hit by more radical change.

This reflects above all a change in the *composition* of employment and the centralization of Tobacco Division headquarter functions on Bristol. Whereas hourly paid and supervisory employment locally fell by 37 per cent over this period, roughly in line with national decline, salaried and managerial staff actually *increased* by 14 per cent compared with a drop, nationally, of around 13 per cent. Decline in production employment was thus offset to a considerable degree, numerically at least, by salaried and managerial employment, reflecting Bristol's enhanced role in corporate terms. This has been mirrored in the decline in salaried, and particularly managerial, staff elsewhere. Managerial staff in Liverpool and Nottingham, previously operating unit headquarters, fell by 58 per cent (29) and 52 per cent (115). Subsequent changes including the further centralization of functions such as R & D have, moreover, reinforced this pattern.

Bristol has been left, then, with a disproportionately high share of managerial and administrative staff. Whereas in 1984 it had 32 per cent of the Division's total UK employment, it had only 23 per cent of hourly paid and supervisory staff; however, it had 52 per cent of salaried and 67 per cent of managerial staff, emphasizing its corporate function. Employment decline was thus accompanied by a marked recomposition of the workforce in occupational terms.

These changes reflected a combination of new investment, management restructuring, rationalization and relocation, and negotiated agreements on manning levels and productivity. For the Division as a whole, the company was able to estimate with some confidence that, out of total employment reductions of 2,600 over the three years to mid-1984, 900 reflected the introduction of new generation machinery (effectively, 'technical change'), 250, negotiated agreements ('intensification'), and 1,450, declining sales ('rationalization'). In the case of Bristol, investment in technical change plus changes in work practices were particularly important through the 1970s, with rationalization, including the closure of the cigar factory, becoming increasingly important in the early 1980s.

Job loss Employment decline and recomposition in Bristol has been achieved through a combination of natural wastage, early retirement, and voluntary redundancy co-ordinated with a major redeployment of staff from older premises to the new complex. A freeze on recruitment combined with normal turnover plus retirement achieved some reductions. More significantly, an early-retirement, voluntary redundancy scheme was initiated. This also affected the new factory, which included the majority of employment by this time, in order to make way for transfers in from the cigar factory and other older premises that were being closed down. No compulsory redundancies took place. Over a twelve-month period 1982–3, normal turnover accounted for a quarter of total employment decline (716) and early retirement or voluntary redundancy for the rest. Staff at the cigar factory and other older premises (mainly hand-rolling tobacco) which were closed were given the option of transferring to the new factory with retraining as appropriate. Out of 700 working there, 440 were re-employed and the rest took early retirement or voluntary redundancy. Staff reductions at the new factory made space for the transfers in.

Job loss and female employment As noted earlier, tobacco was a major source of female manufacturing employment. Job loss, however, impacted on female employment in particular, which fell by 39 per cent (1,700) over the decade to 1981 compared with a 20 per cent drop in male employment. In the twelve months to October 1983 (during which time the cigar factory was run down), female wage-earners accounted for 59 per cent of the total job loss of 550, and women overall for 72 per cent. The differential decline of male and female employment reflected a strategy of non-replacement, early retirement, voluntary redundancy, and redeployment, combined with the impact of rationalization and technical change on traditionally established male and female jobs.

In the first place, a strategy of non-replacement impacts in particular on female employment, given higher female turnover rates. Second, women, particularly older and part-time workers, are often more likely than men to opt for early retirement or voluntary redundancy, feeling that they should make way for younger, possibly full-time, workers who 'need the money more'. With the closure of the cigar factory employing mainly women, and the transfer of other work out of older premises, the prospect of redeployment to the new factory, and possibly retraining, further encouraged a significant number of women to take redundancy terms or early retirement, particularly part-time and older workers, for whom the disruption to established activity patterns and a longer journey to work was an added disincentive.

Finally, certain tasks, including the making and packing of cigarettes and the weighing and packing of hand-rolling tobacco, are exclusively 'women's work', as opposed to setting and adjusting machines, which is 'men's work'. This appears to have been established historically when women were employed to perform specific labour-intensive tasks for which their supposedly greater manual dexterity suited them. Labour costs were also a factor. As functions have been mechanized, some from an early date, women have retained tasks most equivalent to those which previously they performed manually—handling machine-made cigarettes, feeding packing machines with weighed hand-rolling tobacco, removing packed products from the machines. These distinctions have survived major waves of new investment, relocation, and redeployment, including the move to the new factory.

New investment, however, has impacted on female employment in particular. In part this is simply because women outnumber men—about 2:1 in cigarette production and 8:1 in hand-rolling tobacco—so that proportionate reductions have a greater absolute impact on female employment. Additionally, however, the ratio of women to men has fallen because 'women's jobs' have been more heavily affected than 'men's'. Two more general observations can be made. First, this was not a case of women giving way to men in any direct sense. Traditional gender divisions have been maintained, with neither management nor (male-dominated) unions wanting to challenge traditional divisions. Second, by no means all the women who chose voluntary redundancy or early retirement in preference to redeployment intended to give up paid work. Indeed, the company made efforts to find alternative employment for them as part of the closure process. As with many women displaced from manufacturing, however, the company reported that applicants far outnumbered vacancies, and most job opportunities were in sales, catering, clerical, and retail work—mostly part-time and with lower wages.

Recruitment The emphasis over recent years has obviously been on employment reduction, with minimal recruitment since the mid-1970s and a general freeze on production staff. Only essential recruitment has been undertaken, for example where redeployment within the site or in some cases the Division as a whole has proved impossible. In 1982/3 only three production workers were recruited. On the staff side, mainly head office, recruitment has related primarily to normal turnover, with around 50 taken on in 1982/3, mostly related to sales, where there is always some turnover. About 40 YTS trainees were taken on in 1984 in a range of areas including maintenance, catering, and clerical as well as the factory, but the chances of permanent employment are minimal.

Conclusions

Tied to the fortunes of one major employer, the locality has since the early 1970s suffered major reductions in tobacco employment which (up to 1981 at least) declined more rapidly in Bristol than in the country as a whole. Job loss has impacted in particular on female employment. The Tobacco Division remains, nevertheless, a significant source of manufacturing employment in general and female employment in particular. Much of its labour force is moreover drawn from south Bristol, parts of which are marked by high and rising unemployment.

Despite the scale of job loss, corporate restructuring has consolidated and centralized higher-order management and administrative functions in the locality with the establishment in Bristol of the Tobacco Division's head office. This reflected, first, the fact that Bristol was the traditional centre of gravity of the Group as a whole; second, the availability of suitable premises resulting from earlier investment decisions; and, third, the attractiveness of Bristol to managerial and administrative staff. This has resulted in a recomposition of the Bristol labour force, with a shift in the balance of employment towards salaried and managerial staff offsetting to some extent the decline in the number of production workers employed.

Future employment levels are tied in particular to the level of sales. The decline in UK cigarette sales paused in 1983, but continued marginal shrinkage is anticipated in the longer term. More dramatic decline could again follow any major increase in taxation. Competition in the UK market from foreign-based producers remains very strong, requiring continuing high levels of sales and marketing expenditure and generating continuing pressure for productivity gains. In mid-1984 the company did not foresee major restructuring in the short term, at least not for eighteen months. It anticipated at least maintaining its own market share. By mid-1985, however, a further round of employment reductions had been announced: 2,000 jobs were to go in the Tobacco Division as a whole, and the Newcastle cigarette factory was to close, with other losses spread across the remaining production sites. In Bristol the projected loss of 200 jobs was in fact proportionately less severe than elsewhere. The company blamed loss of sales, although the unions claimed that productivity increases arising from new machinery were partly responsible for excess capacity. Cigarette production is thus being increasingly concentrated on the main, Nottingham and Bristol, sites. With Newcastle closing, Swindon, also a smaller factory, producing only cigarettes, might be vulnerable to further capacity cuts, although the company noted that the Swindon workforce had proved highly productive and flexible—mindful perhaps of their vulnerability.

In Bristol, marginal shrinkage of employment is likely to continue, mainly on the production side, reflecting some remaining new investment mainly in hand-rolling tobacco and continuing productivity increases, including increased output from new generation machines. The company has commented publicly that the search for employment savings remains a continuous process. The scale of investment in Bristol and the emphasis on centralized administrative functions is such that the city is likely to be less vulnerable to longer-term change than other production centres. It was indicated, however, that improvements in productivity would continue to be sought in activities where comparison with other sites was not entirely favourable.

Paper, Printing, and Packaging

Paper, Printing, and Packaging is, like Tobacco, a long established manufacturing sector in the locality. Still important in employment terms, it has however experienced major job losses. Employment locally was nearly 9,000 in 1981, 3.0 per cent of total employment compared with 2.4 per cent nationally. This however followed a decade of dramatic job loss locally in which employment fell by over 7,000, representing a 45 per cent drop compared with only 14 per cent nationally. Locally, as nationally, the decline was concentrated on paper, board, and packaging products, which accounted for nearly 90 per cent of total job loss in the sector; the decline in printing and publishing was much less severe.

The remainder of this summary focuses mainly on Paper, Board, and Packaging,[3] although printing operations are integral to much of the packaging industry as such. Employment in these industries collapsed over the decade to 1981 from 11,500 to just 5,000, reflecting a combination of closures and major contraction among surviving establishments. Job loss accelerated as the recession deepened, including the closure of a board mill in east Bristol in 1980 which had employed 1,700, and the decline has continued beyond 1981.

Decline locally mirrored but magnified national trends. The Paper and Board industry, in particular, lost almost 33,000 jobs nationally in the decade to 1981, reflecting widespread mill closures and redundancies—sixty-eight mills closed between 1971 and 1982, half of them after 1978 as decline accelerated. Employment decline has reflected a combination of longer-term trends in markets, process and product innovation, and foreign competition, exacerbated by the more immediate impacts of the recession on demand. Local impacts have been a function of specific corporate responses to this combination of factors.

Corporate context

The industrial structure has long established roots in the locality, going back to the nineteenth century in some cases, with a shifting history of corporate and product interlinkage within the sector and with tobacco and other consumer goods industries locally. Virtually all of the plants surviving in the 1970s had been established by 1945. The growth of packaging (and also printing) in turn stimulated the development of engineering activity. Early growth was linked in particular to the tobacco industry. Mardon Son and Hall (see below), a packaging company supplying the Wills Tobacco Company, was absorbed into the Imperial Tobacco Company in 1902; the board mill was established by Imperial and BAT in 1913 to supply the tobacco industry; and Imperial set up a packaging company in 1918 which eventually was transferred to BAT in 1979. The scale and diversity of activity, however, expanded with the development of branded consumer products from the late nineteenth century. This was reinforced in the postwar boom and by the demands arising from advertising and consumer-oriented packaging outlined earlier. A number of companies diversified: by the 1960s, half of the board mill output was going to the record, pharmaceutical, and other industries, and other manufacturers had diversified into new product lines including plastics-based packaging materials and office equipment.

Employment has been dominated by four major multinational companies, which, through a network of subsidiaries, accounted for roughly 90 per cent of the total in the 1970s. The board mill was owned by the locally rooted Imperial Group with major food, drink, and tobacco interests. Mardon Packaging International, jointly owned by Imperial and BAT until the latter assumed full control in 1979, had four major factories in the locality. DRG had five production sites; this group was formed in 1966 from the merger of long established Bristol conglomerate E. S. & A. Robinson with John Dickinson, based in the south-east. Reflecting Robinson's dominant role, DRG headquarters was established in Bristol. A further packaging products factory, partly owned by Robinson until 1954, is now owned ultimately by Courtaulds. By 1971 paper and board accounted for 3,600 jobs, including the major board mill and a wide range of packaging products, in a spread of plants of varying size. In each case, paper, packaging, and board production in the locality represented only a very small part of the total activity and employment of the parent conglomerates. Local activity was confined largely to production and related management. The exception was DRG's corporate headquarters, formally based in London; a large part of Imperial Group headquarters functions are also in Bristol.

Sectoral context

Looking first at Paper and Board, in the longer term, changing comparative advantages have led to major geographical shifts in production. Nordic producers which formerly exported mainly pulp have capitalized on low-cost energy, local raw material supplies, and the ending, in the late 1960s, of tariff barriers which had protected European markets and producers. Investment in integrated pulp, paper, and board mills increased exports of paper and board; and with smaller, high-cost, non-integrated European mills unable to compete, closures were widespread throughout the 1970s.

These trends were exacerbated in the shorter term by the impact of declining consumer demand for paper and packaging products, by the effect of high exchange rates on imported raw materials, and by high energy costs compared with EEC and particularly Nordic competitors—alleged by UK producers to incorporate an element of subsidy. Surviving domestic producers have sought to specialize either in higher-quality products, which use a mix of pulps or local raw materials, thus outweighing the advantage of integrated mills, or in products which are costly to transport, such as tissues, necessitating in many cases significant new investment.

The packaging industry has been affected in the longer term by new demands in the postwar period for branded consumer goods linked to advertising and consumer-oriented packaging. This was emphasized by the growth of self-service supermarket sales and take-away food, market competition increasingly based on product differentiation, and increasing demand for new forms of packaging and new materials, in particular plastics, plastic film, aluminium foils, and laminates. More recently, however, demand for some types of preformed packaging, particularly bags, has declined with investment by producers in more advanced packaging equipment linked to production lines. Domestic producers have also responded to increasing foreign competition in the market for standardized products by largely switching to 'bespoke' products for specific customers, with no production for stock. At the same time, production runs have become shorter as manufacturers' 'own name' products have been added to branded goods; packaging is changed more frequently to maintain market shares; and customers have adopted multi-sourcing of the same products to ensure supplies and promote competitive pricing. Production runs have been halved in some cases. In the shorter term, the contraction in consumer demand rapidly worked its way through to demand for consumer goods packaging materials, while exchange rates cheapened particularly bulk-produced imports of more standard goods and increased competitive pressure. Again, domestic producers have sought both to invest and specialize in a number of existing product lines, and to develop into new areas, introducing new technology.

Production change

Specific corporate responses to longer-term pressures and the more immediate impacts of recession resulted in a complex pattern of reorganization, capacity cuts and closures, new investment, and acquisitions. These affected different sectors to differing degrees and in combination produced a particular spatial pattern of capacity and employment effects nationally and locally.

Paper and Board employment was virtually eliminated by the closure in 1980 of the major mill, which had employed 1,700. The plant used imported woodpulp from Scandinavia and wastepaper from the UK and was one of the largest such units in Europe. Although it had diversified, folding board was still a major part of its output, with customers including the local cigarette industry and local packaging companies. Closure followed increasing trading losses through the 1970s as the industry as a whole suffered the effects of Scandinavian competition, high energy costs and exchange rates, and the impact of the recession on consumer demand. Job loss in Bristol thus reflected the rationalization of the industry on a UK and, indeed, a European scale.

The specific corporate context was, however, itself unfavourable. Paper and packaging was a relatively minor component of the Imperial Group, whose major interests were in tobacco, brewing, and food. The Group as a whole ran into serious difficulties in the late 1970s which led to major restructuring—this, and its specific impacts on tobacco employment, have already been outlined. In this context the Group's strategy involved almost complete withdrawal from its historic paper, board, and packaging interests, as opposed, for example, to reinvestment and consolidation. In 1979 it also sold its 50 per cent interest in the paper and packaging conglomerate Mardon Packaging International, including two Bristol companies, to BAT, in order to finance its diversification strategy. The remaining mill in the locality specializes in high-quality coated papers, one of the more profitable areas in which, as suggested earlier, non-Scandinavian countries have been able to retain some degree of advantage.

Declining profits in other sectors of the industry have led to a complex pattern of rationalization, reinvestment, and intensification of the work process. Local production relates in particular to the food industry and has faced intense competition within a static market. Older and/or less profitable lines have been phased out and capacity in some cases closed. One company, for example, shut down the production of corrugated board in Glasgow and

plastic cups in Liverpool, and in Bristol cut the capacity of rigid box and cal-
endar and diary production. Another company phased out the production of
standardized plastic bags in which foreign competition was particularly
strong. BAT's takeover of Imperial's interest in Mardon Packaging International was followed by management changes involving greater autonomy
for operating units but within more stringent financial targets, accompanied
by rationalization, closures, and reinvestment. There was general pressure to
cut activities not directly involved in production. In one case, inspectors were
largely eliminated and quality control passed to production workers themselves. In another, the personnel department in particular was cut back.

New investment has been undertaken selectively to increase productivity
and competitiveness in the surviving production for mature mass markets
where competition is intense. Increased flexibility has been sought in the face
of shorter production runs in the bespoke market. There has been substantial
investment in litho-printing, multi-colour capacity, and computer-controlled
equipment for carton production and printing. Some basic functions have
changed little, with new investment leading essentially to faster and more
flexible production, and a significantly lower labour input. New investment
has been limited by the high capital cost of much of the new machinery, particularly when existing equipment has many years of physical life left. This
has encouraged cost-cutting in other areas through the intensification and
squeezing of non-essential work areas.

Some new investment has also been channelled into expanding specialist
activities estimated to have good growth prospects, including medical packaging and some forms of plastic containers. Bristol benefited to some extent,
with DRG basing its medical packaging operations here and investing in
plastics production locally, building in both cases on existing capacity. Partly
for this reason, net job loss in the company locally was only 18 per cent in
1978–83 compared with 37 per cent in the UK as a whole, new product
investment offsetting to some extent losses in the traditional packaging operations. Investment to increase competitiveness in existing mass markets is
traded off somewhat against diversification into new packaging products and
in some cases more widely into, for example, office equipment and technology.

Reorganization of management structures has been an important component of change. This has included in a number of cases the decentralization
of day-to-day control and financial accountability together with increased
central co-ordination and long-term strategic planning. This is in marked
and deliberate contrast to earlier tendencies towards increasingly centralized
control and accountability and has resulted in some reduction of headquarters staff—affecting employment in the Bristol head office of one of the
companies. Modified 'matrix' structures have been instituted, designed to
reduce formal hierarchical control and encourage greater autonomy in
response to market forces.

Employment

As we have seen, major job losses halved employment in Paper, Packaging, and Board over the decade to 1981, to just 5,000. In terms of composition, the industry has a high proportion of manual workers and particularly skilled manual workers. From 60 per cent to 80 per cent of the workforce are generally classed as 'operatives', depending on the extent to which particular plants also have administrative or managerial responsibilities for other production sites. Women account for about 30 per cent of total employment, markedly higher than, for example, aerospace. Typing, secretarial, and clerical work accounts for a significant proportion.

Operatives, however, are predominantly male: in one plant only 6 out of 280 were female; in another, 4 out of 173; while in a third, 15 out of 750 operatives and 50 out of 200 staff were female. Female operatives are confined largely to specific tasks such as gluing and dispatch, or bag-making, which are institutionized as 'women's work'. One plant which, unusually, employs 33 per cent women produces pre-formed plastic bags for the 'downmarket' end of the business, on older machinery. Another has established a small unit physically separate from the main plant employing women producing winebox liners. This separation was designed to insulate the unit from the heavily unionized main works.

Male employment is predominantly 'skilled', in traditional craft unions, and qualified in the printing and engineering trades, effectively excluding women from most areas of shopfloor work. The lifting and carrying was said to exclude women from other, less skilled, areas of work. As with tobacco, these gender divisions were historically established but have been preserved since. Most operatives work two or three shift systems, with minimal part-time work.

Job loss   The outright closure of production sites accounted for a significant share of total net job loss including 1,700 redundancies at the board mill plus other jobs lost through a series of smaller closures. Job loss in surviving production sites has been very heavy in some cases, however. Nationally, one company reduced employment by 4,000 over the eighteen months to July 1981, of which 2,500 related to continuing businesses. In Bristol one plant reduced its workforce from a postwar peak of around 900 in 1965 to 580 by 1980 and halved that again to 270 by 1984; another has cut its workforce by 400 from 1,330 to 930 since 1980, and another from 520 to 400. In one group, 1,400 jobs were lost locally in a range of plants and 250–300 jobs were created through diversification into new product lines over a period 1981–4, leaving total employment locally at 5,000 out of 12,000 nationally. National employment fell from 20,000 to 12,000, indicating that in this case the burden of job loss was greater outside of Bristol, affecting most heavily, in fact, the South-East, where plants were specialized in weaker market sectors.

Heavy job loss in the 1970s has thus been tempered by a relatively slower decline more recently. Although the precise importance of different factors is hard to pin down, much of this reflects capacity cuts or the closure of particular product lines at production sites where other activities have survived. Technical change affecting existing product lines was estimated in one case to have accounted for around 20 per cent of job loss. The remainder results mainly from the demanning of surviving production lines and a fairly ruthless elimination of 'non-productive' staff. It was suggested that in many cases rapid employment reduction represented an overdue 'shakeout', reflecting the urgency injected at plant level by new management strategies including increased local responsibility in the context of central appraisal systems. New product lines, while compensating to some extent, are generally characterized by lower labour content and higher productivity, contributing more to output than to employment. Plants described themselves by 1984 as at 'rock bottom' in terms of employment and production levels, the downward trend having 'bottomed out'.

Job loss and new investment has been reflected in a recomposition of the labour force in terms of skill, age, and to some extent gender. New technology, including computer-controlled printing presses for packaging products which control colour balance automatically, are eliminating some of the last craft skills in the industry. Form-making, for example, which relied on carpentry skills, has been replaced in one instance by computer-controlled laser cutting. In many cases traditional craft skills have been gradually eroded and their relevance undermined. Machine operators nevertheless continue to be defined and paid as skilled workers. There are instances of new areas of work that have evolved where operatives, including women, are engaged in equivalent machine-minding tasks but are *not* accorded equivalent status.

On the other hand, demand has grown somewhat for new skills such as electronic engineering and computer-controlled process operation, some of which are in short supply. Craftsmen have in some cases been specifically retrained to perform these new tasks. In the case of administrative personnel, the squeeze on 'non-productive' labour plus the impact of new office technology is expected to shift the ratio in favour of operatives.

In terms of age structure, early retirement and voluntary redundancy plus a general recruitment freeze has concentrated the remaining workforce in the 30–50 age range. Most of those who left employment were reported to have been over 50. Female employment has been hit slightly more than male—it fell by 61 per cent over the decade to 1981 compared with a 53 per cent drop in male employment. This reflected in part the elimination of particular product lines and activities defined as 'women's work' such as bag-making. In one case, of 600 women who were employed in bag-making up to the late 1950s, all have now been displaced by the shift away from pre-formed bags to printed film produced (by men) on capital-intensive equipment and supplied direct to manufacturers.

Recruitment Following drastic reductions in the numbers of employed, companies generally described current staffing levels as relatively stable. Recruitment was however still confined to the occasional replacement of essential employees only, necessitated by the tight manning levels achieved by earlier cutbacks. Most companies were still looking to trim staff at the margins. Only a handful of skilled operatives in key positions, or workers in sections where turnover was high were generally being replaced. Turnover was highest among less skilled workers, particularly women, and lowest among skilled male operatives.

Skilled workers include NGA or SOGAT members; these unions have considerable influence over the recruitment and selection process, and all skilled recruits have to have a union card. Fitters are often recruited through local informal networks or, failing this, through the local and national press. Informal networks readily meet needs for female employment: one firm reported that 'you only have to let it be known that there's a place and they're queuing up.' External recruitment of management personnel is through national press adverts. A handful of more technical needs related to the increased use of electronic control systems also have to be met by outside recruitment. The Youth Training Scheme has been favourably received by employers as a potential recruitment channel for unskilled and semi-skilled employees, but has met union opposition in some cases. Only one firm in the study had used Jobcentres; others found that they tended to send unsuitable people.

Labour markets and labour relations Shopfloor labour in particular tends to be very local to particular plants. The supply was generally considered to be adequate in terms of quantity and quality although not always in terms of calibre or motivation. Many workers had been with companies since leaving school, and were considered by outside managers to be somewhat unaware of what the latter saw as the 'harsh realities'. Management reported difficulties in tightening up on work practices and introducing a competitive edge.

As nationally, the industry is heavily unionized; the NGA and SOGAT '82 cover skilled printing and related employment, and the EEPTU, ASTMS, and SLADE are also important. Local workforces are thus linked in terms of pay, conditions, and bargaining to national unions deriving much of their power from Fleet Street. Reflecting this, wage rates for skilled and semi-skilled printers were relatively high for the Bristol area, particularly for plants with very localized workforces. Other pay rates, for example for clerical work, were however comparable with local norms.

Views on unionization and labour relations differed. Increased plant-level responsibility plus a growing concern among customers in the bespoke market about the ability to deliver has increased the salience of industrial relations issues at the local level. Unionism *per se* was not generally seen as a major problem. High rates of pay and financial compensation to a relatively small group of central workers tended to secure negotiated co-operation and change over many issues, including new technology.

Despite common negotiating structures, Bristol is acknowledged to have a milder industrial relations climate than Fleet Street and other centres. As one production manager put it, 'you wouldn't believe you're in the same world.' There are however some qualifications. In one case, new investment was said to have been channelled to plants in Scotland, where unions had proved more flexible. This had subsequently put pressure on the unions in Bristol and encouraged flexibility in the introduction of new technology. Management was clearly able to play one site off against another. In another company, central personnel management suggested that Bristol was to some extent losing its easy-going, West Country image and becoming more militant as it started to feel the recession. In places like London, Liverpool, or Glasgow, however, labour relations had improved considerably: the company had achieved high productivity in both Liverpool and London and could get 'just about any changes' if they were prepared to pay.

Overall, it was apparent that the restructuring strategy which combined rationalization with new investment in both existing product lines and new initiatives was strongly conditioned by the need to secure union co-operation. More flexible local management structures were part of the strategy to secure this consent. The introduction of new technology and the process of employment reduction was largely seen by the unions as inevitable. On the whole, unions and management appeared to have co-operated in what was generally, if not in all its details, seen as a mutually beneficial adaptation to external circumstances.

Conclusions

The sector as a whole has been under major competitive pressure nationally and, indeed, on the European scale, reflecting both the comparative advantage of Scandinavian producers and the shorter-term impacts of the recession and exchange rates. Job loss in Paper, Packaging, and Board has been considerably more severe locally than nationally, however—56 per cent compared with 26 per cent for the country as a whole in the decade to 1981. To some extent this difference reflects the major board mill closure, but job loss in packaging has also been well above the national norm. The rationalization of continuing operations as well as outright closure has been a major factor. Significant new investment has also taken place, however. This has partly updated existing production lines, with subsequent impacts on employment requirements. There has also been some diversification into new product lines with limited job growth against the general trend. The specific corporate responses to national and international pressures and their particular legacies of productive capacity have shaped the pattern of local change. Thus, the Imperial Group adopted a strategy of tactical withdrawal from virtually all its paper and packaging interests, breaking its historic links with the sector locally. The two paper and packaging conglomerates, on the other hand, pursued a policy of vigorous restructuring, including withdrawal from less profitable markets, new investment to secure profitability in some continuing product lines, and diversification into a number of new areas. This was accompanied by the introduction of new management strategies emphasizing operational autonomy within corporate financial plans.

This process of job loss left the locality with workforces trimmed to the bare essentials. Both major conglomerates represented locally and the film conversion plant experienced a recovery in profits and were under less immediate pressure. Output was expected to be maintained or to increase marginally, while employment remained stable or declined at the margins. Any upturn in demand would be met in the short term by increased shift working and overtime and in the longer term, by accelerated investment, rather than increased employment. Fundamental problems remain for some sections of the market, however. Having drastically trimmed workforces, a failure to compete in the future is likely to mean further closures. The current situation, then, may well represent a temporary respite rather than an effective counter to longer-term competitive disadvantage, and the trend towards a smaller, more specialized sector locally may well continue.

Aerospace

Originating with the early years of aviation, consolidated by rearmament and postwar reconstruction, and sustained by subsequent investment and diversification, aerospace has been a dominant component of manufacturing industry in the locality since before the Second World War. In 1981 it employed nearly 22,000, over a quarter of manufacturing employment and over 7 per cent of total employment locally compared with 0.9 per cent nationally. Bristol in fact accounted for nearly 12 per cent of all aerospace employment nationally.

Aerospace employment locally fell by some 9 per cent over the decade to 1981. This however tempered to some extent the collapse of manufacturing employment as a whole, which fell by 22 per cent, and was in marked contrast to other traditionally dominant sectors including Tobacco, which shrank by over 30 per cent, and Paper, Printing and Packaging, which declined by 45 per cent. Job loss since 1981 of around 12–15 per cent mainly reflects the redundancy programme of one of the three main companies, Rolls Royce Aero Engines. The industry is very much male-dominated, with only 10 per cent female employment in 1981.

Corporate context

The main complex of companies occupies adjacent sites on the northern conurbation fringe. Rolls Royce employs approximately 9,500 locally (1983) in the development and production of aero-engines and components. The company employs over 42,000 nationally; the other major centre is at Derby, and there are a number of smaller sites. Two divisions of British Aerospace (BAe) are represented locally, operating as autonomous units within the overall corporate structure. BAe Aircraft Group employ 4,800 involved in airframe assembly and component manufacture. BAe Dynamics Group employs 4,770 in the design, development, and assembly of guided weapons and electronic systems and related activities, with some Space and Communications Group activity on the same site. Nationally, the Aircraft Group employs over 54,000, and Dynamics, 23,000.

There are a number of smaller companies also engaged primarily in aerospace and related activities including R & D work and the production of, for example, composite material-based equipment, avionics equipment, pilotless aircraft, and rocket motors. Beyond the immediate travel-to-work area, Westland Helicopters are based at Yeovil and Weston-super-Mare, while Smiths and Dowty, producing avionics equipment and instrumentation, operate in Cheltenham and Gloucester to the north, making up a substantial sub-regional aerospace complex. This represents a major complex of advanced technology industry including electronics, avionics, and engineering-based R & D and production, much of which is tied to central government defence procurement and related activities and to civil and military export markets.

Sectoral context

Aerospace markets at national and international level were to some extent sheltered from recession until the end of the 1970s, in part by continued defence expenditure. Orders for civil airliners slumped in the early 1980s, but with military markets still largely insulated, owing to long-term contracts, manufacturers have become increasingly dependent on defence contracts. With domestic defence markets still showing some growth but likely to stabilize in real terms, companies are looking to consolidate military exports and hoping for an increase in orders for the new generation of civil airliners, particularly outside of Europe and the USA. Static markets are likely to be reflected in pressure for employment reductions arising from increased productivity.

In order to spread escalating development costs on major new projects, standardize defence equipment among allies, and extend production runs by accessing a range of national markets, there has been a major move towards collaborative projects for guided weapons, space, aircraft, and aero-engines. These have included BAe's involvement in the Anglo-French Airbus; the Rolls Royce RB 199, produced with Italy and Germany, which powers the Tornado, itself a collaborative project involving BAe with German and Italian manufacturers; the Anglo-American AV8B Harrier development for the US Marine Corps; and the projected European Fighter Aircraft being developed with Germany, France, Italy, and Spain. Earnings from military markets generated resources through the early 1980s, while an anticipated expansion of civil markets in the 1990s has provided the incentive for product development and wide-ranging restructuring.

Increasingly competitive markets plus the internationalization of development and production also focused domestic concern on the industry's lack of competitiveness. The UK government commitment to increased competition for defence contracts will emphasize this. A 1981 survey ranked Rolls Royce twenty-fourth and British Aerospace twenty-eighth out of thirty-one NATO aerospace companies in terms of productivity (Hartley 1983, p. 108). Rationalization and new investment have been directed specifically towards increasing productivity, and there have been major changes from the late 1970s in government–industry relations, new management strategies, product and process innovation, plus corporate restructuring and rationalization.

A dominant feature of the sector as a whole is its reliance on defence markets, and the particular relationship with the government that this implies. Defence products have in turn been a major component of export sales. In 1984 the Ministry of Defence (MoD) accounted for 63 per cent (by value) of British Aerospace's total sales of guided weapons and related military equipment and 29 per cent of its sales of military aircraft, with virtually all the balance being for export—together, these accounted for.72 per cent of 1984 turnover, with civil aircraft representing a further 23 per cent and space and communications the rest (British Aerospace, 1985). Military sales, similarly, account for around 60 per cent of Rolls Royce turnover, and exports, around 46 per cent.

The nature of the market relationship to the government, as well as its scale, has been significant. Military projects typically extend over many years, with follow-on sales, development, and modification as well as sales support, maintenance, and spares. Development costs for projects have been financed in part by the Ministry of Defence while a proportion of sales have been on a, cost-plus or non-competitive basis. Military exports are largely of products developed under contract to the MoD with a levy payable to the Ministry. Civil projects, notably Concorde and the Rolls Royce RB 211, have also received major public sector financial support. More recently, the government has provided launch finance for BAe participation in the A320 version of the Airbus.

Again, export markets, which accounted for 87 per cent of BAe's civil aircraft turnover in 1983, are crucial. The government places particular emphasis on support for both military and civil export sales including export credit guarantees, soft finance, reciprocal trade agreements, and ministerial sales missions, and on achieving the benefits of collaborative arrangements. The sector as a whole is thus underpinned in a major way both by government defence procurement and the linkages built around this and, although less important than in the early 1970s, by government support for civil aerospace.

Production change

The specific impact of this overall context on the Bristol locality has been reflected in corporate strategy, restructuring, and the division of work between the various sites operated by the three main producers. This section therefore looks at production change within each of the main producers in turn.

Production change has related to the particular pattern of activities and capacity already established at the different sites. Activities have included responsibility for the assembly of specific projects which can therefore be identified with a particular site; manufacture of components and sub-assemblies for projects possibly based at other sites; and corporate functions such as R & D and computing or specialist manufacturing, for which 'lead sites' are designated.

Rolls Royce The Bristol site of Rolls Royce established a key role in component manufacture and assembly in relation to military and supersonic engines from the late 1960s, with work on the Olympus for Concorde, the RB 199 collaborative project for the Tornado, and the Pegasus for the Harrier. Bristol's quasi-autonomous role within Rolls Royce enabled it to sustain significant R & D activities. Resources of fixed capital and experienced labour, accumulated over the previous decade, were such that it could capture a substantial share of continuing work, even though employment was declining through rationalization and technical change. There has been major investment in machine tools, computer-aided manufacture, and some production methods, particularly in relation to component manufacture and, to a lesser extent, assembly. Following restructuring in 1983, Bristol includes a major part of the company's Military Engineering Group, accounting for almost half of Bristol employment. Other activities include component manufacture for this and other sites, which accounts for a further 37 per cent of employment.

With the creation of the new matrix management structure, a Corporate Engineering Group was established as an R & D resource for the company as a whole, split between Derby and Bristol. Building on established capability, Bristol's R & D role has if anything been marginally strengthened; the greater part of higher level staff are locally based, and the locational preferences of R & D staff were said to favour Bristol over Derby. Significantly as well, the corporate Systems and Computing Group is located in Bristol.

BAe Dynamics The establishment locally of BAe Dynamics has been centred around the postwar development of guided weapons. The market success of the Rapier in particular, continuing with later versions, has underpinned the expansion of employment at the site and this is expected to continue. Bristol, sharing work mainly with Stevenage, was allocated specialist roles in relation to ground-based equipment and the design and manufacture of electronic components and sub-assemblies. It also became a major producer of electronic components, sub-assemblies, and systems for other sites within the group producing other weapon systems, navigational equipment, and satellites. The site's role in the Space and Communications Group, split between Bristol and Stevenage, developed on the basis of this capability, initially subcontracting to US companies and more recently being involved with the emergence of a European satellite industry and with civil and military projects. Investment in the early 1980s has included a new printed circuit manufacturing unit.

Corporate strategy to consolidate the company's position in the missile and satellite markets and to increase identification between product groups and sites has emphasized Bristol's role in three main areas: the Naval Weapons Division; the production of components including Rapier ground equipment for the Army Weapons Division and of electronic equipment for the group as a whole; and the development of electronic systems, much of it for other divisions. Electronic and related systems in particular are a fast-growing area. An increasing emphasis on research has also been consolidated at Bristol with the establishment of a research centre to 'serve as the high-technology lead-centre for the whole of the Dynamics group' (BAe 1984, p. 14). Satellite production under the Space and Communications Group is to increase with a specialist assembly hall opened in 1979. A major emphasis has been placed on process innovation in manufacturing. Computer-aided design and manufacturing and robotics have been extensively introduced; the use of numerically controlled machine tools has increased continuously since the mid-1960s; and flexible manufacturing equipment has been introduced. Much of the volume production of electronic components and assemblies has been automated. A number of areas remain more labour-intensive, including the assembly of ground equipment for guided weapons, the production of electronic systems, and other wiring tasks.

BAe Aircraft Group Following the Concorde project on which the Bristol site had been largely dependent, and faced with an acute shortage of work, major efforts were made by the Group to diversify. This was coupled with a significant redundancy programme as part of a rationalization strategy. Work was allocated to the site in order to preserve capacity, and a number of new contracts were secured on the basis of competitive costing, particularly for labour-intensive activities. Corporate strategy was to preserve both existing expertise and major fixed capital in the form of production facilities, assembly hall, and runway. Major components of the package of activities include the conversion of VC 10 airliners into RAF tankers, the 'relifing' of

UK-based American F 111 aircraft, central fuselage assemblies for the BAe 146 'hush jet', and parts of the wing assembly for the Airbus. Corporate restructuring in 1984 placed Bristol in a new Civil Division linked to Hatfield, Chester, and Prestwick, all of which had been involved with Airbus work.

Most recently, Bristol has been designated the management centre for all UK Airbus activity, with management and some design work being transferred from Hatfield; it will also have a greater share of assembly work for the new A320, with associated new investment. This was motivated partly by existing management capacity at Bristol plus the increasing workload at Hatfield on the BAe 146. It will also give more coherence to work at Bristol following a period of rationalization and preservation. Process innovation has taken place in component manufacture, but much work involves primarily labour-intensive skilled assembly tasks. Investment in new production technology has been more modest here than in Rolls Royce or BAe Dynamics.

Company strategies have impacted on different activities locally in different ways. Overall, however, they have consolidated the national importance of establishments in Bristol which have tended to maintain or expand their share of UK activity and their place in the corporate hierarchies. Accurate information on output and productivity change for the individual Bristol sites was not available. It would seem however that, whereas output by value in the BAe Aircraft Group has certainly fallen since the early 1970s, and more recently in the aero engine sector, it has risen significantly in BAe Dynamics, reflecting both the scale of output and product diversification. Substantial gains in productivity over this period across all sectors have resulted from rationalization and intensification in response to declining markets, and also from the desire to increase international competitiveness, particularly in aero-engines, dynamics, electronics-based activity, and major investment in process technology. Thus, nationally,

The number of Rolls Royce employees in the UK, which fell by 5,900 in 1981, was further reduced by approximately 7,600 in 1982—a decline of 23 per cent in the two-year period. These reductions resulted not only from the fall in demand for civil engines but also from the continuing development of advanced manufacturing systems and methods in all the Company's factories. [Rolls Royce 1983].

Productivity has not, however, improved significantly relative to foreign competitors.

In terms, then, of the main dimensions of change, there has been some rationalization and scaling-down of existing workforces in aero-engine and aircraft activity, with some reduction in capacity in the case of aircraft. Restructuring of the BAe Aircraft Group did involve the closure of one site, at Hurn. Particular emphasis has been placed on the intensification of work, and on cutting back 'indirect' or 'non-productive' labour.

It is difficult however to distinguish rationalization as such from the simultaneous effects of intensification, and particularly process innovation and investment. The latter has been particularly important in aero-engines, guided weapons, and electronic systems. Guided weapons and related activity have been characterized by a combination of increased productivity, rising output, and generally rising employment related both to product and process innovation and to the increased scale of activity. This contrasts with other manufacturing sectors such as Tobacco, where process innovation related to existing products has been reflected in higher productivity but lower employment. The Aircraft sector has been characterized more by a simple scaling down of the workforce from its peak during the Concorde project, *in situ* rationalization, in particular.

Employment

Overall, an employment decline of around 9 per cent over the decade to 1981 and a further 12–15 per cent drop up to 1984 disguises different patterns of employment change reflecting the impact of restructuring in the three main companies. Both Rolls Royce and the BAe Aircraft Group have undertaken major redundancy exercises and have secured further employment reductions by natural wastage, whereas BAe Dynamics have expanded throughout with only a pause in the early 1980s. Job loss in aircraft work through the 1970s was marginally offset by continued expansion in guided weapons and related activity. Major reductions in aero-engine employment, further reductions in aircraft, and a pause in guided weapons and other activity were, however, reflected in a more rapid decline in the early 1980s. By 1983, Bristol accounted for around 9 per cent of BAe Aircraft Group employment, 20 per cent of Dynamics and 22 per cent of Rolls-Royce.

Job loss Under a national survival plan, Rolls Royce initiated major employment reductions in 1979 which resulted in the loss of around 4,000 jobs, 31 per cent of the 1979 total, towards the end of the exercise in 1984. This was achieved entirely through voluntary redundancy combined with a major process of internal redeployment. The company retained discretion over which staff were accepted for redundancy terms in order to preserve an acceptable employment structure in terms of skills and experience—necessary staff were not allowed to leave under the scheme unless their place could be filled by internal redeployment. The scale of local and national job loss was roughly comparable; Bristol in this sense neither lost nor gained, although in functional terms it has if anything gained through its role in Corporate Engineering. Job loss affected clerical and manual grades more than technical and managerial staff—29 per cent of the reduction was in clerical grades which made up only 16 per cent of total employment initially, and 50 per cent in manual grades (40 per cent initially). Roughly half of those accepting redundancy terms were over 55.

Aircraft employment was affected over a longer period by a series of redundancies through the 1970s which, together with natural wastage, have halved employment from a peak of 9,000 in the early 1970s which was almost entirely related to Concorde. This involved some compulsory redundancies in the 1970s, along with voluntary exercises which continued into the 1980s. The earlier impact of recession and cutbacks resulted in part from the specific effects of the Concorde project but also from the more general reliance on civil markets. As already suggested, these contracted somewhat earlier than military markets, which sustained the aero-engine sector locally through the 1970s. To some extent, however, the contrast in timing illustrates how the fortunes of different sites have been tied to the success or failure of a small number of major projects. Company employment as a whole, although dipping in the 1970s, was marginally higher in 1981 than a decade earlier. In terms of corporate context, then, Aircraft Group employment in Bristol fell in relation to overall group employment and company employment.

Employment on guided weapons and related activity, on the other hand, has expanded in Bristol, as in the company as a whole, mainly through product innovation and diversification. This has countered any tendency towards job loss from productivity gains through process innovation on existing product lines.

Recruitment The dominant impact of restructuring in employment terms overall has been job loss, and at times two of the main companies have placed a general embargo on recruitment. There has nevertheless been a certain amount of recruitment where promotion or internal redeployment was unable to meet needs created by normal turnover and, in the case of BAe Dynamics, to cater for some expansion and development needs as well. Moreover, all the companies have aimed to maintain their intake of apprentices in order to cater for an anticipated longer-term need for skilled labour. At least one company also recognized the value of securing union co-operation in its redundancy programme. Another company took on 1,200 apprentices over the four years up to 1984 while simultaneously shedding over 30 per cent of its existing labour force. By 1984, with major redundancy schemes completed in two of the companies and expansion restored in the third, overall recruitment was starting to pick up. By 1985 BAe Aircraft group, for example, was advertising externally for jig and tool draughtsmen and toolmakers for A320 and BAe 146 work, while the Dynamics Group was advertising a wide range of electrical and electronics-related posts.

Apprentices are recruited as school or college-leavers with CSEs for craft apprentices and four 'O' levels or CSE equivalents for technical apprentices. One company had instituted an intermediate 'craftician' apprentice scheme, finding traditional craft skills increasingly inappropriate to modern production techniques. Apprentices are recruited via speculative applications, encouraged by contacts maintained with local schools and careers officers. Most are drawn from the locality itself, many from the immediate neighbourhood. Companies receive more than enough applications without needing to advertise. Previously, many recruits would have had family connections with existing employees, but with decreasing recruitment this process has become less significant.

Other vacancies which arise are initially advertised internally within the company concerned and frequently are filled by this means, so that the new intake is mainly via apprenticeship or at the bottom of the relevant grade. The recruitment of skilled and experienced manual workers may be achieved from speculative enquiries, or through extended informal networks—as one employment manager put it, 'we have 4,500 recruiting officers on site and they often know about vacancies before we do.' Failing that, companies will advertise in the local press. They rarely recruit from the unemployed, and, apprentices apart, almost invariably seek experienced and qualified personnel, frequently with specific skills. Clerical intake, however, had increasingly been via the Youth Training Scheme which allows on-the-job assessment before actual employment.

Particular recruitment needs relate to technically and professionally qualified engineering and particularly electronics personnel, including graduates and experienced employees. Guided weapons, electronic components, and sub-assembly manufacture draw heavily on skilled electronics personnel recruited on a local and national basis through the general and specialist press and to some extent through specialist agencies. Competition is strong from a wide range of companies beyond aerospace as such, and while the sector in general has been characterized by job-shedding, shortages of specific qualified staff have been experienced. While competing locally with a number of firms with similar needs, the attractiveness of the locality to more qualified technical and professional staff recruited from beyond the South-West is recognized as a positive factor. This is reflected in the consolidation of R & D activity in Bristol, including BAe Dynamics' new research centre, the local importance of Rolls Royce Corporate Engineering Division engaged in company-wide R & D, and Airbus design work and project headquarters functions.

Aerospace and the wider employment market   With the growth, albeit modest, of electronics companies in the locality, aerospace companies have suffered some loss of personnel, although this has not been a particular problem. Aerospace has more generally represented a source of experienced personnel including wirers, electronics engineers, and highly skilled manual personnel for a range of companies. The locality is also regularly targeted by firms from elsewhere in the UK and also the USA seeking to recruit electronics, aero-engineering, and airframe personnel. Pratt and Whitney, the US aero-engine company involved in collaborative projects with Rolls Royce, periodically place prominent adverts in the local evening paper overtly targeted on Rolls Royce. Lucas Aerospace was advertising in 1984 for design and development engineers for electronics systems work relating to aircraft and missiles in which it is in direct competition with BAe Dynamics, and Honeywell were seeking electronic and mechanical engineers for aerospace and defence work at its Wiltshire plant.

Conclusions

There have been major job losses in the aerospace sector overall, both in the decade up to 1981 and in the 1980s. These have reflected a different mix of restructuring impacts in the different sub-markets and companies. Rationalization in the face of declining markets, mainly on the civil side, has affected aero-engine and airframe employment; intensification, and particularly investment in new process technology, have reduced the labour content and increased productivity across the board, particularly in aero-engines, guided weapons, and related products; the impact of intensification and new investment has been tempered, in guided weapons and related activities, by the continuing buoyancy of existing markets, especially defence products, and by new product development and diversification.

These changes have been reflected locally in major job losses in airframe and aero-engine-related employment, particularly on civil projects, with greater stability and some growth in other sub-sectors. Airframe capacity was preserved, albeit with much reduced employment. This resulted partly from local management initiative, coupled with a corporate strategy of allocating a number of specific projects and part-projects to the site when the prospects looked decidedly bleak. The Aircraft Group now has a much higher degree of corporate purpose with its Airbus role. Aero-engine employment was cut back significantly, in line with the company's national recovery programme, but suffered less than airframe jobs. Employment growth in guided weapons and related activity compensated to some extent for job loss in the rest of the sector.

Despite significant job loss, Bristol has conserved and to some extent consolidated its position in terms of corporate functions and hierarchy including R & D activity and project management. In terms of composition, the proportion of professionally and technically qualified staff has been increasing, and the balance of employment as a whole has shifted in the longer term towards electronics-based skills and experience. Clerical and other lower-grade white-collar labour has declined proportionately, as has less skilled manual labour. There are some indications that traditional craft-based apprenticeships are becoming less relevant to company needs.

The continuing strength of aerospace employment in the locality has been crucially dependent on domestic defence procurement, related support for R

& D and production manufacture, and the export capability to which this gives rise. This has essentially underpinned a major advanced technology sector which, despite rationalization and the drive to greater productivity and competitiveness, continues to dominate manufacturing employment. This has been reinforced by support for specific civil projects.

As we have seen, major programmes of rationalization, restructuring, and reinvestment have been undertaken in the sector since the early 1970s. Much of the sector remains, by its nature, dependent on the success or failure of a small number of major projects. Restructuring is however, for the short term at least, largely complete, with marginal reductions likely but no major contraction of employment foreseen. Employment and technical innovation are now more in tune with anticipated markets and product development, compared with the disequilibrium which developed from the early 1970s. Greater emphasis in the spreading of costs and risk through international collaboration is likely to give individual companies and projects greater stability. Additionally, a more conscious strategy, within the Aircraft Group in particular, of spreading work between sites and avoiding the sort of dependency which developed in Bristol with regard to Concorde is reducing the extent to which the fortunes of specific sites are tied to particuar projects. Airframe employment in Bristol will depend to some extent on the success or otherwise of the Airbus.

Overall, however, the prospects are for relatively stable employment, underpinned in particular by the continued success and further development of guided weapons, electronics systems and related activity, and the leading edge of high technology in the locality and indeed in the M4 corridor as a whole.

Electronics

The electronics industry is at the heart of the M4 corridor image and national hopes of high-tech-based economic revival. Bristol itself is heavily identified with specifically electronics-based economic activity with Inmos, Hewlett Packard, and the up-market Aztec West development, boasting a clutch of computer 'names' among its occupiers, looming large. Electrical engineering overall, in fact accounted for a relatively modest 1.5 per cent of total employment (4,400) locally in 1981 compared with over 3 per cent nationally. Having peaked in 1975, employment actually fell by around 19 per cent (1,000) up to 1981.

Electrical engineering as such, however, encompasses not only electronics-based products but also, for example, heavy electrical machinery and electrical domestic equipment. Electronics more narrowly defined,[4] including computers and electronic capital equipment, accounted for only 0.7 per cent of employment locally in 1981, a mere 2,100, half the national level. Of these only 18 per cent (400) were women. So, despite the image, up to 1981 at least, electronics was actually much *less* important locally than nationally. Moreover, like much of traditional manufacturing, it provided primarily male employment.

Two qualifications have to be made. First, electronics employment did in fact expand rapidly over the decade to 1981, adding over 1,200 jobs. This growth rate appears to have continued since then, adding approximately 400 jobs in the survey companies by 1985. Second, as indicated in the previous section, a significant proportion of 'aerospace' employment is engaged primarily in the design and production of advanced electronics components, systems, and sub-assemblies. Electronics-related employment within the aerospace sector, around 3,000 in BAe Dynamics alone, is actually higher than in electronics as officially defined, and has been expanding almost continuously. Taking the two together, the locality has closer to the national average share of electronics employment.

The remainder of this section focuses on non-aerospace electronics. The growth of electronics activity rooted in the traditional aerospace sector should however be kept in mind. It has, moreover, been an important factor influencing the development of non-aerospace electronics.

Corporate structure and production change

The electronics 'sector' as such is heterogeneous and, in the case of Bristol, thinly spread across a range of different activities tied to different markets and embedded in different market structures. A distinction can be drawn between primarily marketing, sales, and support activity on the one hand, and manufacture and assembly on the other. Research and development can to some extent be separately distinguished. This section focuses in turn on each of these three broad areas, before concentrating more specifically on locational factors. There is no large-scale component manufacture in the locality, although the aerospace company has a major printed circuit board facility, Dupont is to manufacture electrical connectors locally, and a range of smaller manufacturers provide ancillary equipment such as wiring harnesses and cabinets.

Sales, marketing, and support   Falling into the first main group, the Aztec West group of companies (numbering five at mid-1984) are engaged primarily in marketing, sales, and support. They include ICL, Systime (based in Leeds), US-owned Digital, the Canadian-owned GEAC, and Benson Electronics, US-owned via a French company. Products include computer installations, particularly minis and small networks, and computer-based systems including flexible manufacturing systems, computer-aided design and drafting, and dedicated systems for libraries and financial institutions. Firms selling dedicated systems commonly base these around other manufacturers' equipment which is bought in, the two being sold as a package. One of the local companies selling computer equipment in fact sells computer hardware to such 'own-equipment manufacturers', although local market linkages were not significant. With intense competition, this mix of activities reflects the growing trend towards selling total packages tailored to customer requirements with extensive support services as a means of securing markets for both hardware and dedicated software.

For three of the companies, Bristol is a base for essentially regional marketing, sales, field service, and support functions, with comparable centres (from four to twelve) covering the rest of the country. No assembly work as such is carried out, although one company puts together the hardware and software and provides some software support and customer training. One firm maintained only its service centre at Aztec West, with other functions based in a city centre office block.

The companies serve a broadly defined south-west region. This was variously defined, including in some cases Slough, Swindon, and Portsmouth as well as the rest of the South-West and South Wales. They are in a sense 'dependent' on the regional economy (going well beyond the Bristol locality), but their scale of operations reflects the specific characteristics of the market in this area. The general buoyancy of the regional economy, including a large proportion of the M4 corridor, is one factor. More specifically, several companies referred to the concentration of defence equipment and aerospace manufacturers in the region, both in Bristol and beyond, as an important component of the market. According to one, 'aerospace, primarily, accounts for the success of this branch; and another commented that 'the major growth market is in manufacturing, especially aerospace.' Other government establishments were mentioned including GCHQ, the Admiralty design office in Bath, and the Signals and Radar Research Establishment at Malvern. Public sector customers, including universities and local authorities and parts of the expanding service sector, were also mentioned as important.

The other two companies are also engaged in marketing, sales, and support but represent single outlets covering UK and export markets for their particular line in dedicated computer-based systems. Both are to some extent engaged in software tailoring and development in Bristol. One company also assembles and tests installations to customer specifications from sub-assemblies imported from its parent manufacturer or bought in from other producers. It has software development and support teams for particular UK-based product lines located in separate but nearby premises, together with UK and European finance and administrative functions—although, together, these employ only 33 people. All five Aztec West occupants in early 1984 accounted for little more than 200 employees: by early 1985 one estimate suggested that this had risen to nearly 700. This however included a significant number of staff working in the field rather than at the site itself.

Manufacturing and assembly Three companies in particular are engaged in the manufacture and assembly of electronics capital equipment, including computer peripherals, avionics and control systems, and equipment for manufacturing microchips. Between them, they employed around 600 (mid-1984) and were producing for both the national and export markets. Two are completely new to the locality since 1980 and the third, initially based in Wales, has rapidly built up a network of semi-autonomous companies over the same time period. The three companies represent instructive and contrasting case studies in their own right, and are worth looking at in a bit more detail.

The computer peripherals facility was set up by a major US multinational to manufacture and market disk and tape storage devices for the European market. Setting up an initial base in a spec-built unit on the city's northern fringe, in 1984 it moved into purpose-built 125,000 square foot premises on a part of a 165 acre green-field site, allowing for significant expansion. A European R & D facility is also being established on the site, the first outside the USA. Employment in the peripherals plant is expected to build up to around 200 with an equivalent number in the R & D labs. The company was actively decentralizing manufacturing so as to locate closer to national markets and was setting up an onshore European base. This was partly for cost reasons in terms of freight, duty, and labour costs—the availability of assembly labour in California was becoming impossible—and partly to justify market expansion by providing employment, described as 'social responsibility' and winning local acceptance.

In choosing to locate in Bristol, conventional factors, such as transport costs, site availability, and local suppliers, were all weighed up, but 'high on the list was whether it was an attractive place in which to live and work . . . if we couldn't attract and retain bright PhDs we'd have been making a big mistake.' The company also needed a broad spectrum of skills and experience down to basic assembly workers. The presence of the aerospace complex locally was a factor in terms of labour supply expectations; more generally, the area had a good tradition of technical and engineering activity. Aerospace was not a factor in market terms.

A package of financial assistance was put together by the local authorities and Department of Trade and Industry including rates relief, site purchase on advantageous terms, and financial support towards R & D costs (see Chapter 6). This was described as not unwelcome, but land and capital costs were not a high priority. Financial assistance was not reported to have been a decisive factor. It was however indicated that the local authority made a good job of selling Bristol (going to California to do so), came up with a site, and were co-operative over planning permission.

Nor was there real pressure from central government to set up in a development area, recognizing that this was not an acceptable alternative. South Wales was considered but rejected, as were existing UK operational bases including South Queensferry (Edinburgh) and the Pinewood (Middlesex) software, sales, and service facility. The main alternative considered was Lyons, where a site was in fact purchased. However, the overall economic and political outlook was thought to be more favourable in the UK. An English-speaking location was considered to have some advantages, although there is already a manufacturing complex in Germany. Similar location factors related to the R & D lab, to labour market factors including the attraction of top-grade technical and research staff, and also to the existence of manufacturing capacity and to the site itself. It was clear that location alongside existing operations was desirable; South Queensferry was considered 'a bit inaccessible', and Pinewood lacked room for expansion.

The second example is a production unit set up on the city's rural fringe by a major UK electronics conglomerate, to develop and manufacture power conversion and control units for avionics, other defence, and offshore (oil production) applications. Employment, originally announced as building up to 1,000, had reached 220 by mid-1984 and, with market expectations being revised downwards, expansion was not anticipated.

In selecting Bristol, the company referred to the area's excellent communications and technological facilities, its proximity to London, the availability of skilled labour, and the city's attractiveness to technical and managerial staff, including a core of existing staff and potential new recruits. Proximity to aerospace customers was also a factor—avionics and defence applications account for the major part of the company's activities. It also followed parent company policy of dispersing activity to avoid competition for labour between its operating units. Recruitment and turnover was becoming a problem at existing sites.

In this case there was considerable Industry Department opposition to a non-assisted area location, and there was a delay in the granting of an Industrial Development Certificate. Backed by the lobbying of the local authorities and local MPs, the company maintained it would expand in the USA as an alternative, although with no existing US operations this may well have been a bargaining strategy. Acceptance by the government (following the Conservative victory in May 1979) was seen by one MP as 'a very significant development in government policy', and another commented that 'The way is now open for Bristol to develop into Britain's Silicon Valley.'[5] With the deepening recession, however, the project was delayed almost to the point of abandonment.

The third example is a network of semi-autonomous small companies primarily involved in manufacturing advanced 'plasma'-based etching, and deposition systems used in the production of microchips. The company is at the boundaries of technology in this area and is heavily involved in R & D. Customers include major international components manufacturers such as Motorola, Texas Instruments, and National Semiconductors, and leading UK electronics companies. About three-quarters of the firms' output is exported, including significant sales to Japanese manufacturers. By mid-

1984 UK employment totalled around 340, including about 100 in Wales and the rest mainly in the Bristol locality, plus about 50 overseas sales and support staff. Output has been expanding rapidly, with turnover increasing threefold during 1982–4, and employment expanded significantly in 1984–5.

The group originated in South Wales in 1968 with a company set up by three current directors who have been centrally involved in subsequent expansion and product development as 'technical entrepreneurs'. They had left the South Wales plant of a major US electronics company, where they had been involved in semiconductor development, and set up in a Special Development Area near Newport. From this relatively small base, the group expanded to the area west of Bristol with six component and manufacturing companies on different sites. A central administrative, sales support, and additional R & D facility, forming the core of the organization, has been set up on another separate site, moving into purpose-built premises in 1984 and employing around 35. Five separate sales companies relate to different market areas worldwide. Four companies remain in Wales.

Initially, older, less profitable, lines were left in Wales but components and sub-assemblies are supplied to the English companies and new products are being developed there including non-semiconductor equipment. Promoted by physical separation, each company is designed as an operationally independent and autonomous profit centre, specializing in particular product lines or processes, incluing component and sub-assemblies and the assembly of completed installations.

The central administrative and research facility, although within a few miles of central Bristol, is in a relatively isolated rural location. The firm considered Aztec West but it was more expensive and the firm 'distinctly did not want to be a shop window'. The initial expansion from South Wales was prompted by Bristol's electronics image; labour availability, including both skilled manual workers for high-quality specialist engineering and fabrication and high-level electronics graduates; a desire to set up a network of separate but accessible units; and communications with markets and in particular Heathrow which accounts for 90 per cent of exports. Poor industrial relations in Wales reinforced the expansion into the Avon area and the structure of interlinked small companies. Bristol was seen as having major advantages in labour market terms. For production workers such as wirers and high-quality machinists and other metal workers, the presence of the large aerospace companies was a major advantage. The locality was also attractive for qualified technical staff including people coming out of the local universities.

Other companies, illustrating the diversity within the sector, include a range of smaller manufacturers, many of them involved primarily in subcontract work. One, for example, employing 14 people, manufactures electronics equipment from specialist test rigs for aero-engines and mid-range computers to individual circuit boards. Customers have included all the main aerospace/defence contractors in the locality, which have been the basis for growth, and the company also produces short production runs of computer hardware for one of the Aztec West companies when the demand arises. The production manager himself had previously worked in aerospace locally. Production is essentially labour-intensive, much of it relatively low skill. Another company employs around 50 people producing microchip-based intruder alarm systems. Production involves basic assembly labour, pre-dominantly female, inserting components in printed circuit boards, and automatic flow soldering. This was described as a 'high-tech product with traditional low-tech production'.

Research and development. At the other end of the scale, there has been a small but significant growth of advanced R & D in the area. Much of this is specifi-cally related to product development, both hardware and software, or to tailoring products to customer requirements. This has essentially expanded with the manufacturing, sales, and support activity with which it is in some cases closely integrated; R & D related to particular product lines will com-monly be located alongside production, sales, and support of current pro-ducts. More divorced from existing product lines, Inmos established its R & D facility in Bristol in 1979, and a European research lab is being set up alongside the peripherals factory. In both cases the possibility of attracting top-grade R & D staff to the area was a prime consideration. Inmos in fact wanted to locate its microchip facility in the city as well, but government pressure to locate in a Development Area resulted in this prestige project going to Newport—virtually the closest Development Area location with an adequate labour supply and motorway access to Bristol.

Locational factors Looking finally at the sector as a whole and at its relation-ship to the Bristol locality, the local aerospace industry has been a key influence on the growth of other electronics-based employment. It has played a specific role in its influence on the labour market, and a more general part in the locality's reputation for technologically advanced activity. Both were clearly important to the majority of electronics companies locating in the area. The availability of both skilled and unskilled production labour, reflect-ing the strength of aerospace and the presence of other major manufacturing companies, *combined with* the attractiveness of the locality to higher-level tech-nical staff, has been a particular attraction. For a smaller group of com-panies, aerospace has also represented a significant market and a source of subcontract work. The development of sales and marketing outlets has partly reflected the strength of aerospace and other defence-related activity in the locality and the region more widely.

The availability of suitable sites and premises was a secondary advan-tage—although important, it is not clear that Bristol is strongly differentiated from many other localities on this basis. Availability has been facilitated by the overall planning framework and policy decisions relating to particular sites, although the authorities have been more than willing to swim with the tide, and no major policies such as green-belt designation have been seriously challenged by individual cases.

The city's specific advantages at the micro-level are the combination of major sites on the northern fringe, adjacent to the M4/M5 interchange and the fast rail link from the out-of-town Bristol Parkway station. Aztec West offered relatively low-cost prestige premises and 'a good shop front' with excellent motorway and rail access, although the specification of spec-built premises and the lack of services was criticized by some occupants. The ability to come up with major sites on the northern fringe for single occupants as well as estate-type developments has been important in some instances—the adjacent local authority-owned sites sold to the peripherals company and offered to Dupont were clearly influential in that both had fairly exacting requirements.

In terms of specific economic development policy, the attraction of inward investment in particular by US-owned electronics companies has been a central plank of promotional efforts led by Bristol City—what might be called the 'Hewlett Packard Strategy' (see Chapter 6). In trying to pin down the role this has played, it is hard to distinguish specific impacts from more general influences whose causal effects are impossible to disentangle.

With regard to the companies discussed earlier, there do appear to be a couple of significant cases of new arrivals in which the local authority is particularly implicated. Even here, the precise effect of its involvement is hard to assess. As indicated earlier, the peripheral company reported that the local authority played its role effectively, but it was not suggested that it was a crucial determining factor. The financial assistance package was welcome but not essential, symptomatic perhaps of the company's bargaining strength and the desire of the local authorities to secure the move and express their 'goodwill' in a tangible fashion. All five Aztec West companies were in fact established in Bristol before moving to the new site, and predated the development of the local authority's strategy after 1976, as was Inmos. The expansion of the company from Wales was similarly unrelated to local economic development policies. The local authority did add its voice in lobbying against the refusal of an IDC for the avionics company, but this was not seen as in any sense crucial, nor was it described as a factor in the initial choice of Bristol itself.

More generally, to the extent that local authority policies overall are implicated in the quality of the urban environment and infrastructure, the authorities have played a part in preserving and enhancing the attractiveness and image of the area. This in turn has been important in the ability of companies to attract and retain high-grade technical and managerial staff. Central government's role in the provision of transport infrastructure is again relevant. In terms of regional policy, IDC's may have actually steered some growth of electronics companies away from the area in the 1970s, although evidence of specific instances is, apart perhaps from the Inmos case and the avionics company's delayed IDC, flimsy and somewhat apocryphal. Such pressure became in any case merely a token in the 1980s—as we have seen, central government in fact added to the financial package offered to the peripherals factory.

Employment

Electronics employment has grown rapidly since the early 1970s and continues to grow. Existing firms have expanded and new firms been established in the area since 1981. There are examples of rapidly enlarging firms at the boundaries of technology and concentrations of advanced R & D activity. Regional sales and service functions have been sustained by relatively strong markets in the locality and beyond.

In absolute terms, the scale and expansion of electronics are nevertheless very modest compared with shifts in other employment sectors. In terms of composition, it is apparent from the case studies that electronics draws on a marked diversity of occupational labour markets, ranging from high-level production and software specialists to basic semi-skilled assembly work. Relatively low-skill manual assembly and production labour in particular is a major employment category in many companies, belying to some extent the high-tech product image. Women are, with a few exceptions, employed in typing, secretarial, clerical, or administrative posts, or on basic assembly work.

Recruitment The electronics sector has been concerned specifically with the management of recruitment rather than with job loss. Different occupational categories are however characterized by different supply–demand relations, and are recruited through different channels and on different geographical scales. They range from top-level software and electronics engineers or technical sales staff generally in short supply, forcing companies to adopt a variety of strategies to meet their needs, to relatively low-grade assembly workers, where the task is to sift out recruits from a large volume of actual or potential applicants. Managerial grades are commonly recruited internally within the larger companies, partly reflecting a desire to maintain career paths. A transition from senior technical staff to managerial responsibility is common among smaller companies.

Much of the industry is characterized by the overlap between technical skills and experience, reflecting not only individual career paths but also the necessary technical content of management and administration. Where companies are established locally by larger corporations, a management core is usually moved in to set up operations. In the case of the US-owned peripherals company, a team of 15 managerial and technical staff was installed to establish the facility and then withdraw, having handed over to largely domestically recruited staff. More generally, aerospace has been a significant source of managerial staff and 'technical staff turned managers' for a number of companies.

Experienced sales staff are a particularly important category, both for those firms with primarily sales and support functions in the locality and for production companies. Regionally based sales staff of national companies are more involved in selling relatively standard product lines and systems, with varying degrees of technical knowledge required. Volume sales are important, and commission may make up a large part of earnings. Sales staff in companies producing more sophisticated or tailored systems are usually required to have technical qualifications and experience, to a very high standard in some cases. Experienced and effective sales staff are generally in short supply and turnover rates can be high. Recruitment channels include national papers and the trade press and employment agencies are widely used, with constant 'head-hunting'. Some companies have responded by initiating graduate training schemes, though recognizing the dangers of such staff moving on.

Software engineers and other high-quality, mainly graduate, technical staff are similarly in high demand and relatively short supply. Software skills in particular are recruited nationally, and from the Bristol-to-Cambridge belt in particular, rather than locally. Companies also concentrate on graduate entry, aiming to build up relations with particular university departments, getting to know staff and identifying potential maths, computer science, and engineering recruits. The major companies co-ordinate graduate entry and other recruitment at the national level. An expanding, locally based company commented that it was fishing in the same pool but did not have the name to give it the sort of access larger firms built up. Reflecting their market position, pecuniary and non-pecuniary benefits for software and other technical staff tend to be high and working conditions may be characterized by considerable autonomy. Again, staff are recruited on a national scale but local aerospace companies have represented a pool of experienced technical staff across a range of areas incluing electronic engineering, systems, material sciences, and related activities.

Manual recruitment ranges from unskilled, particularly female, assembly workers to highly skilled machinists, wirers, and test engineers, with precise work definitions and required standards varying considerably. Engineers attached to sales and service centres are involved mainly in the repair and maintenance of existing installations. Product innovation is increasing modular design, facilitating 'test-and-replace' maintenance. There is some tendency for field service engineers to be less qualified, with qualified staff working in-house. Recruitment is almost entirely local, with aerospace an important source of more experienced semi-skilled and skilled manual workers. Companies expect to train staff for process-specific semi-skilled tasks and in some cases expect little in the way of relevant experience. Word of mouth and the local press are major sources. Jobcentres have been used in some cases, but were generally criticized for their inability to pre-select suitable candidates. A number of firms have however specifically recruited from the Skillcentre.

Clerical vacancies are similarly filled by word of mouth or local press adverts where necessary. Jobcentres are used more for clerical than other vacancies although practice varies—the US-owned peripherals factory, which pursues an explicit equal opportunities strategy, used Jobcentres as a matter of policy and to provide a wide range of applicants to choose from. Informal networks were formalized in one case by a 'refer-a-friend' recruitment scheme.

Management–labour relations   The electronics sector is characterized by a lack of significant unionization. This contrasts with the electronics-based aerospace company, which is heavily unionized along with the rest of that industry. A greater number of individual employees may be union members on the production side, but none of the companies recognized unions for bargaining purposes. Patterns of individual membership to some extent reflect employees' origins, particulrly in aerospace. Basic assembly workers are commonly women and are less likely to be unionized anyway. The particular style of management–labour relations which has developed in the sector reflects the relative importance of quasi-professional technical and sales staff as opposed to manual 'shopfloor' staff; it is also a product of the size of unit, and of conscious 'preventative strategies', facilitated by the general context of expanding employment.

The US-owned firm was characterized by a 'one-status' corporate style reflected in 'open management', open-plan layouts for virtually all functions, and an emphasis on informality, lack of hierarchy, and maximizing contact between management and staff. Pay is relatively high, maintained in the upper quartile, and supplemented by profit-related bonuses. Conflicts rarely take on a collective form, reflecting, as one manager put it 'individual assimilation problems'. This was mirrored in the sales and service outlets, where the emphasis was very much on image and informality and considerable autonomy in work practices. One employee referred to workplace relations in the following way: 'Like a happy family, there are no unions here, people act responsibly. If there's a rush job on they may stay late or come in at weekends. In return they get job satisfaction, good salaries, and the chance to move between tasks.'

The form of expansion adopted by the company referred to earlier, taking the form of a network of semi-autonomous companies, was designed in part to minimize the distance between management and staff and to promote a collective commitment to the specific aims of the individual units, including financial targets. The degree of physical separation of the companies allows for management contact but discourages contact between the workforces themselves. As one manager commented, reflecting the general strategy across virtually the whole sector, 'We have not given them good cause to join trades unions.'

Conclusions

Electronics employment has grown at a rapid rate from a small initial employment base. Despite the locality's high-tech image, electronics has had little real employment impact in absolute terms. There is little to suggest that the scale of development is exceptional in the M4 corridor or, indeed, compared with many localities throughout the country. There is no real sense as yet in which an integrated network of advanced electronics-based companies is becoming established in the Bristol area. In overall terms, electronics-related activity rooted in the traditional aerospace sector and its subsequent diversification overshadows more recent inward investment. And much of the more recent growth has been influenced by aerospace in terms of both labour markets and product markets.

As we suggest later, the locality's high-tech growth image is largely a product of promotional hype and political hopes. Future employment growth depends on the employment trajectories of existing companies plus the impact of further inward investment—new firm formation is unlikely to be important in absolute terms. A number of existing employers will continue to expand—several have specific plans for future growth. Realistic estimates based on current plans and trajectories do not however suggest that employment growth will exceed a few hundred over the next three to five years.

Grossly inflated claims for future employment creation have been central to the hype surrounding a number of developments. This is reminiscent of the avionics company for which initial press job estimates in 1979 were 1,000–1,400 but which was employing only 220 by mid-1984 with no plans for significant expansion. As this example illustrates, except in the short term, employment estimates are very much dependent on product markets and developing corporate strategy, which are, in the nature of the sector, volatile. Employment totals in terms of thousands have been associated in press reports with both the computer peripherals company and Dupont. On current, relatively firm, expansion plans, total employment in the former is unlikely to exceed 500 including the R & D laboratory, while initial plans for Dupont suggest a modest plant employing around 200.

Inward investment is harder to predict. The locality remains attractive in terms of its specific attributes, although research in the USA for Bristol City Council has suggested that these are not widely known among potential relocators. In this sense, the 'herd instinct', and the attention drawn to the locality by names such as Hewlett Packard and Dupont, may conceivably turn out to be the hoped-for catalyst. So far, at least, there is however little sign of the stampede.

Insurance

Financial services have been a key component of service sector growth, locally as nationally. In fact, Insurance, Banking, and Finance expanded locally by some 73 per cent over the decade to 1981, to nearly 9,500 in absolute terms, representing more than twice the national growth rate. A major part of this increase—40 per cent—was accounted for specifically by insurance employment. This doubled over the decade to 1981, an increase of almost 4,000, compared with 10 per cent growth nationally, a dramatic growth rate, albeit from a relatively small base. By 1981, insurance accounted for 2.6 per cent of all employment locally, over 7,500 in absolute terms, compared with only 1.4 per cent nationally. Over 45 per cent of total employment (3,500) was female, which has expanded at roughly the same rate as male employment.

Having said that, the insurance industry as a whole is not particularly concentrated in Bristol, which accounts for little more than 2.5 per cent of national employment—compared with, for example, 19 per cent of tobacco employment and 12 per cent of aerospace employment. Much of insurance employment is relatively evenly spread over the country in local and regional offices. Nevertheless, Bristol has emerged as a major centre of insurance employment, second only to London, with higher-order headquarters functions strongly represented. Employment growth was achieved, furthermore, in a context of rising productivity, with output increasing significantly faster than employment. There has been a sharp increase in new business per employee and a significant reduction in wages and salaries as a proportion of total management expenses in recent years.

Corporate context

Much of this growth is attributable to the relocation of insurance employment from London. Four UK companies—Phoenix, Sun Life, Clerical Medical and General, and London Life—moved their administrative headquarters to Bristol between 1972 and 1983, and the NatWest Bank established its insurance subsidiary in the city. Other departments of the same bank also relocated, and Welbeck Finance has set up more recently.

These moves resulted in the generation of significant local employment along with the relocation to Bristol of existing staff. By 1983, employment in the five relocated companies totalled over 4,000, suggesting that they account for well over half of total insurance employment in the locality. The remainder is in area and branch offices of companies headquartered elsewhere in the country, or in insurance brokers and related activities. Given the importance of national administrative functions, a large part of insurance activity represents 'basic' employment, a direct and obvious gain to the 'local' economy. These companies are 'exporting' services to the rest of the country rather than simply depending on local or regional markets. Overseas markets are relatively unimportant.

Of the five companies which relocated, three are 'life' companies dealing in long-term life assurance, pensions, and life-linked investment, and they operate only in the UK. One is a 'composite' company, combining long-term and general insurance, and it does have major overseas business. The fifth company provides primarily broking services for the parent bank's customers.

In the longer term, insurance has been an expanding industry in terms of both turnover and employment. More recently, the recession has had a major impact, particularly in general insurance markets. Demand in non-UK markets for general insurance has been particularly weak, and competitive pressure has increased both at home and abroad. Long-term business, on the other hand, though increasingly competitive, has continued to expand, albeit more slowly. It is inherently more stable and predictable and much less subject to overseas competition. Three of the Bristol companies are thus operating in the more resilient, long-term, market. The composite company, however, had been suffering more severe pressure, mainly from its 'general' business; with share prices depressed, it was taken over in 1984. The implications of the takeover are yet to be seen, and this summary relates to the pre-takeover situation.

Market conditions overall are generating strong pressure for cost-cutting and, with labour a major component of total costs, increased productivity. This is reinforced by the importance of price and performance-based competition in the attempt to retain or expand market shares. However, the predominance in the locality of long-term business, in which there is still some growth, may give employment an element of stability.

The spatial structure of the four insurance companies was broadly similar. The Bristol headquarters, with over half of the company's UK employment, would typically include all central administrative functions and departments and some principal managers. The London office, accounting for up to 5 per cent of UK employment, would include the boardroom, general manager, and some principal managers. Property, equity, and other investment, and possibly some marketing, legal, tax, and actuarial activities, remain tied to London, partly for functional reasons such as access to markets and networks, but also owing to the locational preferences of top-level professionals and managers. The remainder of employment, say around 40 per cent, is in offices throughout the country, with branch, area, and possibly regional tiers.

Beyond the big four, employment in branch and area offices of companies headquartered outside of Bristol includes relatively important subsidiary offices in the context of national structures. One company employs 300 in the city and services the 'Western' area taking in West London, Reading and Southampton. The bank insurance subsidiary employs nearly 500 in an autonomous unit; other sections of the same bank, also relocated to Bristol, account for a further 800. In addition, there is significant employment in a cluster of local óffices of insurance brokers and other insurance-related activities.

Production change

With a strong emphasis on cost-saving and productivity increase, management strategies have involved a combination of rationalization of branch and area networks, continued technological change, and above all in the Bristol case, relocation. The overall aim, particularly in the case of long-term business, has been to accommodate future growth in business while maintaining current employment levels, unlike, say, tobacco, where management strategy in the context of shrinking markets has led to major job loss.

Rationalization Most companies have carried out some rationalization of branch and area networks, contributing savings in staff terms and centralizing employment to some extent on larger area offices and administrative headquarters. Some rationalization of head office functions has also accompanied technical change and relocation. Overall, Bristol has if anything marginally gained in employment terms. Where companies are locally headquartered, centralization has tended to favour Bristol: one company removed a regional office tier with the loss of 200 jobs, but with 100 new jobs being established at the Bristol headquarters, 40 filled by internal transfers and 60 by new recruitment. Where companies are headquartered elsewhere, the concentration of activities on to larger branch and area offices has sustained and in some cases has increased employment locally in comparison with smaller urban centres, and the city's role as a regional centre has been consolidated.

Technical change With mainframe computing having been established for bulk operations for some twenty to twenty-five years, technical change in most companies has been a matter of incremental rather than dramatic change. Most if not all major functions are now on mainframes. Companies are at different developmental stages, but most area offices now have, or soon will have, on-line terminals to administrative headquarters. Several companies are installing mini-computers in main area offices, linked to mainframes, while stand-alone micros have proliferated in administrative headquarters. Word processing as such is fairly limited, since many standard letters are bulk-printed from mainframes.

Companies which relocated generally took the opportunity to introduce new systems, including mainframes. Relocation was thus combined as a strategy with investment in technical change. This was generally followed by a lull in such investment. There was no evidence that technical change had 'enabled' decentralization, as has sometimes been suggested. The technical capacity to operate away from London already existed. The major impact of technical change appears to have been to allow the handling of an increasing volume of business with little if any increase in employment. This has been reflected in significantly increased productivity. Much of the impact has been at branch and area levels, where new systems have facilitated rationalization. There was evidence, however, that in some cases total employment in companies which relocated to Bristol was lower after the move, attributable in part to new systems and work practices. Overall, companies were anticipating relatively stable or marginally declining employment in response to technical change. Major impacts on total numbers employed were not anticipated, particularly given the continued expansion of business.

Relocation   As we have seen, the predominant factor in terms of employment change was relocation from London. Four companies moved over the period 1972–6, three of them in more than one phase. The most recent move was in 1983, by which time the overall rate of office dispersal from London had slowed considerably.

The dominant and consistent motive for moving out of London was the cost of premises. Cost differentials compared with alternative locations offered major savings on real or, where premises were owned, opportunity costs. This was reinforced where companies occupied older premises in London, unsuited to the development of appropriate work-organization and technology, were outgrowing existing space, or wanted to integrate dispersed operations resulting from past expansion. Prime West End office rents in the early 1970s were two to three times higher than suburban locations such as Croydon, and four to five times those of provincial centres such as Bristol; City of London rents were even higher: the insurance subsidiary was paying City of London rents twelve times the then current Bristol level.

The differential cost of premises was reported to have been sufficient on its own, other things equal, to promote relocation. In fact, labour market pressures in the late 1960s and early 1970s, when most of these moves were initiated, although insufficient on their own, certainly reinforced the incentives. This was reflected in high turnover rates, low quality, and actual shortages, at a time when companies were still increasing employment—one company reported overall turnover rates of 30–40 per cent, higher for lower clerical staff and typists.

It was Bristol's ability to satisfy a combination of necessary criteria relating to the cost and availability of premises, proximity to London and general accessibility, attractiveness to key staff, and local labour market characteristics which attracted at least some of the companies dispersing from London.

Sites and premises   The relative cost of sites and premises was, as already noted, particularly important, although these were no lower in Bristol than in other major provincial centres such as Birmingham. Bristol rents had however been depressed in the early 1970s by speculative oversupply, which if anything has intensified—agents Knight, Frank and Rutley (1983) spoke of supply and demand in Bristol as 'badly out of touch', so much that, 'despite Bristol's attractiveness and its dual role as a main provincial centre and a recipient of relocation firms, it still has rents at levels not above those in other major provincial office centres without relocation appeal.' One company spoke of catching the Bristol market 'on its knees'.

The city's locational attractions are in a sense 'undervalued' in terms of rents and values. Also, it had both sites and premises available to suit the specific needs of the relocating companies—two rented from the large range of speculative accommodation on offer, two acquired sites and had premises built, and the fifth occupied a part-owned speculative development. The specific need for a site with room for expansion and no problems in obtaining planning permission was accommodated in one case.

Communications   Access to London in particular, and to a lesser extent the rest of the country, were key factors. A hundred miles or about one hour by train from London were rough criteria, which, given motorway links and the High Speed Train, Bristol just about met, allowing staff to meet on a day-trip basis in London or Bristol. Senior management and administrative staff may make the journey several times a month by rail or road. Administrative and management links with the rest of the country and centralized training in Bristol are also facilitated. In terms of access, Bristol was, as one manager put it, 'ideally situated'.

Attractiveness to key staff   Companies had to persuade a critical mass of key staff to relocate with them, and without having to pay too much by way of compensation, in order for a move to be viable. One described this group as 'medium to senior staff with experience . . . 50 per cent of the staff' and another more candidly as 'all males who had been with us for over five years . . . a good sweep of people down to the more modest jobs'. These were long established London workforces with all that entailed in terms of staff's locational preferences; and, early on at least, the London employment market was buoyant. But as one (relocated) manager summed it up, the Bristol area 'has a quality of life, the recreational facilities, everything you can think of, housing, the seaside, the country, it's a very attractive city.' Others referred to 'ambience if you like, reputation', and 'a city with character, good housing, arts, education'. Commuting times from green-belt type locations (where many staff chose to live) were perceived as minimal compared with London. Relative housing costs were attractive. Finally, proximity to London facilitated contact with relatives and friends. Combined with Bristol's image, it also reduced perceived separation, tying in the locality to London and the South-East 'heartland'.

Local labour market   The scale of the labour market and the quality of the educational infrastructure were important to companies' immediate and continuing recruitment needs. Bristol was reckoned to offer an adequate supply both of typing and secretarial staff and of O- and A-level school-leaver recruits to clerical grades. As one manager put it, Bristol 'was a bit like the Home Counties', with the possibility of recruiting 'the sons and daughters of professional classes with a tradition of office employment, people with professional qualifications, and a fair number of graduates and the like'. With the large blue-collar population, there was thought likely to be a good availability of 'lower-grade female labour, the sort of people who were not going to move with the company'. A number of managers specifically mentioned the attractiveness of the area to computer staff, who were particularly hard to recruit and retain in London.

An insurance centre   The development of Britol into an insurance centre itself came to be seen as a positive factor. The experience of early movers encouraged subsequent relocation, and the build-up of a pool of insurance experience and employment in the city was seen, on balance, as advantageous. It offered 'cross-fertilization', a pool of existing talent and an insurance community including good professional branches and facilities for taking professional exams. The possibilities of poaching of staff between companies was a minor problem and, in any case, worked both ways.

None of these factors was sufficient in itself to narrow the choice down to Bristol. Nor indeed did they uniquely identify Bristol; although the concentration of relocations to the city was remarkable, other financial companies relocated to a range of urban areas, mainly in the South-East. All these factors, apart from Bristol's emergence as an insurance centre, were however necessary conditions. Possible alternatives were rejected on the basis of these same criteria. Croydon, for example, was seriously considered by one company, but rejected because rents were still relatively high, it was still part of the London labour market, and accessibility for existing staff was poor unless they relocated. Peterborough was seriously considered by at least two companies: one rejected it on the grounds that it was 'not the sort of place for our staff to live . . . the type of housing and the New Town environment'. Another company met heavy staff opposition to Stevenage for similar reasons—'the housing was totally wrong for our people'—and Basingstoke failed for similar reasons. Places like St Albans, Aylesbury, Reading, and Northampton were rejected partly because they still came within the influence of the London labour market. Wales, the Midlands and the North—Cardiff, Birmingham, Glasgow, or Newcastle, for example—were essentially non-starters in terms of where staff would move to—one manager referred to these areas as 'different cultures'. They were largely discounted also on grounds of distance from London.

Companies expressed a very high level of satisfaction with their locational choice of Bristol, referring to the move as 'an unqualified success' and 'the best thing that ever happened to the company', the pay-off point coming significantly earlier than expected for at least one firm. No real problems were experienced in persuading key staff to move to Bristol, and in general, recruitment and personnel problems had 'disappeared overnight'.

In terms of public policy impacts, specific economic development activity had little influence on relocation, but it may have smoothed the process. The reported 'amenability' of the planning environment may in fact have been more relevant in some cases. Lack of any effective control over office development allowed speculative overprovision, and a depression of rents. The role of the local councils as planning authorities, and more generally in promoting an attractive environment and urban milieu in practice and by reputation, has contributed to the magnetism of the area for financial services, specifically through the preferences of key staff. Finally, the importance of accessibility by motorway and High Speed Train emphasizes the role of nationally planned infrastructure provision.

Employment

As indicated earlier, insurance employment doubled over the decade to 1981, to over 7,500, of whom 45 per cent were women. More detailed, company-level information indicates that a large proportion of employees are relatively young and are on fairly low salaries, carrying out basic clerical tasks. In one case, 79 per cent of employees were under 35 and 65 per cent earned under £8000 p. a.; clerical employment, covering a wide range of activities and responsibilities, accounted for 69 per cent, managerial grades 18 per cent, and data processing 14 per cent.

Employment structure is heavily asymmetrical in gender terms, with women concentrated in typing and the lower clerical grades. In one case, women accounted fo 70 per cent of the bottom three clerical grades but only 25 per cent of the top three, despite the fact that virtually all recruitment is at the bottom of the scale and roughly equal by gender. There were virtually no women in the managerial or senior technical grades which make up 20 per cent of the total, whereas typing was the usual female ghetto.

Gender differentiation in clerical grades related to a number of factors. Turnover rates are much higher among female staff, particularly younger women on lower grades. There were also suggestions that women were less career-oriented and less inclined to seek the post-entry professional qualifications which are increasingly important to career development. This ties in with other findings (Crompton and Jones 1984) that female clerical workers have lower aspirations and that there is less expectation and encouragement in relation to post-entry qualifications. Much of this relates to anticipated career breaks. Gender differentiation in insurance thus displays both 'horizontal segregation' (Hakim 1979), in which women perform different tasks (typing), and a strongly developed 'vertical segregation', in which men and women do the same jobs but women are concentrated in the lower grades.

The impact of relocation   As we have seen, growth in insurance employment in the locality is largely attributable directly to relocation. About half of those employed in the companies which relocated moved with the company and about half were recruited locally. This suggests that about 2,000 jobs were 'relocated' into the locality and a further 2,000 'new' jobs were filled by local recruitment. Bristol's gain was thus, in a sense, London's loss, with new jobs being created in place of those who did not relocate with their company. In fact, overall employment was generally lower in Bristol after moves were completed than it had been in London. As already indicated, companies used the opportunity to introduce new technology, management structures, and work practices—and, in the words of more than one manager, to 'shake out the dead wood'.

There were marked differences between staff relocating and those locally recruited. Staff who relocated tended to be older, male, on higher salaries, and on higher clerical grades, managerial, or technical positions. In one case, only 9 per cent of those relocating were under 25 compared with 60 per cent of locally recruited staff; 61 per cent earned at least £10,000 as against 10 per cent of local recruits; 33 per cent were in managerial positions compared with only 3 per cent of local recruits; and 77 per cent of those who relocated were male compared with 44 per cent of local recruits. This pattern reflects company strategy, which was to persuade more experienced staff to move while expecting to recruit lower clerical, typing, and ancillary staff locally, a strategy that was facilitated by the inability or unwillingness of many lower-grade staff to move from London. Comparable relocation terms were generally offered to most staff, but benefits geared to incomes were much less significant, in absolute terms, to lower paid staff. It was also clear that certain types of staff were encouraged and expected to contemplate moving more than others.

Relocation has, then, led to significant job creation, although mainly in lower clerical, typing, and ancillary grades. This included job opportunities for women which, although towards the lower end of the scale, were nevertheless full-time with relatively good pay and conditions, unlike much of rapidly expanding female service employment.

Recruitment   Major recruitment needs were associated with relocation. Subsequent recruitment has virtually all been to replace normal turnover plus a few specialists as needs have arisen. Quoted turnover rates of around 8–10 per cent suggest that overall needs may have risen to roughly 600–700 vacancies annually in the sector as a whole—figures for individual firms, although substantial, suggest somewhat less overall.

Most clerical staff have been recruited as school-leavers. Relatively high qualifications, four O levels or two A levels, mean that companies cream off some of the best school-leavers and exclude the majority. The major source of applications is individuals writing in, prompted to some extent by links between schools and the companies. General publicity plus school visits and other initiatives boosted speculative applications at the time of relocation. Recruitment is increasingly of A-level entrants, partly because more pupils are staying on after O levels. Companies had in some cases consciously shifted towards A-level recruitment, taking advantage of labour market conditions to take on the best available candidates. Some however expressed the need for 'a good steady flow of people with O levels' for 'more routine' clerical work, conscious that career prospects could not be assured for all entrants.

Graduate entry operates on a national scale and may be linked to specialist training, with entrants channelled towards, say, actuarial, data processing (DP), or sales work. Specialists and experienced insurance personnel are recruited as needs arise, possibly from people who have written in but mainly from adverts in the local, national or specialist press. Typists, secretarial, and ancillary staff are found via the local press or, failing that, the more costly alternative of private agencies. Jobcentres or Professional and Executive Recruitment (PER) are rarely used and have provided very few staff. Private agencies are avoided if possible on cost grounds, although one company placed all its vacancies on relocation with agencies which met a large part of its needs.

Companies have generally found little difficulty finding most grades of staff, even given the heavy recruitment associated with relocation, thus confirming the anticipated attractions of the local labour market. Some specific problems were associated with recruiting and retaining good-quality specialists in a variety of fields, but this was not a problem specific to Bristol.

The internal labour market   The clerical hierarchy, finely graded in terms of job content, runs from entry grades to relatively senior posts with promotion based on ability plus seniority. There are separate management grades and systems, and DP staff will often be on a separate scale. Management staff are commonly recruited internally from the upper clerical grades but with more external recruitment than in the past. At the other end of the scale, career paths from typing grades are minimal and do not connect with clerical grades.

There are signs of a growing polarization between what might be called 'career' or promotionally oriented clerical staff and others, particularly women, engaged on more routine clerical tasks with less expectation—on their own part and the company's—of progression up a career path—'our shopfloor workers', as one manager described them. This partly relates to technical change and the need for bulk inputting and handling of routine information. One manager distinguished between the need to recruit staff and carry out lower-grade clerical tasks, essentially servicing policies and higher-level decision-making, and staff who are going to progress up to supervisory grades and beyond.

The maintenance of career opportunities was seen as necessary in order to retain staff and reduce turnover. Given the pyramid structure of the job hierarchy, this objective relies on relatively high drop-out rates lower down the scale and on differentiation within clerical staff in terms of career prospects and aspirations. As we have seen, this operates partly on gender lines, reinforced by the fact that, with higher female turnover rates, there is a throughflow of women in lower grades while men are more likely to progress up the hierarchy.

At the other end of the scale, certain specialist insurance activities such as actuarial accountants or experienced underwriters, and other professional skills such as legal, accountancy, investment, or sales and marketing, have tended to emerge as specific segments, separated off to some extent from the clerical hierarchy. Problems of turnover and professional rather than company loyalty have led to individualized salary scales and incentives. These labour market segments are tending to become more open, and more liable to 'poaching' by other companies. There is, consequently, more recruitment of experienced staff as needs arise. The same has been true of data processing and systems staff, who again have transferable skills, until recently in high demand. As shortages nationally have abated, so the power of this particular group to achieve relatively high salaries has been eroded and turnover rates have fallen, although demand remains relatively high in the Bristol region and the M4 corridor generally.

Tasks have also become more routinized with less need for specialist staff. Companies have sought to train DP staff internally and to integrate DP personnel more firmly with the overall workforce and company by blurring the divide between DP and other groups. More specific needs have been increasingly met by contract staff or the use of tailored software packages rather than highly skilled staff employed on a permanent basis. These findings are consistent with Rajan's (1984) findings relating to financial services more generally, of an increase in professional and technical staff, and of increasing differentiation within clerical grades, between career and 'non-career' staff.

Conclusions

With insurance employment in the Bristol area doubling over the last decade compared with a 10 per cent growth rate nationally, restructuring has obviously benefited the locality. Relatively high-quality jobs have been created, particularly compared with much service employment growth. To this must be added the wider economic impacts for the area, mainly through the demand for local goods and services from those working in the sector. Wages and salaries account for around 80 per cent of operating costs in the industry, and total wages and salaries in the sector paid locally amount on a rough calculation to at least £70 million in 1983.[6] More than half of this is attributable to relocated companies. Bristol offered relocating companies a combination of major savings in office costs, proximity to London, and general accessibility, plus attractiveness to key staff and an appropriate local labour market. Added to this, it has consolidated its position as a regional insurance centre.

Short-term stability and marginal decline in the longer term as a result of technical innovation are the likely employment prospects in the absence of further relocation. Bristol, however, remains very attractive, with a range of relatively cheap high-quality office space and sites available, and no signs of overheating in the labour market, should other firms be seeking to relocate. Dispersal is obviously well down on the early 1970s. Pressures of expansion have lessened and, given the scale of earlier dispersal from London, fewer candidates for relocation remain. Jones, Lang, and Wooton (1983), however, suggested in June 1983 that twelve office moves involving over 100 employees were likely in that year with a further 20 in prospect. Bristol remains a likely recipient, whether of insurace and other financial services or of other activities responding to the same factors.

Notes

1. Census of Production output and productivity information does not cover the Insurance sector. Other measures indicate, however, that growth in output has generally outpaced continuing employment growth, indicating significantly increased productivity (Rajan 1984; Central Statistical Office 1981).

2. The panel included: the three major Aerospace companies, accounting for virtually all employment in that sector, plus an avionics equipment and a composite materials company tied to the Aerospace sector; all four Insurance companies and the insurance subsidiary of one of the clearing banks which relocated to Bristol, and the regional offices of two companies headquartered elsewhere, accounting for around 60 per cent of insurance employment locally; the single Tobacco sector employer; in the Paper, Board, and Packaging sector, the head office and one major production site of a locally headquartered multinational conglomerate and two other packaging companies; ten Electronics and Computer Products companies including all the occupants of the Aztec West development; and three Engineering manufacturers. Interviews were conducted mainly in the period January–June 1984, and in most cases involved a number of visits to each company and discussions with a range of general and personnel managers. Interview material was returned to respondents for comments and validation. Unattributed quotes in the text are drawn from these interviews.

3. Census of Employment, Minimum List Headings (MLHs) 481–4.
4. MLHs 364–7.
5. *Bristol Evening Post*, 11 July 1979.
6. Multiplying total employment locally by an estimate of average income for the sector as a whole, derived from a number of company annual reports.

4

The Anatomy of Job Loss and Job Creation

The previous chapter described the detailed processes at work in five leading industries in Bristol. This chapter draws on that evidence to present an explanation of the particular pattern of recent restructuring in Bristol. The first section draws out the different forms of production reorganization in the five industries to show that, although job losses and gains emerged from a variety of processes, the corporate strategies which lay behind them shared many central features. The second section identifies the critical characteristics of the Bristol economy which have accounted for its locational advantages in the context of these strategies. The third section moves on to survey the structure of the Bristol economy as a whole and the connections between its different components. The final section then reviews some different explanations for Bristol's relative buoyancy, in the light of this analysis.

Production Reorganization and Corporate Strategies

Employment change is a deceptively simple category (Massey and Meegan, 1982). Jobs may be lost or created for a variety of immediate reasons. Job loss may arise because output per employee increases faster than total output, or because total output falls. Output per employee may rise without any major change in the technology of production, so that the capital–labour ratio is unchanged, and there is an intensification of the labour process. Alternatively, output per employee may rise as a result of investment in new production processes. Job loss associated with a fall in output may simply reflect rationalization (a simple scaling down of both output and employment), or it may reflect technical change (and an increase in productivity). Conversely, new jobs may be created because rising output is achieved simply by scaling up activity (extension or 'simple expansion', the inverse of rationalization). Alternatively, output may rise as a result of technical changes in the production process which can be associated with an increased demand for certain types of labour.[1]

The industries examined in Chapter 3 offered examples of all of these possibilities. They also showed that some new jobs were brought into the city region through the relocation of establishments from elsewhere. We found no indication that relocation was a significant cause of job loss overall.[2] In most cases, however, more than one form of production change has been taking place simultaneously. Indeed, one form (such as technical change) sometimes provided the conditions for another (such as intensification). Each case was complex, and the overall picture could not be reduced to any simple generalization.

There were clear indications in a number of cases that work was being intensified and shared among fewer employees. Output per employee was increasing as a result of reductions in the time spent waiting between the performance of tasks, changed work procedures, or greater effort. However, these changes were often associated with prior or contemporaneous technical changes in the production process. There were no obvious examples of 'pure intensification' on its own, although this does not mean that this has not been important elsewhere in parts of the Bristol economy.

In the Insurance sector, for example, throughput is expected to increase steadily in the foreseeable future, and this is to be managed without increases in employment or changes in technology, implying an increase in the productivity of most clerical grades. However, this is possible basically because the employment effects of existing technologies have not yet been fully absorbed. The effective workload may increase as unused capacity, in terms of existing mainframe and microcomputers, organizational structures, and staff resources, is taken up. In the Tobacco sector there has been a marked intensification, especially in cigarette making and packaging. Formerly each woman unloaded and conveyed a pallet of 3,000 cigarettes every three minutes, but an increasing number now do the same every minute. Similar changes have been brought about in the hand-rolling tobacco section, where new machinery has displaced the traditional manual task of weighing tobacco, while simultaneously increasing output. In these cases, however, increased workloads are directly related to technical changes in the form of the introduction of new generation machinery.

The Printing and Packaging industry provides further examples of increases in workload, especially in traditionally labour-intensive sections such as packing and dispatch, where there have not been major changes in the capital equipment used. Intensification in these cases is related to technical changes elsewhere, because the work flow has been increased by investment in new technologies upstream. For example, the workload in packing and dispatching finished products has been pushed up as a result of the installation of new generation printing equipment.

Increases in productivity as a result of an intensification of work were visible not only on the shop (or office) floor. Lower management levels have been heavily affected in many companies. Intensification here is associated with increased effort, changed working practices, and also changes in the technology of production and in management structure and style. Indeed, it appears that one of the fields of work most affected by recent restructuring is the management labour process. Some of the implications of this are taken up in the next chapter.

Intensification arose in some cases where job loss was associated with increases in output. But jobs were also lost as a result of rationalization and the reduction of output. In a general sense, rationalization was a major source of job loss in the city region as a whole, since many jobs were lost through closures or large-scale redundancies (Bassett 1984, p. 889). In the Printing and Packaging industry, for example, the disappearence of whole sets of activities (such as paper bag manufacture—see Chapter 3) was due to the abandonment of some product markets which have been penetrated by imports or displaced by substitutes. In the Aerospace sector the decline in production for some markets was matched by a fall in manual employment (the effect, for example, of the run-down of the Concorde project in the mid-1970s).

Some shopfloor jobs in the Tobacco sector were shed as part of a nation-wide rationalization of production. The net impact of rationalization on Bristol was, however, more complex than this would suggest. Where rationalization took place in a large corporation with a number of sites, it led in a number of cases to an increase in the share of employment in Bristol, and in some instances employment in Bristol increased as a result. The main examples were in certain occupations in the Tobacco and Aerospace sectors. Rationalization and closure in the Bristol-based tobacco company led to the transfer of administration work to Bristol. Similarly, storages of work in the Aerospace sector led to the closure of a British Aerospace site at Hurn (Bournemouth), which had worked on projects shared with Filton. Some of the remaining work was transferred to Bristol in order to preserve trained labour and consolidate the major site of Filton. (Some employees were also transferred.)

The introduction of new technology has been a major source of job loss, as was shown throughout Chapter 3. New generation microprocessor-controlled machinery has been introduced in the machining of aero-engine components, the assembly of guided weapons components, the insertion of components in multi-layer printed circuit boards, the making and packing of cigarettes and hand-rolled tobacco, the printing of flexible packaging, and the handling of data in the insurance industry. In most of these cases, technical change was directly associated with an absolute reduction in the demand for labour. However, changes in the technology of production have generally been incremental and unspectacular. There has been no sudden quantum leap in any of the firms studied, nor apparently in the local economy as a whole. Where new equipment has been introduced, it has usually been installed alongside older plant, which has continued in use.

In some cases the equipment necessary for computer-aided designs (CAD) and computer-aided manufacture (CAM) has been installed over a number of years, but some time is expected to elapse before it is linked together in a co-ordinated system. The reason is that the cost of major items of new equipment is so great that employers cannot afford to introduce it across the board, whereas a number of smaller innovations and modifications may be introduced without major disruption. In addition, the introduction of new technology, especially in the older manufacturing companies, has frequently been conditional upon agreement with trade unions.

In all cases, the introduction of technical change has been heavily influenced by local labour market considerations. Sometimes the adaptability of labour to alternative forms of productivity increase appears to have delayed technical change (for example in smaller electronics companies, and some of the cases of intensification mentioned earlier); consequently, the overall decline in employment arising from technical change has been gradual. Despite many technical changes on the shopfloor, employment has generally fallen less than in other sections, because many management strategies have focused on cutting over-manning in non-productive areas. The bulk of shopfloor losses were often in departments downstream of those in which new equipment had been installed (as in Printing and Packaging, above).

In other cases technical change has been associated with increasing employment, especially in occupations arising out of the need to install, operate, and maintain the new technology. After a brief pause, the main 'high-technology' employer in the city region has resumed recruitment, leading to employment growth on a trend of about 5 per cent per anum, mostly in the form of recruits with electronics or mathematical skills.

In some cases employment has risen because existing production processes have been extended; that is, more people have been taken on without any associated change in technology. Several companies were expecting to expand in the near future by recruiting additional staff to utilize existing capacity. Some of these (notably in electronics) had excess capacity arising out of over-optimistic investment in the late 1970s based on expectations of market growth, and they expected to recruit as markets revived without introducing major technical changes in produce or process.

Some companies already use new technologies, including robotics, in production, but intend to scale up the amount used only in line with employment as output increases. For example, a manufacture of computer peripherals employs some automated equipment and robotics, but intends to increase this only pro rata with employment as the plant works up to the intended scale of production. The simple extension of production in this manner appears to have been the dominant process behind the growth of employment in the Miscellaneous Services sector, and especially personal services. Output and employment in this cluster of activities has risen by taking on more employees, apparently without major changes in capital equipment.

It is not possible to identify any one sector, and often not any single firm, with any single form of production reorganization. The Insurance sector, for example, has created jobs in Bristol through rationalization, relocation, and the consolidation of headquarters locations, but it may be expected to reduce the labour input relative to output through the assimilation of technical change. In the Aerospace sector jobs have been lost through rationalization and, more especially, technical change. Jobs are also, however, being generated, as a result of rationalization and the consolidation of activities on Bristol sites. Technical changes in both product and process also resulted in some job creation. In the Tobacco sector jobs have been lost through technical change and rationalization, but at the same time some jobs have been brought to Bristol as a result of the way these same processes have impacted unevenly on different locations. In the Printing and Packaging sector, rationalization and technical change have resulted in an absolute loss of jobs in Bristol but an increase in the share of jobs remaining, as work has been relocated and marginal plants in other locations have been closed. Finally, in the Electronics sector the major part of new employment appears to be related to the expansion of existing forms of production.

In general, job creation and job preservation in Bristol have owed less to any radical technical transformation of the workplace than to the advantages of retaining existing work, and locating new work, in Bristol as opposed to other locations.

Corporate structures and strategies

Lying behind changes in the organization of production have been significant developments in terms of corporate strategy and structure. These strategies shared a number of common elements, and in relation to these a Bristol location acquired a particular significance.

In many companies a new strategy was consciously adopted in response to the deepening of recession from the late 1970s. In some cases a clear strategy, in the sense of a decision to move to a new state of affairs, was itself a novelty. An increased awareness of the urgency of increasing competitiveness was precipitated in a variety of ways. Sometimes new guidelines arose following changes in ownership. For example, a major packaging company was forced to rethink its investment strategy when its ownership was transferred to a parent company which imposed financial targets on each unit. In other companies the fragility of existing markets was dramatically brought home when strikes interrupted production and allowed competitors to expand their footholds. In the Tobacco sector the crisis was accentuated by a combination of changes in EEC and domestic government taxation.

In all cases, the new strategies have been heavily conditioned by labour market considerations, and in some cases these have explictly played a major role in determining which of a number of investment possibilities would finally be chosen. Management strategies have often been influenced by the labour market because they have aimed to change labour market practices. In different ways, many of the companies have been consciously restructuring their working patterns. Although this has often been accompanied by the introduction of new technology, it is not reducible to it. As noted, technical change in most cases has been gradual, yet the changes in related labour processes have been quite radical.

These changes may be summarized as moves towards the greater individualization of the work process as managements have dismantled, to varying degrees, pre-existing centralized structures. Payment and promotion prospects for both manual and non-manual employees in manufacturing and large service employers have generally become more closely related to performance. Workforces on different sites are also tending to become more independent of each other, as work has been redistributed to create new site specializations by product.[3] In the Aerospace sector 'centres of exellence' have been created. A major investment programme has been launched to restructure the British Aerospace Filton site in order to faciliate the separation of activities and workforces in the different divisions.

A shift towards a more 'individualized' work process is often evident at the level of the individual worker. Assessment and appraisal schemes are widely used at all except the most basic levels. Management and administrative grades are especially affected, the HAY–MSL system being widely used in determining final salaries. Assessment schemes are becoming increasingly important to career and salary advancement. There is a growing emphasis on line management in industries as different as aerospace and insurance. Occupations in the Insurance sector in which it has been possible to 'get away without doing much' are becoming fewer.

At the same time, employment in many lower management positions is being reduced by the drive to minimize the proportion of 'non-productive' workers. In many cases responsibility for recruitment to basic-level grades has passed more thoroughly to local site level and to line managements. Some corporate recruitment and promotion practices wich emphasized conformity to codified rules, such as internal labour market ladders based on seniority, have been curtailed by a greater emphasis on results in terms of production. There appears, then, to have been a general shift towards forms of labour management which provide finer detail in monitoring of individual employees (Groom 1984).

These changes are bound up with a decentralization of management. In one case a major corporation completely reversed its 1970s strategy of centralization of functions. The role of central management in this and other companies has been slimmed down and confined to service and strategic functions; a matrix organizational structure has been introduced to encourage individual companies to exercise greater autonomy; and this has resulted in a reduction in central employment such that the company headquarters no longer occupies eight of the twelve floors in its office block. In another case a company has expanded by 'cloning' new offshoots, which have been established as separate companies linked through common directors and corporate R & D services. In the large aerospace companies, where matrix management structures have been used for some years, profit centres have been defined at establishment level in order to increase responsiveness to the outside market.

These changes in the labour process have often been associated with a particular spatial pattern. In many establishments in Bristol, tasks associated with 'conception' are undertaken on the same site as those involving 'execution'. Investment in the manufacturing sectors has been designed to consolidate or create R & D and headquarters functions alongside basic production. This is also visible among large employers in the services sector. The office complexes created by relocating insurance companies were neither subordinate 'part-process' units nor 'clones' (Massey 1984), but complete central units, including all the major strategic, executive, and production functions except those few (employing a handful of people) which need to be retained in the City of London.

As a result, different functions have in many cases been juxtaposed, rather than separated by space, as some have suggested (Keeble 1976; Massey 1984, p. 190). There seem to be a number of reasons why this juxtaposition has been so prominent in Bristol. In some cases it is the result of technical imperatives. In aerospace and electronics, for example, much of R & D is in fact development, whereby innovations are constantly being incorporated in the product. In this situation close contact between design and production teams is essential. Second, in some companies the juxtaposition has arisen as a result of labour market policies which emphasize site specialization by product, so that individual sites undertake both the 'conception' and the 'execution' of specific products. This is seen as a way of providing individual managers with maximum autonomy while inhibiting or breaking up collective organization within the workforce across the company as a whole. In other cases juxtaposition is only partly related to technical requirements or labour strategies. In insurance, for example, it was also financially advantageous to locate 'shop-floor' staff alongside high-level employees for reasons of property management.

In general, it appears that the Bristol area specifically offers suitable labour market conditions for companies which wish to juxtapose different functions. The balance of motives for this overlaying of functions varies, but Bristol's comparative advantage as a location for such juxtaposition emerged as a common feature across a range of industries.

Locational Factors

Companies regard a Bristol location as advantageous for a number of reasons. The major factors are accessibility, the costs and supply of premises (especially offices), the composition and size of the local labour force, and the area's attractiveness to élite labour groups. These functions were at the root of decisions to relocate into Bristol, or to increase the share of work allocated to Bristol plants. Some of these features can clearly be traced to the previous history of economic activity within the city region, i.e. to 'past rounds of investments'. Others originated elsewhere; Bristol's position in the transport network, for example, is a consequence of national public investment in the 1960s and 1970s. The accumulation of specific skills and characteristics in the labour market derives from a number of particular historical influences. Prominent among these is the influence of defence spending. It is convenient to start by looking at this, since it has been unusually important in the Bristol region.

The role of defence expenditure

Defence expenditure has played a major role in the Bristol region since the mid-1930s. The zone stretching between Cheltenham, Swindon, and Yeovil, with Bristol at its centre, is probably the most defence-dependent region in the UK (Lovering 1986). This zone receives a disproportionate income from three forms of defence expenditure: Ministry of Defence procurement of defence equipment, arms exports, and the wages and salaries of Ministry of Defence civilian and service personnel. Bristol itself contains the largest concentration of defence–aerospace activity in the UK, and the area also includes major defence and aerospace industries in Gloucester–Cheltenham and Yeovil. These three complexes alone account for one-fifth of national employment in the aerospace industry, and are important in terms not only of size but of function, in that they are important R & D locations. Other companies with major defence interests include Thorn-EMI at Wells, and Honeywell Defence Systems at Corsham. Rocket motors and explosives are manufactured at a Royal Ordnance Factory at Bridgewater, and rocket fuels at Weston-super-Mare.

Major non-industrial defence establishments in the area include GCHQ in Cheltenham, the MoD warship design department in Bath, the MoD Hydrographic Department at Yeovil, and a number of military bases. At a fairly conservative estimate, between one-quater and one-third of male employment in manufacturing in Bristol has been in defence industries throughout the postwar period, some three times the UK average. Total defence expenditure per capita in the South-West region as a whole is around 50 per cent above the second highest region, the South-East, and the proportion in Bristol may be considerably higher.

The Bristol aerospace industry has been heavily dependent on defence markets throughout the postwar period, with the prominent exception of the Concorde project between 1962 and 1978, and it has become even more dependent on defence in the 1980s. Bristol-based aerospace companies were involved in several of the most advanced military projects from the 1940s to the 1980s, and their position has been consolidated by the combination of industrial concentration and international collaboration. Defence expenditure has also been important for other components of the Bristol economy, including for example engineering companies manufacturing nuclear sub-marine handling gear, and others in the plastics and clothing industries.

In the mid-1970s (the only period for which such information is available), Ministry of Defence spending on the procurement of equipment accounted for about one-ninth of the income and output of the South-West region (Table 4.1). This however considerably understates the real significance of defence industries in the Bristol area for a number of reasons. First, the Bristol region accounts for a disproportionately large share of the South-West's defence production. Second, these figures refer only to Ministry of Defence procurement, but arms *exports* are also of major importance, particularly to the locally represented defence companies. British Aerospace is one of the largest UK manufacturing exporters and the Rapier missile, for which ground equipment and components are made in Bristol, is its biggest single export. Rolls Royce aero-engines are also exported on a major scale.

Third, defence spending is concentrated in the most technologically advanced sectors. Bristol has been developed as a key site in the defence capital goods industries, such as the emergent command, communications, control, and intelligence (C3I) industry since the 1970s. Fourth, defence spending relative to manufacturing output has risen sharply at the national level since the mid-1970s. In money terms, British government expenditure on defence equipment rose by 111 per cent between 1978 and 1984, and over the same period arms exports rose by 130 per cent, while manufacturing out-put rose by only 42 per cent. Defence spending rose from 10.5 to 11.5 per cent of public expenditure (HMSO 1985). This implies that defence spending has played an increasingly important role in Bristol's relative buoyancy.

The spatial significance of defence procurement is that it is large and extremely unevenly distributed. As a result, the Bristol region has received a major inflow of public spending and this has been directly implicated in the relatively slow decline of overall manufacturing in Bristol. Major defence contractors have, moreover, tended to develop close relationships with government, which have consolidated their position and have tended to induce a self-perpetuating market dominance. Thus the Bristol aerospace companies have remained major defence contractors through a series of different product demands since the mid-1930s. This means that they have been able to provide relatively stable and immobile employment.

In the influence of defence spending, Bristol may seem to share something with southern California (Saxenian 1983; Malecki 1984). The parallel is superficial, however, for Bristol does not resemble Silicon Valley in any detail (Boddy and Lovering 1986). Although defence spending has been an important component of incomes and employment in Bristol, it has not generated the kind of regional agglomeration economies which proved so important in Santa Clara County in the 1950s and 1960s. The demand generated by the defence industries and government establishments has

Table 4.1. *Defence procurement and regional assistance by region, 1974/5–1977/8* [a]

Standard region	Net manufacturing output £m	Regional assistance[b] £m	Defence procurement £m	(Procurement ÷ output) × 100 (%)	Regional assistance + procurement £m	(Assistance + procurement) ÷ output × 100 (%)
North	10,478	476	573	5.5	1,049	10.0
Yorkshire and Humberside	15,393	89	245	1.6	334	2.2
East Midlands	12,047	10[c]	744	6.2	754	6.3
East Anglia	4,673		264	5.7	264	5.7
South East	46,726		3,674	7.9	3,674	7.9
South West	**9,078**	**26**	**889**	**9.8**	**915**	**10.1**
West Midlands	20,531	2	599	2.9	601	2.9
North-West	23,920	250	949	4.0	1,199	5.0
Wales	7,448	239	112	1.5	351	4.7
Scotland	14,225	424	549	3.9	973	6.8
Great Britain	164,519	1,516	8,598	5.2	10,114	6.2

[a] = Sum of totals for financial years 1974/5–1977/8 in current terms.
[b] = Regional Development Grants plus selective regional assistance.
[c] = Includes assistance not split between East and West Midlands.

Source: Regional Statistics, CSO, net manufacturing output and regional assistance; Short (1981), defence procurement.

influenced the regional market for computer equipment but, overall, the defence industries remain as enclaves lacking major direct links to other activities in the area. Nevertheless, defence work has attenuated the loss in jobs in manufacturing overall and it has also had a major impact on the local labour market. This has exerted an indirect but important influence on activity in other sectors.

Geographical location

Bristol occupies a strategic position in the major road and rail networks, with rapid access to Wales, the South-West, the Midlands, and the London region. Companies indicated that this has two distinct aspects. Bristol's position in relation to the national and international transport networks is important for certain types of activity, while its position as a regional centre with a large hinterland in the South-West and Wales is important for others. In particular, the city's location plays an important role in the composition of its labour market.

Bristol's proximity to Heathrow and London has exerted a major influence on a variety of companies, including manufacturing exporters, office-based companies which have relocated out of London, and companies with their corporate headquaters in London or abroad. Manufacturing companies relied heavily on the motorway network for access to markets in the rest of the country, and also on the Continent. Access to Heathrow is the major factor in some cases, especially for manufacturers of high-value, small-bulk items in the electronics sector.

For many manufacturers, the critical factor is access to the east coast docks rather than Heathrow, but all depend heavily on the motorway network. A manufacturer of automobile sub-assemblies sold on international markets reckoned that the extra transport cost arising from Bristol's westerly position were insignificant, and were heavily outweighed by advantages in terms of labour markets. The completion of the M25 was expected to reduce still further the effective distance between Bristol and Europe. R & D staff from this company were required to keep in regular close contact with European customers such as Ford and Volvo and relied on access to Heathrow.

In the service sector, access to London is also important, but for different reasons. In many of these companies, higher-grade staff need to be within reasonable travelling distance of London. This is particularly marked in the insurance sector, where relocated companies have left their specialist functions in the City. This factor also played a role in other service sectors. In these cases the key feature of Bristol's location is that it is possible to travel to London, attend a full-length meeting, and return the same day. In the insurance sector senior staff may need to do this several times a month, and several relocating companies limited the choice of locations to towns not much above one hour's travelling time from London (see Chapter 3). Bristol represents the western boundary of this region, largely as a result of the British Rail High Speed Train service which reached full operation by the late 1970s. Through-trains reach London in little over an hour and bring Bristol within commuting distance. This facility has been widely used, and British Rail have progressively expanded their commuter parking facilities.

In some cases the provincial airports have also exerted an influence. A relocated electronics manufacturer with other major sites in the South-East regularly used the Bristol (Lulsgate) airport for business journeys to its head-quarters site (which has its own airfield). Another electronics manufacturer regularly imports its components through Cardiff airport (Roose), which is only a little further in travelling time than Lulsgate from Bristol's northern fringe.

A critical feature of Bristol's location is that while it is near enough for higher grades to commute to London as necessary, it is far enough away for commuting times and costs to be prohibitive for other grades. This is per-ceived as a major locational advantage, since the local labour markets for these groups are insulted by distance from those of London. When insurance companies sought new locations they rejected towns nearer London, such as Stevenage, Reading or Northampton, largely because these fell within the influence of the London labour market. Bristol's location in the national transport system is therefore doubly important; it is accessible from London (or vice versa) for higher-paid groups who can afford to commute, yet is not so accessible that it has ceased to contain an independent urban labour market for other groups.

For some companies the critical aspect of Bristol's location is the access it provides to regional markets. The city's regional nodality appears to have increased in the 1960s and 1970s with the opening of the Severn Bridge and the completion of the M4 to Wales and the M5 to the South-West and Birmingham. These two motorways intersect four miles north of Bristol, and the regional access they provide has been critical both to companies and to certain groups of employees. It has had a particularly marked impact on service companies exploiting regionally defined mar-kets. In these cases the operative region is based on market size and trans-port patterns.

In the computer industry, for example, the region served from Bristol extends well beyond the South-West of England; in many cases it ranges from mid-Wales to Berkshire, taking in South Wales and the South-West. One company said that most of its customers are close to the M4, M5, M3 or M27. The regional structure of the insurance sector is similar, if somewhat less broad, and several Bristol offices performed regional functions for the whole of the South-West of England and parts of Wales. These corporately defined regions enhanced the advantages of locations in or near Bristol. Many com-panies serving the regional markets lie adjacent to the local motorways, including the major warehousing activities in Avonmouth and in Bristol itself. The Aztec West industrial estate, which includes several regional sales and service facilities, is situated by the M4/M5 intersection.

The regional centrality of Bristol is important in both the private and public sectors, and is reflected in the distribution of government departments and public corporations. Media services for the South-West, and often Wales as well, are concentrated on Bristol, including Harlech Television (HTV) and a large regional branch of the BBC. The increased nodality of the city was symbolized by the migration of some regional headquarters from Cardiff to Bristol following the opening of the Severn Bridge, for example the Central Electricity Generating Board (CEGB) (Warren 1976).

Bristol's regional position has also been an important factor in the general attractiveness of the location. Easy access to the tourist facilities of Wales or the South-West has clearly enhanced its life style attractions. It is possible not only to attend meetings in London on one day, but also to relax in the mountains of Wales, or the coast of Devon, on the next. Many companies identified this combination of access to city and country as a major element in the appeal of Bristol to élite employees, and this has been an important indirect influence on economic restructuring.

In short, Bristol has been brought closer to London, but not so close that the advantages of the local labour market have been damaged, and at the same time it has grown more central within the South-West and Wales. Just as the development of its aerospace sector has at times been critically dependent on government defence spending, so these changes in access have also been related to government transport policy. Two of Bristol's major locational features are therefore related to past rounds of investment in the state sector.

Bristol's image

Bristol is an élite location in the sense that it is possible to attract labour market groups which are scarce on the national level. The reasons for this are not all as obvious as the locational advantages. Several employers said that the image of the area is a selling point when recruiting higher grades. All the companies agreed with the area's largest employer's claim that 'we've never had any problems getting applicants to come to Bristol, from all over the country.' This company recognizes the attractiveness of Bristol to the extent that its recruitment advertisments explicity stressed that successful candidates would have a choice between a location in Bristol, the Midlands, or the London area. Electronics and insurance companies shared the view that Bristol is a popular location for professionals, managers, and high-level technologists. It is also attractive to entrepreneurial groups. Two manufacturing companies which had opened up in the Bristol area said this was partly because Bristol was 'somewhere we would be happy to live in'.

Bristol's attractiveness owes something to its geographical position and accessibility, and something to the physical character of the city. Relatively cheap housing in the executive market (especially in dormitory villages surrounding the city), and the environment and cultural amenities of 'a real city', which is 'not too far out from London' and the rest of the South-East, are important. The physical environment, including the stock of buildings, the old city docks, and the closeness to surrounding countryside, have been profoundly influenced by the form of past industrial activity. Bristol's relatively late adaptation to the industrial revolution meant that many of its traditional roads and buildings were retained despite the explosive transformation of the urban environment elsewhere. Landowning patterns and the political traditions of Bristol, Somerset, and Gloucester councils had the effect of imposing sharp limits on Bristol's urban expansion to the South and West, and this preserved woods and farmland within sight of the city centre.

More recently, Bristol has been less afflicted by redevelopment and dereliction than other urban industrial areas, and it has not accumulated many visible symptoms of decline. This has been due partly to the nature and relative stability of traditional employment until the late 1970s, but also to planning practices, as noted below in Chapter 6.

However, it is evident that Bristol's attractiveness is not fully explained by its location and its built environment. Less tangibly, but importantly, Bristol is seen as part of the English heartland and a suitable place for the 'good life'. Many employers said their élite employees felt Bristol to be 'part of the Home Counties' or 'almost part of London'. This perception, or evaluation, was highlighted when employers contrasted Bristol with other localities which they did not regard as having comparable virtues. South Wales, for example, is 'not the sort of place the people we want would like to live in'. Many of the companies which had moved out from London felt that cities in the Midlands or the North had such unattractive images compared to Bristol that many of their higher-grade employees would not have been willing to relocate to them. These images relate to both the social environment and the work culture. One company which had originated in South Wales and extended into Bristol referred with some distaste to 'the eccentricities of the Welsh' in contrast to the familiarly English work and social environment of Bristol.

As Bristol has a social cachet to élite labour groups which is not entirely reducible to material factors, there appear to be deeper social and cultural factors at work. For some groups a Bristol location constitutes part of the status and non-monetary income attached to their employment (Massey 1984, p. 142). This of course refers predominantly to white English males in their early or mid-career. A fuller explanation of the attractiveness of Bristol to them would need to unravel the sociological and ideological influences underlying their attitudes and locational preferences (Massey and Miles 1983).

Overall, Bristol's geographical location has exerted a pervasive and favourable influence on the impact of economic change. Bristol has become increasingly nodal in the sense that it provides producer and headquarters services in its market area to private sector firms and non-profit and governmental sectors (Stanback and Noyelle 1982, p. 132). At the same time, it has effectively been brought closer to London and to Heathrow so that its environmental and other advantages have become more salient. Location has been a factor making it possible for employers to tap the local labour market profitably. It has also been a more positive influence through the locality's attractiveness to élite groups in the labour market.

The Bristol labour market

The specific character of the Bristol labour market has been a major influence on the outcome of corporate responses to economic change. Its distinctiveness is related to the fact that it is the largest independent urban labour market on the M4 corridor.

It is helpful here to split the labour supply into two broad groups. The first of these, and the larger by far, consists of the economically active residents in the area; the second consists of employees who may be attracted to work in Bristol. The influences which have been discussed above have affected this pattern of potential supply. Other factors, however, such as the historical patterns of female employment, have also played important roles. In principle, there are three critical dimensions to labour supply: availability, costs, and militancy. Bristol effectively offers advantages to employers on all of these dimensions.

Many employers identified Bristol as the first large labour market west of London in which the supply of the main categories of basic labour is effectively independent of the influence of London. The major occupational groups in question included routine clerical labour, secretaries and typists, unskilled manual labour, and semi-skilled manual production labour. The *in situ* skilled labour force is distinctive in terms of the availability of skilled manual workers, including for example a range of groups specialized in skills pertaining to the printing and aerospace industries, and non-manual groups with a range of engineering and drafting skills. An incoming multinational company observed that these are the types of labour 'for which Bristol has a reputation'. This is underlined by frequent recruitment advertisements placed in the Bristol press by US aerospace and electronics companies.

To a large degree, the availability of these categories of labour is a consequence of the size and longevity of the major industries in the area, especially aerospace. Several electronics employers explicitly acknowledged the role of aerospace: 'a big advantage of this location on the production side is as a result of the effect of large companies such as British Aerospace training wirers.' The aerospace companies shared the view that they had been instrumental in creating the labour market conditions suitable for electronics activity which helped to bring in certain multinationals to Bristol. They generally welcomed this as contributing to the growth of 'an electronics community'.

The aerospace sector has not, however, been the only factor influencing the composition of local labour supply. Demographic change, and a historically low female participation rate, created substantial reserves of female labour which service sector employers have tapped in recent years for clerical occupations, personal services, and other tasks conventionally defined as 'women's work'.

It was noted earlier that Bristol is a location to which it is possible to attract 'élite' employees, and many members of some of these groups are also resident locally. A Bristol location enables employers to gain access to the limited national supply on relatively advantageous terms. Key groups include data processing staff, software engineers, draftsmen (who usually are men), design engineers in a range of occupations and technologies related to aerospace and electronics, plus the legal and accounting professions, other professional groups (media, arts, etc.) and small-scale entrepreneurs.

However, although Bristol is attractive to these élite groups, it would be misleading to place great weight on this factor alone. Many employers commented that they would find it as easy, and in some cases much easier, to recruit these employees in other cities and towns in the South-East. Electronics companies said that if they had wanted only 'high-technology' employees they would have been better suited in Hertfordshire. The relocating insurance companies believed their key staff would have been almost as willing to go to other towns such as Stevenage or Peterborough, although these were rejected in the end (see Chapter 3).

In terms of its ability to attract these élite groups, therefore, Bristol is only one corner of a wide zone, stretching roughly from Cambridge to Southampton and including the other M4 towns, which has been described as the British 'sunbelt' (Massey 1984, p. 141). Its uniqueness lies less in the access to technologists, graduates, and experienced specialist engineers who are scarce on the national level than in the juxtaposition of these élite groups with a large, relatively isolated, urban labour market with a distinctive skill composition. Bristol lies at the centre of a regional market for skilled manual labour (especially in electronics assembly) stretching from Bridgewater in the south to Swindon in the east and Newport in the west. It also contains unskilled manual and clerical labour (including female and part-time workers) in sufficient quantity to meet the requirements of all but very large employers.

The fact that production, design, and administrative groups may all be recruited in the Bristol area on acceptable terms means that Bristol has labour market advantages as a location for activities in which R & D production and administrative functions need to be adjacent. These labour market features have been sufficient to overcome disadvantages in other respects, such as the absence of regional grants and loans. In other cases, labour market advantages have supplemented other advantages, such as the availability of land and premises.

The advantages in locating production and design activities near to each other have been particularly important in the defence industries, where the divide between experimental and routine production is less rigid than in mass-production consumer industries. This salience of the specific combinations of labour available in Bristol has also been reflected in the services sector. Insurance companies relocating to Bristol found it possible to recruit all the grades they required, from office support staff (cleaners, caterers), through clerical grades, up to senior managers and professionals. They were able to find an immediately available local supply of suitable office labour because Bristol was 'big enough not to worry' and had a good long-term supply of school-leavers of what is seen as suitable quality (see Chapter 3), while at the same time their senior staff were willing to move to the city. Moreover, they were able to find this combination of labour market features in a city which had ample office space at a relatively depressed price.

Many employers commented favourably on the industrial relations reputation of Bristol workers. Large companies with sites in other locations contrasted the stable and orderly atmosphere of industrial relations in Bristol with the more problematic conditions in their other plants. Bristol workers were said to be 'slow to rouse', especially when compared with London or the North: one large aerospace employer said 'in Bristol they *like* working for us, unlike in Lancashire.' An incoming electronics company said that one reason the area had been chosen was that 'labour relations are very good.' A multinational company in the printing and packaging industry commented that Bristol has traditionally been part of 'the easy-going West country', and its industrial relations have traditionally been 'little more than a debating society'. Bristol workers have been seen by employers in general as less militant, as having a generally relaxed approach, which also means that they would be less responsive to financial inducements, especially when compared with London.

Some employers, however, were rudely awaken in mid-1984 when a dispute in the aerospace sector led to an unprecedented series of strikes and a prolonged factory occupation. A management spokesman protested symptomatically that 'it's just not Bristol' (Lawrence 1984). In the same period Bristol print trade unionists were actively engaged in the national dispute concerning the Messenger newspaper, and there were repeated industrial conflicts in the docks. At least one multinational corporation feels that these are symptoms of a wider change in the industrial relations environment. Bristol is becoming separate from the surrounding localities in the South-West, and 'more like other big cities'. In recent years 'things are a bit more difficult', and industrial attitudes are becoming 'a lot more militant than they used to be.'

The Structure of the Bristol Economy

The previous section drew out four features—defence spending, location, image, and labour market structure—which distinguish the Bristol locality and which have been influential in the restructuring of its major industries. However, this still leaves a large part of employment change unexamined. It was shown in Chapter 2 that the bulk of new employment has been in the service sectors, and between 1978 and 1981 the major source of new jobs was the Miscellaneous Service industries. The relationship between growth in these service sectors and restructuring in the industries examined in Chapter 3 depends on the interrelationships within the local economy.

This section looks at the way different parts of the Bristol economy interact with each other, determining how changes in any one part are transmitted throughout the system as a whole. The analysis is necessarily less detailed than that of the dominant industries covered in Chapter 3, because it was not possible to explore other industries in any detail, not least because the service sector consists of an extremely large and heterogeneous group of employers. Nevertheless, the survey evidence and other sources did indicate the main features of the relationships within and between the dominant industries and other sectors, and it is possible to draw some fairly reliable conclusions.

The structure of the regional economy may be analysed in terms of the distinction between 'basic' (or 'export') sectors and 'dependent' (or 'residentiary') sectors of the local economy (Stanback and Noyelle 1982, p. 19). The basic sector consists of establishments whose markets lie outside the region, while the dependent sector consists of those whose markets are formed by producers and consumers in the local market. Since the spending power of these groups is in turn governed by the basic sector, this means that the growth of the dependent sector is determined by what happens to the basic sector (Fothergill and Gudgin 1982, pp. 33–4). The industries we examined in Chapter 3 lie mostly in the basic sector, selling in national or international markets. The analysis in this chapter suggests that the relative stability of the basic sector may be traced to Bristol's distinctive advantages in terms of defence spending, image, geographical position, and labour market.

The case studies suggested that different establishments within the basic sector in the locality are in general entirely independent of each other. There are a few strong or systematic linkages between establishments, and small companies are generally of marginal importance to the major firms, with the possible exception of some producer services such as small-scale software provision and some financial services. Where suppliers and subcontractors are based in Bristol, they tend to specialize in low-value activities. In the Aerospace sector, for example, local subcontractors are used for sand-blasting, silk-screening, cleaning, and some transport and catering; the major contractors for high-value activities and suppliers of large-quantity items are 120–150 miles away. The insurance industry looks to local suppliers mainly for catering, maintenance, and some printing services; and much the same pattern prevailed in the other industries. Similarly, although some computer sales and service outlets in the Bristol area are heavily influenced by demand emanating from large firms and public sector establishments in the region, and a few small manufacturers in Bristol are dependent on subcontracting to the large companies, these local enterprises do not make a major contribution to their customer's output.

The overwhelming impression is one of a lack of linkage. This is exemplified by the defence industries: although their impact has been very significant in terms of direct employment and income generation, they have effectively remained an 'enclave' in the sub-regional economy. Instead of generating dynamic agglomeration economies, they have grown increasingly separate from other regional activities and from each other, although their overall importance in terms of incomes and employment has not declined. .

The economy of the city region consists less of an integrated production system than of a series of materially unconnected production units which coexist in the same area (Taylor and Thrift 1983). The changes in production in a range of industries in recent years therefore reflect a multiplicity of separate and uncoordinated decisions in repsonse to a range of separate market and corporate influences, and not in any real sense an interrelated restructuring of the regional economy.

However, there does appear to be a substantial sub-set of industries which essentially comprise a dependent sector. The basic sector generates activity in this group through the spending of its employees, rather than of the companies themselves. In other words, the dependent sector consists mainly of personal or consumer services, and such linkages as do exist seem to run through consumption rather than production. The apparent expansion of this sector in Bristol may be a result of demand factors, or it may reflect unusually favourable supply conditions, or both forces may be present simultaneously.

Looking at the demand side, it is not very easy to disentangle the effects of demand generated locally from that of visitors, tourists, and other sources outside the city region (in other words, to differentiate the basic from the dependent sources of demand). However, it does seem that the apparently strong pressures for growth in these dependent sectors have been affected by the growing core of élite employment in the region. Indeed, the personal service infrastructure may be one component of the city's attractiveness to such groups, and the growth of élite employment in turn appears to be a factor in the expansion of personal services. The socioeconomic composition of the region is consistent with a relatively large core of élite groups (Chapter 2), and their discretionary spending may be expected to create a market for a wide range of locally provided activities, ranging from upmarket retailing and the manufacture of luxury goods to restaurants and hotels, entertainment, and prostitution, all of which appear to have been booming in Bristol in the 1980s. The importance of the consumer spending of élite employees (the majority of whom are to be found in the basic sector) for non-élite groups in dependent sectors takes on an added significance if the economic distance between élite groups and others widens as a result of polarization in the labour market (see Chapter 5).

On the supply side, the growth of dependent consumer services has been based largely on the employment of women, especially in part-time work. At the national level, two-thirds of female employment in Miscellaneous Services is part-time. Women in employment in Bristol appear to be concentrated in the dependent sectors to a greater degree than nationally, despite the growth of female employment in some basic sectors such as Insurance.

In employment terms, the Miscellaneous Services group is as important for women as the Aerospace sector is for men, and its relative importance has been growing. Between 1978 and 1981 this sector increased its share of female employment in Bristol by 2 per cent, although its share of male employment rose by only 0.5 per cent. Over the same period total female employment in Bristol fell more rapidly than nationally (2.1 and 1.6 per cent, respectively), while male job loss, on the other hand, was much less severe than nationally (falling by 4.8 and 7.3 per cent, respectively). As a result, employment in Bristol did not become feminized to the same degree, the female share of employment rising at less than half the national rate.

Compared with the national trend, therefore, women in Bristol have been pushed out of the labour market, and the Miscellaneous Services have become exceptionally important for those remaining in employment. This suggests a possible relationship between women's and men's jobs in Bristol. If local consumption linkages are indeed important, then women's employment is becoming increasingly dependent on the discretionary spending of élite groups. But since the latter are largely composed of men, women's employment is effectively growing increasingly dependent on the consumer spending of men. In short, although the regional productive apparatus is highly unintegrated, there are nevertheless important linkages within the region arising out of the spending of groups in the basic sector. The distributional processes in the labour market which are involved in this are analysed in the next chapter.

The highly fragmented structure of the Bristol economy, and the role of consumption rather than production in providing linkages within it, has implications for the way in which changes in one part are transmitted throughout the system as a whole. Changes in a particular establishment tend to remain confined to it, and the basic sector as a whole will exert a significant influence on the dependent sector only if a number of basic establishments simultaneously experience changes in a common direction. As we have seen, in the first half of the 1980s a wide range of employers in the basic sector were influenced in similar ways as a result of Bristol's locational advantages. The net impact was that the basic sector as a whole was buoyant, and this stimulated dependent growth. In the foreseeable future these advantages of the Bristol location will remain, but they are not likely to intensify as they did in the 1970s, The radical changes in the motorway and rail networks of the past fifteen years are not going to be repeated; the future course of defence spending is a matter of considerable controversy (Greenwood 1984; Levitt 1985); and defence is unlikely to provide the levels of employment achieved in the past, even though some part of the Bristol defence sector occupies a niche in the expanding defence electronics field.

Some labour market advantages may also be expected to decline as the Aerospace sector provides a decreasing flow of trained labour, and as other companies absorb the available supply. Bristol's growth in the 1970s and early 1980s has essentially been 'passive', derived from forces originating elsewhere, rather than from any dynamic regional process. The city's ability to claim a disproportionate share of activity in the future is not likely to improve and may even decline. The basic sector as a whole, therefore, is unlikely to expand significantly in the absence of an upturn in economic activity in general. This in turn means that the future of the dependent sector's activities is equally uncertain. Since Bristol's ability to attract employment was not considerable in relation to the need for jobs even in the recent 'successful' period, there are reasons to look to the future with considerable caution.

Bristol in the Spatial Division of Labour

The analysis in this chapter has suggested that Bristol's relatively successful adaption to economic change is ultimately related to the fact that it provides a unique labour supply in a location which is also advantageous in other terms. Property market influences and accessibility have played a role in opening up its pool of relatively low-cost amenable labour to mobile employers, and have affected the élite composition of the labour force. In addition, locational inertia and particular institutional relationships have sustained the established industries.

These processes have combined social, political, ideological, and even physical influences in addition to more obviously economic ones. As a result, explanations which focus exclusively on one dimension are likely to be misleading. For example, in some analyses the central determinant of regional development has been the pattern of industrial ownership and control, and domination by multinational firms is often regarded as a sign of weakness. This does not provide useful pointers in the case of Bristol, where multinational corporations have generated both job loss and job creation. Employment in Bristol appears to be at least as dependent on foreign companies as other locations which have not fared so well (Bassett 1984). Indeed, foreign companies have been a source of relative strength: between 1978 and 1981 employment in foreign-owned manufacturing companies in Bristol fell by 3 per cent, compared with 13 per cent in UK-owned companies. This represents an even better performance of foreign-owned companies than in other regions (Townsend and Peck 1985).

Other analyses have suggested that the size composition of industry has a major bearing on new firm formation, such that a locality dominated by large establishments will tend to have a low new-firm birth rate and small businesses may be rare (Gudgin *et al.* 1979). In Bristol, however, where large firms appear to have been as important as in many other cities (Bassett 1984, p. 883), small businesses have nevertheless played a modest but positive role. It appears that patterns of ownership and scale have been less important than locational advantages.

The availability of land and premises plays a key role in some other analyses. However, the evidence suggests that Bristol's advantages in these terms can be found in many other locations, and decentralization in response to a lack of land and premises has not been particularly significant. The availability and cost of premises has been essentially a permissive factor. There are also examples which run counter to the argument that firms in inner-city locations necessarily suffer disadvantages: several companies in the printing and aerospace industries have remained on their traditional sites and often in multi-level premises. In one instance, for example, the fact that it was especially costly to adapt an old multi-level building to new technologies was mobilized by management to secure union co-operation in the change: employees were offered a choice between partial job loss arising from technical change, or complete closure. This indicates that the importance of physically constrained locations may be conditional on the character of the local labour market, and it would be a mistake to attempt to explain the 'urban–rural shift' of recent years solely in terms of physical constraints in the cities (Fothergill and Gudgin 1982, p. 104).

Some commentators have attempted to relate uneven regional and urban development to the geography of innovation. Most industry is believed to be locationally immobile once it has reached a certain threshold, and the key locational processes are therefore those which operate at the early stages when an initial 'propulsive influence' induces an industry to establish itself in a particular location. By extrapolating from the experience of Silicon Valley it has been suggested that the key locational factors in the current period are high-amenity areas capable of attracting highly qualified people, as it is these groups who give rise to 'truly entrepreneurial industrial traditions' (Hall 1985, p. 15).

The evidence does not suggest that this sort of process has been important in Bristol. New innovation-based establishments are small, few, and far between, and the bulk of innovation has always taken place within the aerospace companies. This sector has grown and remained in Bristol for a variety of reasons, among which its role as a defence industry has been pivotal (Lovering 1986), and the amenity value of the city region appears to have been of marginal significance. If we are indeed about to enter a new expansion based on the coming of the 'fifth Kondratieff' (Hall 1985), Bristol's place in it appears to be based more on the labour market and related factors than on its magnetism for innovation.

It is often held that the fortunes of a locality are associated with its place in the spatial division of labour, in the sense that relatively buoyant employment reflects the dominance of establishment with higher-level, and thus indispensable, functions (Westaway 19874; Massey 1984). Again, Bristol does not fit easily into the schema presented by this approach. As was shown in Chapter 3, there is a marked juxtaposition of different functions in a number of its major industries. In some cases a spatial division of functions is technically unworkable, notably the high-technology defence sector, while in others it is convenient, for reasons of property management and labour control, to combine them under one roof. In a sense, Bristol's advantages could be said to be related to the absence of a spatial division of labour in some key cases.

Putting this another way round, Bristol has advantages as a location for a range of different functions. The locality as a whole, therefore, benefits by not being functionally specialized. This puts the local labour market in an interesting perspective. It was suggested earlier that different elements within the labour force perform very different functions because the local labour embodies features characteristic of both urban and quasi-rural 'sunbelt' labour markets. In a sense, perhaps, the labour force is already so deeply divided by gender, age, race, and skill that employers have found it a favourable location for activities which cannot easily be separated by space.

These observations suggest a way to conceive of the city's emerging place in the national and international division of labour. Bristol provides a location which is simultaneously an accessible foothold in the European market, an area with an ample supply of low-cost offices and factories, and a source of a heterogeneous supply of low-cost amenable labour. It should not be forgotten, as well, that the élite labour in the region is often low-cost labour on the international scale; this is especially true of R & D employees in the aerospace industry (Hartley 1983).

These roles are related to the way of the sub-regional economy operates. The requirements of the groups employed in capital accumulation in national and multinational companies are partly provided through the local market, through which channel they draw on the labour of other groups. These groups provide those requirements at low cost, which in turn sustains the low relative costs (on the international level) of the labour directly involved in accumulation. To reduce this to a formula: capital finds a relatively low-cost and amenable labour supply in Bristol partly because the costs of reproduction of that labour are low. This in turn, is related to the fact that the reproduction requirements of these central workers are provided by other workers who tend to be drawn from less advantaged groups. Powerful allocative processes operate in the labour market, which largely exclude women, blacks, and young people from élite occupations engaged in accumulation on the national and international scale and crowd them disproportionately into those activities which are propelled by the spending of the élites.

Bristol's articulation to the wider international economy, therefore, appears to be bound up with a particular 'internal' arrangement through which production and reproduction are secured. In terms of this conceptualization, the city's distinctiveness is defined by the fact that it is a location where élite labour groups centred in London and the 'sunbelt' zone overlap with a regional capital containing an insulated local labour force. Although other cities in Europe and the UK share some of these features, the precise balance—the degree of accessibility, the image of the location in the perception of élite groups, and the divisions between different groups in the labour market—is unique.

Notes

1. This categorization is borrowed from Massey and Meegan (1982). For completeness, it is worth pointing out that, in principle, jobs could also be created as a result of 'relaxation' of work effort—the inverse of intensification. This seems to be a purely theoretical possibility.
2. In one case an aerospace–electronics company left Bristol, but most of its employees moved to one of the aerospace employers.
3. This reflects a more general trend: 'In the 1970s employers sought to get a grip on their own pay and effort levels by bringing in job-evaluated pay structures, work study, and formal negotiations'; but in the 1980s 'there is pressure to move away from the remote negotiating structures and towards pay rates and working practices attuned to the needs of individual businesses' (Groom 1984, p. 12).

5

Labour Market Dimensions

In this chapter we shift the focus towards the distributional aspects of the recent economic restructuring. Although Bristol as a whole has survived the recession relatively unscathed when compared with other major British cities, large numbers of its citizens have nevertheless suffered as much as many people living in far less 'successful' areas in terms of unemployment rates and other indicators of social stress. Conditions in parts of the old inner-city areas of south and east Bristol, and especially the outer council estates in the north and south, present a harsh contrast to the affluent sub-urbs of Clifton or Westbury-on-Trym. The prosperity of Bristol as a whole has disguised the relative decline in the urban core and drift to the surrounding quasi-rural ring, as in other British cities (Spence and Frost 1983). Some dimensions of inequality were described in Chapter 2. By examining the operation of the labour market, we can begin to identify the processes responsible for these patterns.

The labour market plays a dual role in the local economy. From the point of view of employers, it is the source of labour required in production. The last chapter adopted this perspective, and identified some of the effects on employers of the specific character of the Bristol labour force. From the point of view of residents, on the other hand, the labour market is the source of employment, and the package of incomes, social interactions, and life-chances that goes with it. The terms on which they participate in the labour market therefore have a major impact. In this chapter we shall examine the labour market from this second perspective and identify the processes which underlie the allocation of employment opportunities in Bristol. By focusing on employers, we can trace the way the demand for labour is translated into employment.

This chapter is based on intensive research into a relatively small number of employers and other actors in the labour market designed to unpack particular process in detail.[1] It is therefore more like a series of revealing glimpses through a number of (well-placed) windows, than a definitive and balanced picture. Nevertheless, the findings make it possible to identify some of the major social processes at work in the Bristol labour market.

Relatively little is known, beyond some rather unhelpful generalizations, about the precise ways in which employers arrive at their demand for particular kinds of labour.[2] The first section of this chapter therefore examines the recruitment process in the panel of Bristol employers, and identifies the role of different selection criteria and recruitment channels. The second section draws out the implications for the structure of the demand for labour in Bristol, and the ways in which this may be changing. The third section examines the processes which give rise to institutional discrimination, particularly in terms of gender; and the fourth section reviews some indications that the Bristol labour market is becoming more polarized. The conclusion discusses some theories of inner-city labour markets in the light of this account.

Employers' Practices and the Structuring of Demand

The starting point in an analysis of labour market processes in Bristol in the mid-1980s must be the recognition that labour markets do not 'clear' in the economic sense. In theory, if the supply of labour at the going wage is greater than the amount required, employers have an incentive to lower the wage and increase the number of workers they are prepared to employ. At the same time, the supply offered should contract when the wage falls, and these spontaneous processes should lead the labour market towards balance. In reality, Bristol employers face an apparently permanent excess supply of labour in some markets, and simultaneously a chronic shortage in others. Few employers showed any sign of responding to excess supply by increasing employment or reducing wages, although it is quite possible that some smaller employers have been doing this. In the specialized occupational labour markets where employers face a shortage of labour, their response has generally been equally inflexible.

The rigidity in the demand for labour has meant that Bristol employers have had to devise other ways to manage the supply of labour. They have, in effect, assumed the role of 'gatekeepers', controlling the allocation of a total of employment which is largely independent of the local conditions of labour supply. In markets characterized by excess supply, employers have constructed filtering devices, the effect of which is to remove from consideration a substantial proportion of applicants on the basis of certain defined characteristics. In markets characterized by labour shortage, they have broadened the geographical range of recruitment.

Recruitment and selection criteria

In the recruitment process employers mobilize a set of pre-defined criteria in order to establish the eligibility of applicants. They advertise vacancies to potential candidates through specific recruitment channels, and the choice of channel is influenced by the selection criteria they adopt. Evidence from employers and other labour market actors suggests that these selection criteria can be broken down into two distinct elements, which we here call 'competence' and 'suitability'.[3] A candidate becomes eligible only if he or she is acceptable in terms of both of these. The criterion of competence, which is usually made public by the employer, relates to the objective technical abilities required. The criterion of suitability, which is inevitably less tangible, refers to characteristics of personal and social nature. Whether or not a candidate is seen as suitable depends on how the employer assesses his or her acceptability to potential workmates, responsiveness to orders, ability to exercise appropriate initiative, tolerance of routine, etc. Employers generally use various proxies as indicators of these characteristics.

In markets for scarce labour, recruitment involves *searching* for candidates, and Bristol employers often need to obtain access to people already in employment. The recruitment process in 'excess-supply' labour markets has a different emphasis, being essentially a process of *elimination* of large numbers of candidates. Employers have systematized and routinized the short-listing process by setting up a simple series of indicators, the nature of which is best conveyed by the term many employers and employment agencies in Bristol use to describe them: 'knock-out factors'. In some cases these 'knock-out factors' are formal characteristics such as academic or trade qualifications; in others they are informal characteristics such as previous work record, age, and appearance. (Punk hair styles, for example, were often cited as the definitive negative indicator, and an 'obvious' knock-out factor.) In practice, it is clear that social group characteristics such as gender are frequently used as indicators, although the research did not seek to examine actual discrimination in detail.

Employers in the survey invariably regarded academic qualifications as a strong indicator of an applicant's character, and thus suitability. This could be illustrated by the case of an employer filling a vacancy for a clerical post which he described as a boring 'dead-end' job. The skills required were minimal, so the criterion of *competence* was of limited value in eliminating applicants. This task therefore fell to the criterion of *suitability*, for which educational attainment was taken as a major indicator. Applicants with A levels were discounted as unsuitable on the grounds that 'that kind of person' would soon become bored and dissatisfied. O-level passes, on the other hand, were a positive indicator: the company 'needs a good steady supply of people with O levels, we'll need some at the bottom operating the terminals'. Here the employer had a fairly strong idea of the type of personality he was looking for, and assumed that this was accurately indicated by academic qualifications. This 'credentialist' use of qualifications as indicators of personality, rather than ability, appears to be extremely widespread.

In scarce labour markets, employers may be obliged to accept a *competent* candidate because they cannot hold out for the ideal. In these cases the competence criterion is most important, because employers cannot afford to reduce the potential supply of candidates by adding further criteria of suitability. In excess labour markets, on the other hand, competence alone fails to differentiate applicants, and other criteria are added to increase the 'suitability' barrier. Employers can afford the risk of prematurely discarding

some acceptable applicants. The greater the degree of excess supply, therefore, the greater the significance of the informal criteria which are enlisted as
additional 'knock-out' factors. Recruitment practices in Bristol exemplified
the distinction between those job-seekers who are treated as 'individuals' and
hose who are effectively regarded as 'reserves of labour', this distinction
being entirely contingent on the market context (Massey 1984, p. 144).

The scale of excess supply is illustrated by the case of a new employer who
received 4,000 applications for 400 vacancies (three-quarters of which were
part-time). Other companies regularly face a similar ratio, if a lower absolute
number, of applications. When filling unskilled occupations employers therefore rely on the application of simple and sweeping 'knock-out factors'. Two
of the most commonly cited are track record and location. All the employers
surveyed attached considerable importance to applicants' track records. This
has obvious implications for the ranking of the unemployed or school-leavers
among applicants, as shown below. The emphasis on track-records also indicates a high degree of consensus among Bristol employers as to the qualities
of good candidates. Location is often used as a knock-out factor, particularly
where companies use word-of-mouth channels to advertise vacancies. The
aerospace and print industries, for example, recruit most manual and lower-
grade clerical employees from the adjacent residential areas. In some cases
employers discriminate locationally in order to create or preserve a strong
identity in their locality. Several incoming employers, for example, chose
locations where they could build close links with local schools and the community. Some established companies also prefer applicants living nearby
because this reduces the problems of travel to work (which are severe in some
areas of Bristol).

Recruitment channels

Information about vacancies in Bristol is transmitted through a variety of
well-defined channels including the press, public and private employment
agencies, a variety of word-of-mouth networks, and in-house advertising.
The evidence indicates that the complex network formed by these channels
and institutions has a twofold impact: first, it distributes information to
potential job-seekers unevenly; and second, some of these institutions affect
the selection criteria which come into play.

The press is a major recruitment channel in Bristol, the evening newspaper
regularly advertising several hundred vacancies in a wide variety of industries. The Thursday daily and national press is especially important for electronics staff, and the trade and weekly press are used for many managerial
and professional vacancies. Several employers said that an advertisement for
a clerical vacancy would bring 100 replies the following day, and even a one-
line advertisement is enough to get 'plenty of applicants'.

Jobcentres are used by employers seeking unskilled or semi-skilled staff, especially when they anticipate a large number of applications. Jobcentres are able to specialize in this kind of vacancy because their resources of general labour and their wide network of branches allow them to implement 'knock-out factors' on a large scale. In addition, this is one of the few niches in which they are free of major external competition and internally imposed restraints. This is reflected in their bias towards unskilled and semi-skilled manual vacancies. Approximately one-fifth of the vacancies handled by Bristol Jobcentres in 1983 were in catering, cleaning, and hairdressing, a quarter were in transport and selling, and a fifth in clerical or related occupations. The remainder included a diverse group of processing, repairing, painting, construction, and miscellaneous occupations. Professional and managerial vacancies accounted for 3 per cent of total placements. Jobcentres are believed to account for around one-third of all local placements, although there is no statistical evidence to support this. They are free to the user, while private agencies charge from 10 per cent to over 30 per cent of the relevant first-year salary.

Private agencies dominate in the more 'upmarket' vacancies, and in temporary posts (from which Jobcentres are excluded by policy). The competition between private agencies in Bristol has intensified their efforts to establish their own niches, and the market seems to be in a state of transition. The emerging pattern is influenced by the existence of certain barriers to entry which have given rise to a market-sorting process. Recruitment to technical vacancies, for example, often requires some trade-specific expertise, which is not so important for recruitment to general and secretarial vacancies. This has important distributional implications, because the agencies respond differently to employers' selection criteria.

Agencies in Bristol handling élite vacancies tend to interact more closely with their clients and may refine or negotiate selection criteria with them. Agencies dealing with unskilled or semi-skilled vacancies tend to possess fewer resources of specialist expertise, and at the same time face much more intense competition. Their own market position depends on accepting what they perceive to be their clients' preferences, and on differentiating their service from those of rivals by meeting those preferences as thoroughly as possible. This means that they tacitly impose additional criteria.

Moreover, as they deal with vacancies which require only modest technical abilities, the additional criteria they impose inevitably focus on suitability rather than competence. Thus secretarial agencies, for example, claim to provide not merely good secretaries, but attractive and co-operative ones. This is reflected in the deliberately 'feminine' marketing image presented by most secretarial agencies. As a result, the structure of the agency market has an influence on the recruitment process, and may lead to the imposition of selection criteria additional to those laid down by employers.

A high proportion of vacancies in Bristol are filled without the use of press advertisements or employment agencies. Many companies advertise vacancies exclusively by *word of mouth* or notices at the workplace, and this often provides a large number of candidates. One long-established employer described how news of a vacancy 'leaks' in the local area and people spontaneously 'turn up in droves'. Another said: 'we have 4,500 recruiting agents on site.' Some companies contact candidates individually, especially former employees who have been laid off. The aerospace companies have traditionally recruited from people 'turning up and asking at the door', and after a lapse this practice has picked up slightly. These companies were in the habit of recruiting the children of existing employees, although this has ceased to be practical on a major scale. Nevertheless, one major company said it still does not advertise its apprenticeships beyond Bristol, rejects applicants from outside Bristol, and, 'all other things being equal', favours applicants with relatives already in the plant. Word-of-mouth contacts are also commonly used in recruiting to élite vacancies. Groups such as qualified engineers, salespeople, and professionals are frequently known to each other through regional or national networks, and these contacts play an important role in senior appointments.

In some industries the *trade unions* constitute a recruitment channel. During the recession, skilled printers have been obtained primarily through the local union branch, and the aerospace companies have also tapped 'card-holders' in this way. Although the companies have ambivalent attitudes toward the closed shop, they all recognized its value in providing access to employees of proven quality.

Unsolicited applications from individuals provide a major informal recruitment channel in Bristol, especially in the office sector and the traditional manufacturing employers. The insurance companies find the majority of their school-leaver entrants through this route (one company receiving 1,000 letters from school-leavers in 1984). Company representatives visit schools to make presentations, sponsor sports and other activities, which they described as 'generally sowing the seeds'.

In many cases the link between employer and school is quasi-formal.[4] One manager described his goal as establishing 'a tight relationship where they would contact us and say, We've got a first-class one here'. Electronics companies have also developed personal contacts with local school-teachers, such that, if we needed someone in a hurry we'd phone [the school] and say, Have you got any child who might be suitable? They'll tell the child, who will then apply.' Many of the larger companies employ full-time schools liaison officers. In some cases links between employers and local schools have ironic consequences: computer companies at Aztec West regularly contact the nearby Patchway school simply to maintain good local public relations, but one manager said he felt it was 'a bit funny' talking about careers, 'as there aren't any'.

Many employers identified the *Youth Training Scheme* as an important recruitment channel, and in a number of cases it is the major source of young recruits.[5] This was one of the scheme's main advantages to these employers: 'YTS is useful because the head of the relevant department can monitor trainees *in situ* to see how they go.'

A large part of employment in the major public and private sector employers in Bristol falls within their 'internal labour markets' (ILMs).[6] These provide for the internal advertising and filling of vacancies, and account for an appreciable proportion of recruitment to skilled manual, higher clerical, and managerial positions. Vacancies above entry grades, with the exception of some high-level and technical vacancies, are first advertised internally, and only if this fails is the vacancy filled externally.

Selection criteria, recruitment channels, and discontinuities in the labour market

This interplay of selection criteria and recruitment channels has important effects on recruitment patterns. The base-line criteria for selection are essentially laid down by employers. In most cases the job tasks are not technically demanding and many applicants are adequately competent, so the additional criteria which are added as 'knock-out factors' emphasize non-technical characteristics. In many cases these are supplemented by employment agencies. Even where vacancies are filled through Jobcentres other criteria are often added, such as being able to call in to the Jobcentre regularly or being on the telephone.

In the absence of more pertinent information, employers and agencies frequently base their choice of additional criteria on stereotypes, the more so where there are few technical grounds for differentiating between candidates. Many employers effectively target recruitment on pre-selected groups, the use of particular recruitment channels corresponding with particular selection criteria. Moreover, since the recruits selected in this way are likely to be satisfactory, employers and agents are under no consistent pressures to test the validity of their selection criteria, which tend therefore to become self-perpetuating.

In short, the structure of the labour market and of the recruitment network creates pressures leading to 'qualification inflation', and in most cases these qualifications are conditioned by social convention rather than technical or economic criteria. This gives rise to an institutional labelling process (Becker 1957). Selection criteria tend to be less rigid and arbitrary, and the social labelling therefore somewhat less discriminatory, in scarce labour markets, where technical considerations play a greater role in recruitment.

Industrial Restructuring and the Restructuring of the Labour Market

The overall demand for labour in Bristol is given by the set of specific external and internal labour markets in which establishments in Bristol are

engaged. The Bristol labour market as a whole is therefore extremely heterogeneous, but the evidence suggests that it may usefully be conceived in terms
of three broad strata defined on the basis of labour market type.

The first stratum consists of external labour markets characterized by an
excess supply of labour. It includes many of the occupations which are conventionally defined as unskilled or semi-skilled, both manual and non-
manual, and especially those in small and medium-sized firms. It also
includes similar occupations in larger companies, where these are insulated
from the internal labour markets which apply to other occupations. The typical occupations in this stratum include cleaning, catering, some maintenance, unskilled manual work, many routine typing, secretarial, and clerical
posts, and a variety of jobs in smaller service sector enterprises. Employees in
this stratum are not regularly regarded by their employers as candidates for
other positions in the company. Promotional ladders are non-existent or
minimal, and individual employees therefore have to construct their own
career paths by moving between employers. Recruitment practices are governed by employers' perceptions of the type of employee most likely to accept
the limited intrinsic satisfactions and career prospects available. In some
cases these occupations are being shed from larger companies to smaller to
independent subcontractors, especially in cleaning and catering.

The second stratum consists of the major internal labour markets in large
companies, together with equivalent occupations in smaller companies. (The
majority of occupations in the companies surveyed lie within this stratum,
partly because the research focused on large companies.) It includes a large
proportion of clerical, semi-skilled, and skilled manual occupations. External
recruitment is confined mainly to entry grades, and prospects for promotion
and financial advancement are governed by criteria internal to companies,
rather than the external market. Employment in this stratum is characterized by relative stability, and this provides a degree of security and predicta-
bility for both employees and management. The élite groups in the Bristol
labour market include the occupants of higher positions in this stratum.

The third stratum is made up of external labour markets characterized by
a shortage of supply. It includes expanding occupations in technical fields,
such as data processing staff, experienced engineers, salespeople, and other
occupations involving scarce and transferable skills, such as the professions.
The occupants of these positions form the other component of the labour
market élite. A distinctive feature of the Bristol labour market, as shown in
Chapter 4, is the size and vitality of this stratum. Employers are unable to
find adequate numbers of suitable recruits for these occupations internally,
and often find it difficult to retain them. A manager said of one such group:
'they think of themselves as DP [data processing] men rather than identifying with the company; they don't care who they work for.' Another employer
described these employees as 'spiralling round between companies com-
manding what salaries they can get rather than working up a career ladder'.

This three-layer framework is useful in analysing the relationship between Bristol's labour markets and its economic structure. The larger companies straddle several different strata, while some small fast-growing companies, which are too new or too small to have developed their internal labour markets, operate mainly in the two external strata. Computer companies, especially sales outlets which have no production activities, employ few people in the occupations which are found in the first stratum. The fact that high salaries and attractive conditions are enjoyed by all employees in these 'high-technology' establishments is therefore a poor guide to the conditions of other employees in Bristol.

The strata do not, therefore, correspond directly to industrial divisions. Nor do they correspond directly to distinct social groups. The third stratum includes élite groups whose membership is predominantly male and white, but the technical emphasis in selection criteria in these occupations means that qualified women have been able to establish a foothold. The presence of younger women in certain technical and professional posts is greater, and growing faster, than in some other occupations. The first stratum includes a high proportion of members of traditionally less-advantaged groups, but it also employs some members of advantaged groups. Some of these are participating in the labour market temporarily or partially (such as students working in restaurants, hotels, etc., and part-time employees). The fact that women, young people, and ethnic minorities have a disproportionate share of disadvantage cannot therefore be explained solely in terms of their confinement to a specific stratum in the labour market.

The changing structure of the Bristol labour market

The restructuring described in earlier chapters has had particular effects on the employment practices which underpin the structure of the labour market. The changing demand for labour has initially resulted mainly in job-shedding and redeployment, and the impact on the structure of the labour market as a whole will take some time to be absorbed. The first stratum appears to be expanding in relative terms, and possibly absolutely. Many firms in Bristol are increasing their use of subcontractors, and some are substituting these for in-house capacity. This is most prominent in marginal but regular activities such as cleaning, catering, transport, and routine maintenance. In the third stratum, demand for certain labour groups, especially in technical fields such as electronics, is likely to continue to expand, although at a modest absolute rate. This is the case both in high-technology sectors such as aerospace and electronics and in traditional sectors such as printing and packaging, where a few employees with these skills are required to modify and maintain the new electronics-based production equipment.

In the longer term, many of the larger employers of élite groups in the third stratum are attempting to substitute capital or other forms of labour.

The conditions of work and market position of some high-level technologists in one large company, for example, are being modified as the company moves towards an integrated computer-aided design and manufacturing (CAD/CAM) system. The company expects that it will 'have to discipline the designers, for example to limit their choice of components'. In others, sophisticated specialist software packages are being bought in as substitutes for in-house development by advanced software systems personnel.

The internal labour markets which make up the middle stratum have also been affected by new technical imperatives and new forms of labour management. Technical change in particular has led to a shift in skill requirements, resulting in a decline in the demand for some existing occupations and a less dramatic increase in the demand for other groups. At the level of entry recruitment, it has been possible for employers to respond by devising new trainee entry channels (e.g. 'craftician' apprenticeships, and new categories of graduate entry), while contracting older forms. However, at non-entry grades, and especially the managerial and supervisory levels, adaptation has been constrained by manpower planning and industrial relations factors. For example, the effects of the decline in demand for some categories of middle-range management have been compounded by the fact that displaced staff have generally been redeployed and not laid off. This has created bottlenecks in some higher positions which provide important niches in career structures.

Similar processes have occurred in shopfloor occupations. In many cases, particularly in industries characterized by high skill content and strong unionization, such as printing and aerospace, job loss has been managed through early retirement, but this has had a major effect on the age distribution of employees. Today, a block of employees in the 30–50 age range often occupies the bulk of senior shopfloor positions, and this implies that the flow of mid-range vacancies will be severely limited over the coming decade. Employers recognize that this may threaten the effectiveness of the existing internal labour market as a source of motivation, with the danger that it may become harder to retain experienced staff and maintain harmonious industrial relations. Internal labour markets have also been affected by the increasing demand for skills in which existing employees have not been trained. Some companies are modifying ILM structures at the 'top end' by adding new financial and status rewards for certain occupations, or by tacitly abandoning some part of the internal labour market structure by recruiting élite employees externally.

In many cases the effects of technical change have been exacerbated by new labour management policies which have increased the emphasis on individual performance (see Chapter 4). Thus, in the manufacturing sector some employers have restructured production so as to identify sites more closely with products or functions and to differentiate employees by location. In some cases the transition has been difficult, especially where the separate workforces were formerly closely linked through common collective bargaining and common advertising of vacancies. Changes of this kind appear to have been implicated in the strike in the Aerospace sector in the summer of 1984. In other cases, especially in managerial occupations, the emphasis on a more personalized labour process has been reflected in a growth in the importance of assessment and appraisal schemes. One effect of this is that the insulating properties of traditional internal labour market structures have been eroded, so that individual tasks, remunerations, and career paths have become less stable and predictable. A manager in a large office said that one effect was that: 'there used to be jobs here where you could do nothing, but not any more.'

Some companies have begun to construct new ILMs in order to reduce their reliance on the competitive external markets in the top stratum. As an example, the development of modular computer equipment has made it possible to deskill technical servicing, and to replace skilled qualified engineers by young semi-skilled salespeople. These new employees have been recruited to the bottom rungs of a new internal promotion ladder, although this embryonic internal labour market is very limited in range. Other companies are constructing new ILMs as a result of new pressures on manpower management. Some employers have until recently been able to provide career paths as a fortuitous offshoot of rapid growth, but recent declines in growth have meant that prospects for personal advance no longer lie within the company. In order to prevent a loss of staff to competitors, new promotional ladders are being introduced to sustain morale and commitment.

In many cases the scope for new internal labour markets is severely limited, for example by technical requirements. Some companies, notably in electronics, have responded by adopting other means to maintain loyalty and prevent the loss of staff, including familistic styles of industrial relations, and payment levels closely determined by turnover rates. The truncation and narrowing of some traditional promotional channels, together with the limited range of these new ILMs, implies that the pyramid of occupations within the middle stratum as a whole is tending to become flatter. At the same time, the greater individualization of the work process and increasingly direct influence of the market on those in employment is affecting conditions in this stratum and bringing them closer into line with those in the external market strata.

Institutional Discrimination and Labour Market Structure

The existence of major 'discontinuities' in the Bristol labour market is associated with the uneven distribution of employment among different social groups. A prominent feature of the Bristol labour market is the extent to which women, different ethnic groups, and young people tend to occupy distinctive jobs. This is particularly visible in gender terms, largely because evidence on the dimensions of race and age is less readily available. This section reviews some of evidence, and is followed by an analysis of the underlying processes.

The labour market at the national level is characterized by major cleavages corresponding to the division between the sexes, and these take the form of both occupational and industrial segregation (Hakim 1979; Martin and Roberts 1984). This pattern is replicated in Bristol, where in some respects it is exaggerated (Boddy and Lovering, 1986). Occupational segregation is particularly evident in the older manufacturing industries. In the Tobacco industry, for example, the long standing gender division of labour, whereby some shopfloor tasks are regarded as exclusively 'women's work', has survived despite major investment in new equipment and the transfer of production to a new factory, as described in Chapter 3. Women have retained responsibility for a particular group of tasks identified with the labour-intensive sorting and packing which women performed in the past; so, while men became 'machine-setters', women became 'machine-minders'.

Occupational segregation is equally marked in the Paper, Printing, and Packaging industry, where machine operatives are almost invariably male. Women on the shopfloor are often effectively grouped into female-only enclaves in the more labour-intensive activities such as gluing and dispatch. Here too these occupational gender divisions are sanctified by tradition, and have survived revolutionary changes at the level of product, process, and the corporate context.

The bias in female employment towards labour-intensive activities has meant that job-shedding has had a severely uneven impact on the sexes. In one packaging factory, where 600 women were once employed, there are now only a handful of women, all in ancillary occupations. Occupational segregation in the Aerospace sector has been so marked that it has almost resulted in industrial segregation. The skilled nature of most shopfloor occupations in this industry has been associated with a male bias, and aerospace accounts for over a third of male employment in manufacturng but only one-seventh of female manufacturng employment. Women in the industry are clustered in typing, secretarial, clerical, cleaning, and catering positions. The small number of women on the shopfloor tend to be concentrated in enclaves defined by occupation. There are very few women in managerial, technical, and professional positions, with some exceptions in personnel, PR, and systems/software. The male bias of the aerospace industry is significant in view of the fact that the industry has generally been more stable than the rest of manufacturing.

The Electronics sector associated with 'high technology' illustrates the emergence of occupational segregation by gender even in new and relatively expanding industries. Women in these companies primarily occupy the conventionally female occupations of typing, reception, and secretarial and routine clerical work. In some smaller electronics manufacturing companies women also are the major source of 'unskilled' and 'semi-skilled' labour.

Meanwhile, the overwhelming majority of software engineers, sales people, professional grades, and managers are male. This sector illustrates gender divisions based not on historical practices but on the discriminatory impact of employers' recruitment practices and the structure of the local labour market.

The Insurance industry offers examples of 'vertical' gender divisions whereby female employment is differentiated from that of men not by occupation but by seniority. In a not-untypical example noted earlier (Chapter 3), women accounted for 70 per cent of the bottom three clerical grades but only 25 per cent of the top three, and there are virtually no women in managerial or senior technical grades. Since the bulk of recruitment is to entry grades and is roughly equal by gender, this reflects the unequal career paths followed by men and women after entry. This industry also embodies 'horizontal' occupational segregation, in that virtually all typists and secretaries and many ancillary staff in, for example, catering are female.

The Miscellaneous Service industries exemplify the combination of occupational and industrial segregation. It was noted in Chapter 4 that women entering employment in the Bristol labour market are being crowded into this sector. Nationally, women account for between two-thirds and three-quarters of employment in these industries; one woman in ten works in a hotel, and another one in ten works in a public house. Recreational activities, clubs, and restaurants, where between 45 and 64 per cent of women work part-time, have been the fastest-growing sources of employment for women nationally. This is likely to be even more the case in Bristol.

There are also systematic divisions in the labour market on the basis of age group, and this too is based on both occupational and vertical segregation. In many companies applicants falling within certain age-bands are excluded from all except 'trainee' vacancies and entry grades; and although these companies also provide some unskilled routine occupations, they prefer to fill the latter with older people, especially women. It appears that employers' preferences for older people are based primarily on their unfavourable estimation of the suitability, rather than the technical competence, of young people. Their desire to channel the recruitment of young people through 'trainee' schemes reflects a perception that young people in general need a tighter reign of supervision and training in the social skills of work.

Many employers in Bristol clearly regard the employment of inexperienced young people as a risk. This seems to be magnified in many cases by perceptions based on social stereotypes of young people, and many employers and employment agencies referred to styles of dress and appearance as indicative of their unsuitability—'they come in here looking like that and expect a job!' Many also referred to the desultory attitudes of young people who had been 'sent along by the Jobcentre' and who were obviously 'no-hopers'.

Older people are also seen as a discrete category. Many employers prefer to recruit older female applicants (but not those nearing retirement) for unskilled shopfloor vacancies. Married women returning to work are widely seen as suitable for the most routine non-career posts, the 'dead-end jobs' in some cases. Some employers are very reluctant to employ older men for unskilled vacancies, especially those nearing retirement age. One employer said he would avoid taking on 'old boys' because they give a less attractive image to the company than younger people.

Although the research did not focus specifically on the issue of race, it became very clear that it is highly salient in the Bristol labour market. For obvious reasons this is rarely overt, but many of the public and private employment agencies and many employers acknowledged the pervasive influence of racial discrimination and many said there would be no point in sending a black applicant to certain employers and some localities. None of the employers admitted that there was an explicit racial dimension in recruitment, but the proportion of black people employed was invariably smaller than that in the Bristol population, and where black people were employed they were often grouped together. In general, employers and agencies thought that the smaller 'back-street' firms were the most discriminatory, with some exceptions. Some areas are recognized as particularly racist, especially South Bristol. When the subject of race was raised, employers frequently identified black people with St Pauls, one manager referring to St Pauls as 'the black quarter' (although the majority of black people in Bristol in fact live in Easton and Eastville).

There has been a growing recognition on the part of many leading companies of the degree of racial discrimination in the labour market, especially since the St Pauls disturbances of 1980. This has been an explicit influence on one group, which has developed initiatives to direct employment towards black people. These focus on small business promotion, with a secondary emphasis on improving the racial composition of employment in larger companies. On the whole, these efforts have been focused on St Pauls, as a deliberate response to the events of 1980. Considerable interest was aroused when a US company, which operates a strong equal-opportunities policy in its American plants, announced that it was to set up in Bristol. In the event, the Bristol subsidiary appears to have adopted only a minimal form of anti-discriminatory recruitment and it employs a proportion of black workers approximately in line with that in the local population (a total of less than double figures in 1984). The company claims that UK anti-discriminatory legislation is a barrier to the implementation of a full-blooded positive action policy.

Discrimination and employers' practices: the underlying processes

These social asymmetries in employment could be traced to two underlying processes: (1) discrimination was often a direct consequence of the way in which employers recruited; (2) discriminatory outcomes also arose because different groups of potential employees were unevenly placed to respond to the opportunities offered. In many cases both of these processes were at work simultaneously.

Many employers use 'knock-out factors' which systematically exclude certain groups. The sexes, for example, are often distributed asymmetrically in a company simply because gender itself is a criterion in selection. In very few cases does this reflect prejudice on the part of employers in the sense of a purposive 'desire to discriminate'[7] either on their own behalf or on that of their employees (although in one company it was said that the women were spread around the shopfloor in order to prevent them 'nattering'). More generally, the selection criteria include social factors such as gender because employers believe that these are indicators of relevant competences or suitability.

Many employers held that there are significant gender differences in technical competence relevant for certain occupations. This is most evident in the large manufacturing companies, where the belief that women generally have 'nimbler fingers' is extremely pervasive. An electronics manufacturer reported that 'men don't assemble printed circuit boards because they don't have the dexterity', and another said that women are suitable for soldering and wiring because; 'it's manipulative skills'. A third confirmed that 'women are more adaptable to small tasks; they've got the dexterity', while another employed only women because the work 'needed their dexterity'. The assumption that there are significant gender differences in technical competence is also evident in 'caring' occupations and those concerned with 'dealing with people', which tend to be identified with women. Although the study did not explore this in any detail, women appeared to be disproportionately represented in some medical occupations, and a very high proportion of women in managerial grades were in personnel departments.

In a small number of cases competence criteria worked against women, where they were excluded from occupations because they were thought to be physically incapable of performing the work. Unskilled shopfloor workers in the packaging industry, for example, are nearly all men because the work involves lifting very heavy rolls to load and unload machines; so are workers in the primary area of tobacco manufacture responsible for handling baled tobacco (in an automated process with sophisticated handling equipment) defined as 'dirty and heavy work'.

In general, however, supposed gender difference in competence were far less important than supposed differences in suitability. While many employers regarded men and women as equally capable of the tasks associated with a particular occupation, they often believed that one sex was more 'suitable' than another. It was frequently claimed or implied that women are more suitable than men for routine occupations because they become less dissatisfied with boring jobs, and have lower career aspirations. This was said to explain the concentration of women in routine clerical and repetitive manual occupations. An electronics manufacturer focused his recruitment on housewives because, although the work was extremely repetitive 'painting-by-numbers', he believed women would be content with the chance to earn the money. Part-time work in one large factory was said to suit the women's wish or need to go shopping, together with their lack of interest in career advancement. The fact that the bulk of routine clerical work in the insurance sector is performed by women was said by some employers to reflect the fact that young women want jobs for three or four years before they leave to get married. In many office-based companies the VDU operators, responsible for inputting routine information, are all young women, or, as one manager put it 'little girls engaged in dead-end jobs'. Married women who return to work were said to be especially suitable for the most routine unskilled occupations: the post of filing clerk was said to 'suit a married woman, who just wants a pay packet, better. It wouldn't give an A-level person satisfaction for very long'.

For these reasons, many employers regarded women as particularly suitable for certain jobs but claimed that they were unable to recruit on an explicitly preferential basis. The legal framework poses barriers to this, since it is impossible to indicate a preference for one sex even when it is 'well known' that a job is more suitable for either a man or a woman. Some large companies said that they had problems in recruiting through Jobcentres for this reason, and word-of-mouth networks lend themselves more easily to gender-specific recruitment.

In many cases, however, socially uneven employment patterns could not be traced so directly to discriminatory selection criteria and recruitment channels. This was particularly the case in sectors characterized by vertical segregation, where the selection criteria for promotion are not gender-specific, such as the insurance industry. In these cases uneven outcomes arose because promotion was heavily influenced by the possession of post-entry qualifications, which are obtained through study on a voluntary basis. This gave importance to conditions outside the workplace, especially resources of time, which are evidently distributed unevenly between men and women. Differences outside the labour market appear to play the major role in the gender inequalities in promotion, which have resulted in the fact that the insurance industry has been described as 'a young man's profession'. Interestingly, however, in one company with 55 per cent female employees, 50 per cent of those currently studying were female. This may reflect generational differences in gender patterns, younger women being more able and more motivated to seek careers in the industry. In many managerial occupations promotion is conditional upon geographical mobility, and this also biases the selection process against women. Extra-market constraints of this kind appear to be at the root of cases of 'income discrimination', where men and women performing similar tasks are rewarded differently. One company which employs women on semi-skilled assembly said it would have to pay twice as much if it employed skilled men in the same tasks.

In some cases, therefore, discrimination in the Bristol labour market could be traced directly to constraints outside the market which result in different groups—in this case the sexes—entering the labour market on unequal terms. In other cases discrimination could be traced to the selection practices adopted by employers and agents whereby recruitment is targeted on pre-selected groups. In many cases the socially uneven distribution of employment is reinforced by employers' preferences for applicants with a good track record, including relevant experience.

The widespread use of track record as a 'knock-out factor' tends to reproduce the existing distribution of occupations. It also biases recruitment away from young people and the unemployed. Many of the new positions in the electronics industry, for example, have been filled as a result of recruitment procedures which selected out the 'cream' of applicants on the basis of their track records. The result has been that none were filled from the unemployed, and the average age of clerical and secretarial staff in the industry (30–40) is well above that in other local industries. Priority in recruitment to various shopfloor occupations in the Aerospace sector is often given to 'time-served' workers, and relevant experience is crucial for higher technologists.

In general, the way in which employers in Bristol structured their demand for labour has been closely linked to their perception of the local structure of supply, and the different motivations and supposed abilities of different groups. This structure of supply, in its turn, has been heavily influenced by social attitudes and the distribution of tasks outside the workplace. Under the general influence of excess supply of labour, employers have been under no pressure to revise their expectations of different groups, and as a result their recruitment practices have almost invariably tended to replicate traditional patterns.

There were, however, some important exceptions. Some companies have increased their employment of women in élite positions, most notably some engineering companies which have participated in the Women in Science and Engineering scheme (WISE). This has not always been reducible simply to a shortage of labour, as there has been no shortage of applications for apprenticeship positions. Training agencies have also played an important role. The Employment Rehabilitation Centre (ERC), in particular, has been able to place members of otherwise disadvantaged groups in positions to which they are often effectively denied access. Young unemployed black trainees, for example have been placed in clerical posts in major companies as a result of the ERC inviting employers to visit the centre and observe trainees *in situ*. This has created a small but significant alternative route into employment which has overcome the influence of the dominant selection criteria. However, recent public policy changes have tended to marginalize the

ERC and reduce the scope for demonstrating to employers the validity of alternative criteria.

Polarization in the Labour Market

The structure of the labour market as a whole appears to be growing more polarized as a result of the uneven growth of its three strata. The first stratum appears to be expanding both absolutely and relatively, and this is reflected in the exceptionally rapid growth of the Miscellaneous Services sector and some small manufacturing industries (as shown in Chapter 2). The middle stratum has been affected by major job losses in large companies, which suggests that it may be contracting in absolute and relative size. There are also signs that the employment profile of many internal labour markets has been changing, which suggests that the pyramid of job opportunities in the stratum as a whole is becoming flatter, and the flow of higher-level vacancies is likely to be limited for some years by the low turnover of existing occupants. The third, 'élite', stratum appears to be expanding or at least consolidating under the influence of the buoyant demand for scarce technical and professional skills. When this is set against the prognosis for decline in the middle stratum and expansion in the first, it implies that the local labour market is tending towards a greater degree of bipolarity. The decline in higher positions in the middle stratum, together with the buoyancy of the third stratum, where recruitment is conducted on the regional and national level, also implies a tendency for the proportion to decline of high-level posts in the local economy that are occupied by Bristol residents.

Meanwhile, the impact of technical changes on the demand for labour, and changes in the form of labour management, are imposing increasingly effective barriers between different labour markets. The opportunities open to school-leavers are conditioned increasingly by the academic qualifications they obtain, and also by location and social indicators, leading to a greater differentiation between employees at the point of entry to the labour market. It appears that this differentiation is increasingly reinforced at later stages in employees' careers as a result of the impact of their early work history on their eligibility for subsequent vacancies, and the pervasive emphasis on track records in selection, together with the tendency to channel recruitment specifically on selected groups. Where initial occupations impart only a narrow range of skills, subsequent opportunities for mobility are very limited, so that employees who start in 'dead-end jobs' may find it increasingly difficult to break out of them.

Conversely, occupations for which labour is scarce tend to impart experience and skills which enhance the employees' subsequent eligibility for élite vacancies. Graduate engineers, for example, can often choose between several employers and ocupations when they enter the labour market, and by the time they have gained between five and seven years' experience they are even more privileged, and are widely courted by employers who regard them as 'gold dust'.

The nature of selection criteria and recruitment channels is therefore such that people entering the two lower strata become progressively less likely to move into higher strata later in their working lives. The choices open to individual employees in the lowest stratum, for example, are increasingly limited to remaining in labour markets strongly characterized by excess supply, or to withdrawing from the formal labour market altogether.

Similarly, 'basic' or non-career employees in internal labour markets in the middle stratum become progressively less able to start new careers with alternative employers. Some members of the top stratum also may be likely to move 'downwards' as a result of changes in technology and labour demand which may gradually diminish the privileged position of certain technical occupations, and lead to increasing differentiation within the élite groups. In many respects, the dominant rcruitment processes imply that the institutional barriers to individual mobility may be growing higher.

In short, there are strong indications that the structure of the Bristol labour market as a whole may be growing more bipolar, while the trajectory of individual employees through the labour market is becoming more rigidly determined at an early stage, with differences between individuals heavily influenced by their social group. These structural patterns lie behind the fact that employment growth in Bristol has been concentrated on the lower-paid forms of employment. (Earnings in the growing categories of employment, such as non-manual occupations, are well below the national average.)

On the other hand, the jobs which have been disappearing fastest have been those in which large numbers of employees have been relatively highly paid; manual female employment, for example, where average earnings in Avon in 1983 were 5 per cent above the national average at £91 per week, has generally been in decline. There are high-paying jobs in a number of industries, but these do not appear to be in occupations where the employment of local people is expanding significantly. For example, top-rank printers may earn £16,000 a year, but their numbers are falling: managerial and professional groups in many companies earn between £12,000 and £20,000, and experienced electronics engineers may earn up to £20,000, but they are often recruited outside Bristol.

The cumulative character of advantage and disadvantage

The income differences between occupations are closely associated with differences in other spheres, so that the different dimensions of inequality are cumulative. As a result, income statistics may grossly understate the real differences. Many élite groups, for example, receive substantial non-financial advantages, such as cars, mortgage concessions, and other perks, in addition to higher salaries. But female clerks earning between £3,000 and £5,000, and assembly workers earning £80–£90 per week, do not generally receive additional incomes in kind. Moreover, current income differentials tend to be positively associated with differences in career prospects. The differentiation between 'career' and 'basic' employees is sometimes reflected in pay differentials, with new entrants tipped for career advancement being paid more than others in the same occupations. More generally, low pay tends to be associated with low career prospects.

There are also major differences in the conditions under which different employees in Bristol work, and the inequalities in income and career prospects tend to be repeated in this third dimension. Élite groups, such as R & D personnel, electronics engineers, and salespeople, frequently work in attractive environments, and enjoy considerable autonomy, extending from strictures on dress to working hours. Some electronics companies, for example, offer 'academic' work patterns to their software engineers alongside traditional 'nine-to-five' routines for clerical and secretarial staff. In markets with excess labour supply, hours of work are usually strictly enforced, as are standards of dress and behaviour. In many cases the pace of work is also dictated by the production line (tobacco or packaging), while in others it is maintained by the structure of supervision (electronics manufacturing or insurance). In many cases these differentials in pay, prospects, and conditions are also reflected in the relative instability of employment.

Economic Restructuring and the Impacts of Change

Finally, a number of observations can be made focusing on the distribution of benefits generated by the processes of restructuring and on some of the mechanisms behind this.

Bristol compared with other cities

Despite the existence of major, and possibly deepening, inequalities in the labour market, the evidence suggests that the benefits of relatively 'successful' economic restructuring in the Bristol region have been pervasive. Unemployment has been relatively less severe in Bristol as a whole. The unemployed have to some extent been more likely to find work here than elsewhere, although long-term unemployment has risen towards the national rate. The analysis of labour market processes in this chapter throws some light on the reasons for these outcomes. It suggests that the processes underlying them may be very different from those put forward in some analyses and assumed in dominant policies, and that there is considerably less ground for optimism in the future.

It is generally held that 'successful' economic restructuring in a region will bring benefits for all its residents. The demand for skilled groups leads to an absorption of the available supply, and a demand for others to take their place. As a result, the initial demand stimulus works its way through a hierarchy of labour markets until the effects are transmitted to all employees and job-seekers (Donnison and Soto 1980, p. 129).

This process presupposes, however, that the local labour market is sufficiently integrated for demand effects to ripple across the entire system. The analysis of recruitment processes in Bristol shows that this is not a realistic model of the labour market, at least in this locality. There is no systematic tendency to eliminate excess supply in individual markets, and employers' practices erect major barriers to any diffusion of demand from one labour market to another. There is little indication that the recruitment of scarce groups generates openings for the less skilled in the area to fill their places, especially since élite vacancies are often filled on the national level and result in in-migration. The fact that many employees in Bristol have benefited relative to their equivalents in other cities is not therefore a reflection of the efficiency of the 'trickle-down' process in the Bristol labour market. Instead, it implies that the effects have been widespread simply because employers have targeted recruitment on many different groups.

This dovetails with the discussion in the previous chapter which suggested that employers with several different kinds of labour requirements have found the Bristol area an advantageous one in which to set up, expand, or retain employment. Although the benefits of restructuring in each labour market have been confined to the groups directly affected, this has been a large group overall thanks to the breadth and diversity of the restructuring. The buoyancy of the Bristol labour market therefore appears to have been a result of the heterogeneity of economic restructuring in the locality, and not the flexibility of the labour market as such.

Intra-urban variations

Some mainstream analyses of the urban labour market suggest that variations in unemployment between different social groups and areas within cities are due to the different 'characteristics' of the various groups in the workforce. The relevant characteristics include skill composition, marital status, family size, experience of unemployment, and ethnic origin (Evans and Richardson 1981).

However, the analysis in this chapter confirms that this notion of 'characteristics' is highly problematic (Elias and Keogh 1982; Hall 1981). An examination of the recruitment process shows that these 'characteristics' derive their salience from employers' practices on the demand side. Put simply, employers have few jobs to offer, and they filter out applicants by devising ways to disqualify most of them. The existence of excess supply means that there are no major endogenous forces compelling employers to base their selection on objective economic criteria. This provides a degree of autonomy

in the way in which employers exercise their 'gatekeeping' role, and in practice they incorporate wider social attitudes, often exaggerated through the
use of sterotypes. Employers' practices tend to generate systematic institutional discrimination in the labour market, which thereby reproduces pre-
existing social divisions.

Discrimination

Discrimination in the labour market is often seen as an aberration on the side
of demand, through which employers obtain 'satisfaction' by excluding certain groups (Becker 1957; Chiplin and Sloane 1974). Our account suggests
that this fails to capture the dominant processes in the Bristol labour market.
Recruitment practices in Bristol are discriminatory because employers allocate job opportunities selectively on the basis of their assessment of the
potential labour supply from different groups. On the whole, institutional
discrimination in the Bristol labour market is a result of these perceptions of
patterns of supply, rather than of prejudice in the narrow sense of an exo-
genous 'preference' for some groups. It is therefore primarily the result of
'statistical discrimination' (Phelps, 1972). Some discrimination on the basis
of 'employers' misperceptions' might have been expected, but the degree and
permanence of this could be revealed only by a detailed examination of
actual employers' practices, which creates a basis for persistent erroneous
discrimination on a very large scale. The absence of market-clearing leaves
employers without an economic basis for testing and modifying their perceptions, which remain heavily influenced by social stereotypes which tend to
become fossilized.

It is often suggested that discrimination, especially in relation to gender and
race, may be based on the attitudes and actions of employees, especially
through trade unions, rather than employers. The evidence suggests that it
would be misleading to regard this as the major source of discrimination in the
Bristol labour market, although it has played an important role in specific
cases. Unions have clearly influenced occupational segregation between the
sexes, especially in declining sectors where managements are anxious to preserve harmonious relations with a mainly static labour force. This has been a
factor helping to retain some high-paid jobs occupied by males at the cost of
lower-paid female employment. However, the compartmentalized nature of
the labour market means that there is little reason to believe that the discriminatory impact of employees and organized labour has been more systematic
than this. Trade union actions have not inhibited the workings of a redistributive 'trickle-down' mechanism in the labour market, since there has been little
economic basis for such a mechanism in the first place. The discriminatory
impact of trade unions appears to have been marginal compared with that of
wider social stereotypes operationalized through employers' practices. Meanwhile, trade unionism may have played a 'positive' role by helping to consoli-

date the attractiveness of the Bristol area to employers through their impact on the preservation of a skilled, and generally well disciplined, labour force.

The role of public policy

Public labour market policies in Bristol have essentially been 'passive', and to that extent, as in other localities, they have tended to permit or reinforce discriminatory processes. Public agencies have essentially sought to meet employers' needs without questioning employers' practices. For example, Manpower Services Commission agencies in Bristol, under the impact of central directives, have underwritten employers' selection criteria in a number of ways. Jobcentres have complied with employers' preferences for applicants with good track records, and have often added other criteria designed to increase the Jobcentre placement rate and enable them to compete with private agencies. The effect has been to add criteria which have intensified existing divisions. Jobcentres have been under pressure to recreate a 'hotbox' of favoured potential candidates, and to exclude from consideration the already disadvantaged, such as the long-term unemployed and unskilled school-leavers.

By confirming employers' desire to recruit what they regard as low-risk candidates, and at the same time discouraging job-seekers who do not fall within these preferred groups, public agencies have tended to intensify the process of institutional discrimination. The virtually automatic allocation of the long-term unemployed to the Community Programme, for example, may consolidate their disadvantages by reinforcing the perception, shared by employers and the unemployed alike, that they have little to offer in the labour market. (And, indeed, several respondents pointed out that the long-term unemployed in Bristol are more likely to gain employment if they hide the fact.) The Youth Training Scheme is based on the notion that the position of young people may be helped if they are trained in certain competences. However, the research suggested that employers rarely discriminate against young people on objective grounds of competence, and that notions of social suitability play a far more important role. This explains why the training content of schemes such as YTS has been of minimal significance to many employers who have used them for pre-selection purposes. The bulk of selection and training services offered by the Manpower Services Commission (MSC) appears to exacerbate rather than diminish the inequalities in the labour market by legitimizing and reinforcing existing recruitment practices, and by failing to take into account the real processes of 'discriminatory gatekeeping'.

Other public agencies also play an important role in underwriting 'received' employers' practices, most prominently the local authority education department, especially at the most local level. Many schools in Bristol have been keen to collaborate with employers in providing 'extended internal labour markets'. Some employers commented that some teachers have resisted this, but that those who are 'more concerned with getting jobs for their kids' have often responded enthusiastically. As noted above, the social effect of these links is conditioned by the selection criteria which teachers and employers share.

Public sector agencies have also played a more general role in the local labour market by legitimizing existing criteria. In this context, the emphasis of the local authority on industrial promotion, targeted at incoming high-technology multinationals, is perhaps especially important, since the focus on industrial restructuring deflects attention from the distributive aspects of the labour market. These aspects have been addressed only tangentially, and always from the side of supply. Although local authorities, private employers, and voluntary organizations have introduced a number of inno-vatory training schemes, their impact can be expected to be only marginal, since inequalities arise in the first instance on the side of demand.

In short, public policies in the labour market, at both local and national level, appears to have consolidated the adverse distributional processes des-cribed earlier. They have directly and indirectly endorsed employers' prac-tices, and they have intensified the market-sorting process among labour market agencies, which exacerbates the discriminatory effects of selection. As shown earlier, there have been some significant exceptions in the form of training initiatives which have redistributed labour market opportunities. However, these are generally being marginalized, and the public sector as a whole appears to be offering fewer models of alternative practice.

Future prospects

It was noted in earlier chapters that Bristol has sometimes been seen as a model of future employment patterns for Britain as a whole. In some respects this may be accurate. Some 'high-technology' companies in Bristol exemplify new 'Japanese' styles of industrial relations, where the demand for trade unions is deflected by familistic management and concessions in terms of pay and conditions. Employment in the large unionized companies is generally declining, although less so in aerospace, and the growth of small companies, although marginal in employment terms, reflects the growth of both high-technology and small-scale service employment. Most new jobs have been created in the services sectors, and Bristol is starting to resemble the model of future growth set out in the Chancellor of the Exchequer's speech to the IMF in September 1984: 'We must not be seduced by the wonders of high-tech into overlooking the fact that many of the jobs of the future will be in labour-inten-sive service industries which are not so much low-tech as no-tech' (Rogers and Brummer 1984; see also Kaletsky 1984). This could describe recent employ-ment change in Bristol, where genuinely 'high-tech' jobs have accounted for only a very small part of employment, while the growth of a cluster of labour-intensive service employments has been particularly important.

This chapter suggests that there is another side to this vision of the future. This pattern of growth may create some employment, but at the cost of deepening divisions in the labour market. Access to 'high-tech' and 'no-tech' jobs is distributed unequally, with serious implications for the distribution of economic benefits, and for wider social inequalities. Meanwhile, public policies towards the labour market are characterized by an increasing acceptance of the dominant processes. There are few signs of any attempt to mobilize public institutions along other than market-related lines. In the foreseeable future, the Bristol labour market as a whole is likely to remain relatively buoyant, but the reproduction and deepening of social divisions through the labour market may become increasingly severe. While Bristol is likely to remain modestly 'successful', the benefits may be increasingly confined to certain advantaged groups.

Notes

1. The material in this chapter is drawn from two main sources. Interviews with the panel of firms described in Chapter 3 yielded a great deal of material on employers' requirements, problems, perceptions of the local labour market, and labour management practices. A number of other important actors in the Bristol labour market were also interviewed, including a range of private sector employment agencies, MSC Regional and Area Office managers, Jobcentre managers, Skillcentre and Employment Rehabilitation Centre managers, and private sector training agencies. These provided complementary and cross-cutting information.
2. Despite the considerable body of work which has been devoted to the labour market, especially following the emergence of an inner-city 'problem' in the 1970s, 'considerable ignorance remains concerning the processes at work in the urban labour market, despite the numerous prognostications on the urban problem' (Elias and Keogh 1982, p. 12).
3. For a similar perspective, see Jenkins (1984).
4. These have been described as 'The Extended Internal Labour Market' (Manwaring 1984).
5. This means, of course, that the process of selection and allocation within YTS take on an added significance. Recent research into YTS in Bristol and other areas suggests that these processes have important distributional implications in Bristol (Fenton *et al.* 1984).
6. Internal labour markets have been defined as administrative units such as plants or firms within which the pricing and allocation of labour takes place and which are governed by administered rules and procedures (Doeringer and Piore 1971). They provide both a system of rules and rewards to provide control over labour, and an internalized recruitment channel.
7. Prejudice may be regarded as representing a desire to discriminate which in practice may be unfulfilled, while discrimination is an outcome, which may arise in the absence of a conscious desire to treat one group more favourably than another. For an introduction to the economic literature, see Sloane (1985).

6

Public Policy Responses to Economic Change: Local Authority Economic Development Policies in the Bristol Region

This chapter turns to the development and role of public policy as it has impacted on the Bristol locality, focusing in particular on the development of policies at the local level. We start, however, by looking more briefly at the national policy context, in terms both of explicit urban and regional strategies and the implicit, spatially differentiated, impacts of other forms of government policy and expenditure.

The National Policy Context

Changing central government policies have a variety of regional and urban impacts, both directly intended and unintended. In this sense government policies may act as catalysts to local change or as powerful constraints on local policy development. How have national policies impacted on the Bristol area?

The impacts of explicit urban and regional policies

Explicit urban and regional policies are those government policies that are directly intended to encourage or restrain local economic development. Bristol's experience of such policies has been largely a negative one, in the sense that the area has been almost entirely excluded from the main programme of urban and regional aid but has been affected by government constraints aimed at directing investment to other regions. Thus the Bristol area has never achieved Assisted Area status under regional policy and has never been included in any list of partnership or programme authorities as defined under the Inner Urban Areas Act of 1978. In addition, Bristol has failed to secure major government grants for its port expansion, has failed to get on successive lists for Enterprise Zones, and has failed in its bid for Freeport status. As a result, local authorities in the Bristol area have lacked certain developmental powers granted to many other large cities and have been excluded from important sources of grants and subsidies.

The Bristol experience thus seems to stand in stark contrast to the experience of South Wales, just a short journey across the Severn Bridge. South Wales has had a long history of government aid under successive regional and urban programmes. South Wales ports received development grants which were denied to Bristol, and different areas have secured Enterprise Zone and Freeport status. Assisted Area status has also enabled South Wales authorities to tap European regional development funds. If the South Wales experience has been one of government 'hands-on' policy, then, on the face of it, the Bristol experience seems to be one of 'hands-off' development.

Not only has the Bristol region been excluded from various forms of grant and aid; it has been affected by government policies designed to divert investment to South Wales and other Assisted Areas. Evidence suggests that Industrial Development Certificates (IDCs) were fairly easily available for developers in the Bristol area in the mid-1950s, but became more restricted after 1958 (Bristol City Council 1967). In 1976, for example, an IDC was refused to Toyota, who wished to build a car import and distribution terminal adjacent to the new Royal Portbury dock. Government pressure to locate in Liverpool provoked a local outcry, and even though a revised application for a smaller unit was accepted Toyota subsequently withdrew in favour of expansion at their existing base in Sheerness. Again, in 1979 government pressure succeeded in forcing Inmos, the state-funded microchip producer, to locate its first UK production plant in Newport, even though the management had chosen Bristol for their headquarters and had selected a site for the plant on the north Bristol fringe. Such government pressures in favour of South Wales have provoked much bitterness among Bristol leaders, in spite of the obvious fact that unemployment in South Wales has consistently been much higher than in Bristol.

Not *all* restraint policies have worked to Bristol's disadvantage, however. In 1964 Office Development Permits were introduced to restrict office development in London; later they were extended to cover the southern and eastern counties and the East and West Midlands. Bristol, strategically sited at the western end of the M4, was able to capitalize by attracting new office developments, and thereby established its reputation as a major provincial office centre. Nevertheless, on balance, explicit regional and urban development programmes do not appear to have favoured the Bristol region and in important respects have been positively disadvantageous. It would be incomplete to leave the analysis there, however. It is also necessary to look at the local impacts of a variety of government programmes which are not explicitly aimed at solving urban and regional problems but which can have major developmental impacts. These policies may be described as 'implicit' regional and urban development policies.

The impacts of implicit regional and urban development policies

Here the evidence suggests that Bristol has benefited greatly from a variety of government spending programmes that tend to fall outside of the main categories of regional and urban policies described above. First, government investment in transport infrastructure has greatly increased the nodality of the Bristol area since the 1960s. The opening of the Severn Bridge in 1966 and the construction of the M4 and M5 motorways greatly improved Bristol's accessibility to other regions of the country. The proximity of the M5 became a significant factor in the marketing of Royal Portbury as 'the motorway port', and the area adjacent to the M4/M5 intersection has become an important location for regional and national distribution depots. The M4 link has perhaps been of greatest significance, making Bristol the obvious western end of the M4 corridor, with good links to Heathrow, London, and the South-East. The development of the High Speed Rail link between Bristol and London in the 1970s further strengthened Bristol's ties to this growth corridor. Although road and rail improvements have also been extended across the Severn Bridge and through South Wales, Bristol appears to have strengthened its relative position.

Second, and more important, Bristol has benefited greatly from government spending on defence and the aerospace industry. As we have seen, aerospace has been Bristol's leading industrial sector in employment terms in the postwar period, and its development has been closely tied to government defence and civil contracts from its earliest days. Some estimates of government spending on defence contracts in the region were presented in Chapter 4, and it is revealing to compare levels of defence-related expenditure with the volume of overt regional assistance. Table 4.1 compares government spending in the standard regions on Regional Development Grants and selective regional assistance on the one hand and defence procurement on the other. Wales, for example, appears to have done relatively well in terms of regional aid, compared with the South-West, until Ministry of Defence contracts are taken into account: the relative position of the two regions is then reversed. Over the four-year period covered by the table, the combined 'aid' figure for the South-West totalled £915 million, almost three times the combined figure for Wales. Of course, the South-West region stretches right down to Cornwall, but given that most of the defence industries are located in the Bristol sub-region, the figures give some indication of the scale of impact on the local area.

As argued in Chapter 4, this simple financial comparison may understate the uneven impact of state spending on the different regions. Defence contracts go directly to firms, frequently in the form of front-loaded funding for development and production, and often in conjunction with guaranteed markets for finished products. Defence (and aerospace) contracts may therefore have more immediate impacts on employment and profits than many forms of regional assistance.

In conclusion, although the figures are only crude, they do suggest that the Bristol area has benefited considerably from government spending outside of the explicit regional and urban programmes, to a degree that may have more than offset the disadvantages imposed upon it by being excluded from, for example, Assisted Area status. This whole area of implicit policies obviously needs more detailed analysis before a realistic balance sheet can be drawn up.

Central government controls on the powers and resources of local government

The ability of local authorities within the area to respond to local economic problems has been constrained by central government controls on the powers and resources of local government. In common with other large urban areas, the structure of local government in Bristol was substantially reorganized following the 1972 Local Government Act. Before reorganization, the County Borough of Bristol was the major unit of local government, surrounded by a cluster of urban and rural district councils. Following reorganization, the new unit of Avon County Council was created as an upper-tier authority with a lower tier of non-metropolitan districts. In the process, Bristol lost extensive powers and resources to the upper-tier authority, and in spite of encompassing the major concentration of population in the area was reduced to the same local government status as the surrounding, often semi-rural, areas. This loss of status after a bitter rearguard action by Bristol leaders has left a legacy of resentment that has marred relations between Bristol and Avon, particularly in periods when the two authorities have been controlled by different political parties. As we shall see, these problems have had significant effects on the form and implementation of local economic development policies.

Government financial controls have also imposed important constraints on policy development and implementation by local authorities in the area. The period since 1979, in particular, has witnessed a series of measures designed to limit or reduce local government spending. Revenue budgets have been constrained by the introduction of the Block Grant system, supplemented by increasingly severe centrally determined targets and penalties on overspending. Capital budgets have also been constrained by capital spending controls. Table 6.1 presents figures for local authority spending in the Avon area for the period 1978–9 onwards. This shows that, although grant-borne expenditure increased substantially over this period in cash terms, once inflation is taken into account, rate and grant-borne expenditure in real terms was almost exactly the same in 1984–5 as in 1978–9. In spite of increasing social and environmental problems stemming from the recession, therefore, spending in real terms remained at a standstill over this period. Moreover, this level of spending was sustained only by rate rises sufficient to compensate for the steady reduction in the proportion of total spending covered by central government grant. So, while spending has at least been maintained in real terms, cuts in government grant have shifted the burden of expenditure much more heavily on to local ratepayers, business and domestic alike. The proportion of total expenditure covered by government grant fell from 60 per

Table 6.1. Local authority expenditure and govenrment grant, Avon group of authorities, 1978/9–1984/5[a]

Financial year	Total expenditure[b] in current terms £m	Total expenditure[c] in real terms £m	Government grant as[d] a proportion of expenditure %
1984/5	418.3	319.3	44.1
1983/4	416.5	330.5	45.9
1982/3	405.5	337.9	48.2
1981/2	359.6	321.1	57.8
1980/1	327.3	327.3	57.9
1979/80	268.8	310.0	58.9
1978/9	233.1	319.3	60.2

[a] Aggregated for Avon County plus Bristol, Northavon, Kingswood, Wansdyke, and Woodspring Districts.

[b] Rate and grant-borne expenditure defined as total rate + revenue grant in change in balances.

[c] Based on GDP deflator, *Economic Trends*, Central Statistical Office, base year 1980/1.

[d] Revenue grant as a proportion of rate and grant-borne expenditure.

Source: General and Rating Statistics, Chartered Institute of Public Finance and Accountancy.

cent in 1978/9 to only 44 per cent in 1984/5. This in effect represents a direct loss to the locality of around £160 million over the six years.

Finally, in addition to these general financial constraints, local economic development policies have also had to operate within a limited statutory framework. Local authorities have used powers under a variety of acts but have tended to rely most heavily on general powers under Section 137 of the 1972 Local Government Act to spend up to the equivalent of a 2p rate on projects, in the interest of their areas, which fall outside specific statutory provision. Having been excluded from the additional powers and resources conferred on some authorities under the 1978 Inner Urban Areas Act, local authorities in the Bristol area who have adopted economic development strategies have had to rely for the most part on Section 137 powers.

The local context: socioeconomic change and political processes

The national policy context outlined above provides a broad set of constraints on local policy initiatives. However, within these broad constraints a wide array of political initiatives and policy developments are possible. What policies emerge will depend, among other things, upon the complex array of factors that influence the local political system. This section therefore explores some of the general influences at work on the Bristol political system as a preliminary to the more detailed discussion of economic development policy that follows.

Local political processes cannot be divorced from the wider processes of economic restructuring and social change that go on in the local area. Economic restructuring involves changes in the division of labour and the social relations of production in the area. These changes, combined with national political and ideological factors, changing patterns of consumption, and local cultural traditions, play an important part in reshaping local class structures (Urry 1981). Political interests and political conflicts cannot, then, be read off in any simple or direct way from social class structures. Classes, fractions of classes, and consumption sectors do not emerge in any automatic way as collective actors on the political stage. Nevertheless, such changes in social stratification do modify the bases for the articulation and aggregation of group interests and their political representation. It has been argued, for example, that the erosion of traditional class boundaries may encourage political realignments in voting terms and the growth of non-class-based social movements centred on local environmental or amenity issues. It is clear that a wide range of effects are possible, and these will need to be disentangled in each area. We cannot hope to trace the multiplicity of interactions between economic, social, and political change in Bristol in any detail. However, it is important at least to indicate the salient aspects of political change and point to the major influences at work.

As we have seen, Bristol's prosperity up to the late 1960s was a reflection of the long post-war boom. In spite of rapid service sector growth in the early 1960s, 41 per cent of total employment was still in manufacturing in 1969 and there were more male workers in manufacturing than in services. The continuing importance of traditional, male manufacturing employment helped to sustain traditional trade unionism and Labour Party politics. Industrial diversity and low unemployment helped to maintain low levels of labour militancy.

The old County Borough of Bristol was largely controlled by moderate Labour majorities up to the end of the 1960s, with brief periods of Conservative control between 1960 and 1963 and 1967 and 1972. Throughout the 1960s and early 1970s, both major parties were dominated by their respective leaders, who shared a similar vision of Bristol's future as a commercial, industrial, and port city and took a common view on many planning problems (Clements 1978). The policies pursued by the council were apparently viewed with favour by local business interests. Clements, in a study of 'local notables' and the council in the period 1965–6, attempted to identify a commercial and industrial élite in the city (Clements 1969). The élite appeared to have little direct representation on the council but had developed a network of formal and informal contacts with leading councillors and officers, particularly with respect to planning issues. It is evident from Clements's interviews that council policies broadly coincided with the élite's priorities. When asked to rank the major problems facing the city, 44 per cent of the élite sample referred to industrial growth and port expansion, and 44 per cent mentioned improved roads, traffic planning, and air communications. These were, as we shall see, priorities of the council during much of the 1960s.

Outside of the formal political apparatuses, political organization was sporadic and short-lived up to the late 1960s and focused mainly on housing and conservation issues. Tenants' organizations were active in a series of rent strikes in Bristol in the late 1940s but faded in the 1950s and 1960s. Inner-city redevelopment schemes sparked a brief surge of community opposition in Easton in the early 1960s which had little lasting impact. In the later 1960s, however, following redevelopment schemes in more visually promi-nent locations nearer to the city centre, a more middle-class conservation lobby began to organize. This was to play a powerful role between 1967 and 1971 in opposition to the council's ambitious plans for an urban motorway circuit through Bristol's inner suburbs.

In retrospect, the 1950s and early 1960s look like a period of relative social and political stability with a broad consensus on many policy issues based on the common interests of workers and employers in continuing economic development. This consensus began to be challenged first by middle-class groups campaigning on planning and conservation issues.

From the early 1970s, important changes began to take place in political institutions and political practices as the result of national political and ideo-logical forces and changes in local economic and social structures. As we have seen in Chapter 2, from the early 1970s onwards the region began to experience rapid economic restructuring, the key elements of which can be summarized in the following terms:

(a) a rapid decline in traditional manufacturing employment accompanied by the emergence of a small but growing high-technology sector
(b) an increasing internationalization of the manufacturing sector through the integration of local branch plants into larger and larger global cor-porations, with the increasing dependence of local output on inter-national economic forces
(c) a rapid expansion of the service sector to a dominant position in employ-ment terms, although internally differentiated with sub-sectors subject to a variety of different forces
(d) a relative decline of traditional, male manufacturing jobs and a rapid increase in jobs for females, particularly in certain service sectors which offer lower-paid, part-time, and less skilled jobs.

These economic transformations have significantly modified the social structure of the region. By the early 1980s the Bristol area had a working class comprising a declining proportion of manufacturing workers in tra-ditional industries and a rising proportion of lower-grade service workers, many of them female. Between the working class and a small local bourgeoi-sie lay a growing mass of intermediate professional, managerial, and admin-istrative workers occupying what could be termed 'contradictory class positions' (Wright 1978), subject to diverse political and ideological influences. The size of these groups exceeded the national average. Finally, in common with other large cities, a distinctive 'underclass' of welfare dependents and long-term unemployed had begun to emerge, concentrated in particular areas of the city and bypassed by growth in service and high-technology industrial sectors.

These changes in social structure began to modify the bases of political representation and political action in the city in the 1970s. The decline of the male-dominated manufacturing sector weakened the basis for traditional, class-oriented trade unionism and traditional Labour Party politics. This has been reinforced by the growth of female-dominated employment sectors where trade union organization has been weak. The rapid growth of the large, intermediate, white-collar grouping, subject to diverse economic and ideological pressures and fragmentation into 'consumption sectors', has opened the way to a greater concern with distributional, consumption-based issues rather than traditional, shopfloor, production-based conflicts.

Shaped by such forces, politics in Bristol has become more diverse and volatile since the mid-1970s. Following local government reorganization in 1974, the new County of Avon became Conservative-controlled, while Bristol remained under Labour control. In 1981 Avon was captured by Labour with the Liberals emerging as a significant minority. In 1983 Bristol became a 'hung' council with the Conservatives as the largest party taking control with Liberal support; in 1984 Labour became the largest party, taking control with no overall majority. In 1985, as the result of Alliance gains, Avon in turn became a hung council with Labour as the largest party.

At the same time, there have been important changes *within* the major political parties. From the mid-1970s onwards more collective styles of leadership began to emerge, particularly in the Bristol and Avon Labour groups, centring on leadership groups rather than dominant leaders (Barker 1981). From 1979 onwards the basis for Labour's traditional municipal reformism began to collapse under the pressure of increasing central government controls and expenditure cuts. The collapse of the framework for traditional policies of service expansion and council house management overlapped with the growth of left-wing ideas and representation within the local Labour Party, influenced by new philosophies of radical municipal socialism associated with councils such as Sheffield and the GLC. This was accompanied by attempts to strengthen the influence of the party on the development and implementation of policy by Labour groups on the councils. (See Fudge 1981 for parallel developments elsewhere.)

This momentum towards greater group accountability to party organizations was greatly increased by the election of a number of new, more left-wing, councillors on Bristol Council after 1979 and Avon Council after 1981. These councillors tended to be younger, more middle-class in background, and less aggressively 'Bristolian' in outlook. The result in Bristol was growing divisions in the Bristol Labour Party at all levels, resulting in a series of left-versus-right battles in the 1978–84 period over individual policies, the accountability of elected councillors, and strategies of opposition to Conservative government cuts. Conflicts have often been bitter, with temporary expulsions of left-wing councillors from the Bristol Labour group in 1981 and 1982. The Avon Labour group, on the other hand, more left-wing from the beginning, largely avoided these problems, and the rise of left-wingers to positions of power within the Bristol Labour group by 1985 heralded a period of accommodation (perhaps temporary) between left and right.

The Conservative Party and the Conservative groups have remained more monolithic over most of this period, but the last few years have begun to see the emergence of factional conflicts between, on the one hand, traditional 'shire' Conservatives and 'one-nation' Tories critical of the Thatcher experiment and, on the other hand, the more ideologically motivated Thatcherites anxious to pursue privatization and the extension of market principles to local government.

Outside the political party organizations, there has also been evidence of more diverse forms of political activity. The middle-class environmental and amenity groups, already active by the late 1960s, have become more organized and influential over time, achieving a number of significant victories over development proposals in the 1970s and 1980s (Jenner 1984). Pressure group activity and community organization in more working-class areas continued to be sporadic in the 1970s, but in 1980 the St Pauls area of the city erupted in the first of the inner-city 'riots' that ripped through the run-down, multi-racial areas of Britain's major cities in 1980 and 1981 (Joshua *et al.* 1983).

This eruption of an 'underclass' in an area of high unemployment and ethnic minority concentration surprised the city's leaders and the local political parties and shocked them into urgent action. While the local Trades Council held a public inquiry (after the government refused to hold one), the leadership of the major parties on Bristol and Avon came together with the Bristol Council for Racial Equality to form a Tripartite Committee to launch policy initiatives. The effectiveness of these policies was limited by the lack of resources and the limited channels of communication with the black and Asian population. The St Pauls disturbance was not repeated; it produced limited benefits, and left no lasting political organization in the area. Only in the last year have there been signs of autonomous black organizations beginning to pressure the traditional political parties.

As unemployment has spread to the large council estates in the outer areas, there have been signs of community and tenant activism in more areas of the city in the 1980s. The level of activity and influence is still low, however, and in some cases has been the direct result of encouragement and support by the Labour Party. Tenants' groups in some areas have been nurtured into being over the last year as the direct result of a policy commitment by the Bristol Housing Committee. Some of the major impulses to political activity have come from outside the area. Proximity to Greenham Common

Table 6.2. Phases of economic change and policy development in Bristol since the war

Economic period	Policy characteristics
'Long boom': 1945–late 1960s	Postwar reconstruction to the early 1950s; lubricating the market and prolonging the boom in the 1960s (through infrastructure investment and liberal planning policies)
Transition to crisis: 1970–8	Crisis perception and policy launch (emphasis on manufacturing regeneration and the inner city)
Economic crisis: 1978/9 onwards	Policy-widening and policy proliferation (multi-sectoral and multi-area initiatives)

and the South Wales coalfield generated a great increase of political activism during CND campaigns and the miners' strike. There are signs that the radicalism generated by participation in these issues may have longer-lasting effects in the local area.

In summary, politics in the Bristol area has been changing as the economic, social, and class structure of the area has been changing. Although political activity around local issues remains focused on the councils and operates largely through the traditional party apparatuses, there have been signs of diversity and change within the parties and increased pressures from non-party-political groups. With this sketch as a basis, we can now turn to a more detailed analysis of the specific policy area of economic development.

Economic Change and Local Economic Development Policy in the Bristol Region

The analysis of economic development in Chapter 2 pointed towards three broad phases of development of the local economy in the postwar period; these are summarized in Table 6.2, along with the general characteristics of development policy in each phase. This is not to imply a simple causal connection between economic problems and policy responses. Complex social and political processes mediated between the perception of local economic problems and decisions on appropriate measures of response. It is important to understand how economic problems came to be perceived and interpreted in certain kinds of ways which partly reflected the political and ideological dispositions of the decision-makers. It is also important to understand the constraints on the capacity of decision-makers to respond effectively to the perceived problems. We shall find, in the subsequent analysis, that economic changes, problem perception, and constraints on responses interacted in different ways between and within these phases.

The 'long boom': 1945 to the end of the 1960s

We have already observed that Bristol was well placed to take advantage of the long postwar boom. Although manufacturing employment declined slightly by about 1 per cent between 1961 and 1969, this was below the national average and was offset by rapid service sector growth. Office development transformed the central area of the city, and the construction of the Severn Bridge, M4, and M5 made Bristol a focal point for distribution. The area enhanced its image of growth and prosperity. This was a period of stable two-party politics in Bristol, with Labour the dominant party in most years, although a large measure of consensus existed on many issues based on a common vision of Bristol's future. Only towards the end of the period were elements of that vision challenged by community and conservation groups concerned over redevelopment.

In considering economic development policies during this period, we are concerned principally with the old Bristol County Borough. The actions of a number of committees, particularly Planning and Docks, contributed to economic development, although there was no explicit, overall policy. Three broad areas of policy were of particular importance: industrial policy, port development policy, and central area office development policy.

Industrial policy   Manufacturing industry was still regarded as the basis of Bristol's prosperity, and industrial policy was aimed at maintaining the manufacturing base, encouraging diversity, and rationalizing the distribution of industry through the provision of serviced industrial estates. A number of trading estates were established in this period, the earliest ones in the city centre and south Bristol areas to replace war-damaged sites. In the 1950s and 1960s further estates were developed to provide local employment opportunities near large council estates in the south and east of the city, and in the later 1960s a shortage of industrial land and growing demand for distribution depots prompted the development of new estates at Avonmouth, close to the port and the new motorway system.

Even in the late 1960s, planning was still based on the assumption of continuing manufacturing growth into the foreseeable future, although a note of caution was beginning to enter research reports. Thus, a 1967 planning research report projected a 12 per cent increase in manufacturing employment (+12,000 jobs) between 1965 and 1981 on the basis of past trends, with most growth expected to come in aerospace and electrical engineering and with stable or slightly falling employment in traditional sectors such as food, drink, and tobacco and printing and packaging.

Port development policy   Industrial development was closely linked to the city's ambitious port development policy. Bristol's prosperity in the past had been associated with the development of her port. The inadequacy of the original city centre docks in the late nineteenth century had led to new docks being constructed from 1877 onwards downstream at Avonmouth on the Severn estuary. By the late 1950s however it was being strongly argued that these docks in turn were becoming inadequate to deal with the increasing size of ships. Plans for a major new dock investment on Severnside were first floated in the 1950s, and in 1959 the city-controlled Port of Bristol Authority (PBA) bought land for a site between the existing Avonmouth and Portishead docks. In 1964 Bristol submitted its development plans to the Ministry of Transport. The scheme presented was an ambitious one designed to exploit the city's motorway connections and make Bristol the third-ranking international port in Britain. The first stage involved the construction of nine berths at a cost of £27 million, but the second phase of construction would raise the total of berths to twenty-five.

The scheme received backing from the National Ports Committee, but was turned down by the Wilson government. The decision was justified in a detailed investment appraisal that argued against the scheme on two grounds (Ministry of Transport 1966): first, the container-age investment was better concentrated in existing ports (such as London and Liverpool); and, second, that on the basis of its detailed forecasting model it was most unlikely that the new port could attract sufficient traffic, especially export traffic, to reach commercial viability.

Undeterred, the city drew up a revised plan for a smaller port, West Dock 1, costing £15 million, which was incorporated in a Bill submitted to Parliament in 1968. The scheme was once more opposed by the Ministry of Transport and was thrown out in the Common on a second reading. Undeterred yet again, the city drew up a third scheme, West Dock 2. Although a pale shadow of the first plan, it could still handle six ships of 70,000 tons (three times the size of those able to use Avonmouth), with ample surrounding land for modern handling equipment and industrial development. The crucial difference this time was that Bristol agreed from the outset to meet the full cost itself through borrowing on the money market. The then Conservative Commons approved the new Bill in July 1971.

Bristol's tenacious pursuit of a new dock was based upon an alliance of local interests that began to come apart only later in the 1970s. The successive schemes received bipartisan support from the local Labour and Conservative Parties throughout the 1960s, and verbal backing was forthcoming at crucial junctures from trade unions such as the Transport and General Workers Union. Not surprisingly, some of the most direct expressions of support came from shipping interests in the city such as the Bristol Steamship Owners' Association, but general support was also expressed by wider business organizations such as the Chamber of Commerce.

The campaign for the new dock was also sustained by an ideological framework which enabled widely different interests to come together with a common goal. Local Conservative and Labour leaders often linked the docks scheme to Bristol's glorious maritime history and the tradition of the Merchant Venturers. A Docks Committee chairman described the scheme as 'one of the greatest merchanting ventures since Cabot sailed from this port to discover North America' (PBA 1966). At the same time, the docks project could be looked at in a quite different light, attractive to those less enthused by a maritime past closely entwined with the slave trade. Arthur Palmer, a Bristol Labour MP, gave the project a distinctive socialist dimension by describing it as 'the largest single municipal trading undertaking in the country' and noted that 'in an earlier age it would have been a source of socialist delight' (*Hansard*, 8 July 1968). A project that could be seen simultaneously as a continuation of a glorious entrepreneurial past and an expression of socialist advance was clearly capable of generating widespread support!

The other side of this distinctive image of Bristol's central role in the maritime world was an almost paranoid sensitivity to outside criticism, especially when linked to competing proposals to develop the Welsh ports; and special ire was reserved by the local press and local politicians for the Welsh MPs who were seen as a powerful lobby blocking Bristol's proposals. Richard Crossman's *Diaries* show that this was indeed the case (Crossman 1977, p. 118).

The sense of an embattled city fighting to preserve its maritime greatness was strong enough to resist evidence that suggested that a new port was not essential to Bristol's future prosperity. The Ministry of Transport's own analysis challenged Bristol's forecasts in 1966. The then Minister of Transport pointed out in the 1968 Commons debate that growth rates in the Bristol sub-region had been higher than in other parts of the country over the period 1961–6 even though port traffic had increased by less than average. Finally, the Severnside study concluded in 1971 that 'generally we do not see the Severnside ports as being major stimulants to the economy of Severnside' (Central Unit for Environmental Planning 1971). Nevertheless, in 1971, by a vote in Council, the city committed itself to a massive municipal investment with no promise of government support.

Central area office development policy   While industry expanded and the struggle over the port continued, the most visible signs of economic development were the new office blocks that rapidly began to transform the central area of the city. About 100,000 square feet of office space was being completed a year in the early 1960s, but this increased rapidly to over 250,000 square feet a year in the period 1964–7 (see Figure 2.7 above). Planning permission was readily available under both Labour and Conservative Councils. Finally, the travel-to-work problems associated with industrial estate development and central area office growth were used to justify hugely ambitious plans for large-scale urban motorway construction to provide three circuits at different distances from the city centre with links to the national motorway system. An inner circuit road was largely completed by the late 1960s and a start was made on an intermediate circuit. In summary, in the late 1960s Bristol looked set for continuing growth, with the Council under both parties pursuing development policies that attempted either to reinforce market forces moving in Bristol's favour (e.g. industrial and office development) or to reverse forces that seemed temporarily to be moving against Bristol (port development). If Bristol had much in common with other large cities in its policies on industrial and office development, it stood out sharply through the magnitude of its municipal port scheme.

The transition period: 1970–1978

We have identified the main elements of change in this period in Chapter 2. Between 1971 and 1978 manufacturing employment dropped by 14.2 per cent, the equivalent of 15,326 jobs. At the same time, employment in service industries grew by 14.3 per cent, equivalent to 24,633 jobs. In spite of this rise in service jobs, unemployment rose above the national average in 1972 and once again in the period 1977–9 (see Figure 2.1 above). Although successive increases in unemployment prompted a series of economic policy initiatives, the first part of this period was marked most strongly by mounting opposition to the office development and transport infrastructure policies launched in the previous period but now regarded as a major threat to the character of the city.

The rapid increase in service employment was associated with a new boom in office construction. More than 2 million square feet of office space was added in the six years up to 1978, equal to one-third of the total 1978 stock, with over 1 million square feet having been completed in the peak year of 1974. This office development was mainly speculative and was concentrated in the central area, much of it proving attractive to insurance and banking companies decentralizing from London. However, the recession began to hit the demand for offices from 1973 onwards, and the high level of completions in 1974, 1975, and 1976 led to a massive oversupply and a rise in vacant acommodation. In December 1976, for example, there was over 1 million square feet of vacant office accommodation in the city in units greater than 10,000 square feet.

The boom in construction fuelled local opposition. Even in 1971, Bristol had been singled out as an example of 'the developer's dream gone wrong', with hasty planning decisions leading to the destruction of the central area environment. In 1972 the Conservative leader of the council was forced to defend office development policy in an article headlined 'The Great Office Block Scandal' (*Evening Post*, 2 March 1972). Walker argued that current policy was part of a wider plan. The first stage had been to attract regional offices, the second stage was now attracting national firms decentralizing from London, and the third stage would begin to attract firms operating on a European-wide scale.

After Labour was back in control of the council in 1973, pressure to restrain office growth increased further. The boom coincided with increased pressures on the housing market, and much publicity was given to rising waiting lists ('Boom Town or Heartbreak City?', *Evening Post*, 3 December

1973). The Bristol Trades Council sent a deputation to the city's Resources and Co-ordination Committee to express concern over the imbalance between the rate of office growth and the loss of industrial jobs, and protest reached a peak in the same year when a housing action group took over an empty office block for a week.

The scale of the protests prompted the council to start a full-scale investigation into office development policy, and the new Labour leader was quoted as saying that the preoccupation with Bristol becoming a regional commercial centre had 'gone too far' (*Evening Post*, 20 June 1973). The following month the Planning Committee agreed to freeze office development by deferring consideration of new applications for at least a two-year period, with limited exceptions for cases of clear planning gain. At that point 7.9 million square feet had been completed, 1.5 million square feet was under construction, 2.1 million square feet had planning permission, and a further 2.5 million square feet was 'morally committed'. The ban was therefore largely symbolic.

Opposition to unrestrained office growth overlapped with opposition to the major road improvement schemes linked to the redevelopment of the central areas. The Outer Circuit Motorway scheme was attacked by protest groups led by the middle-class conservation lobby for its destruction of inner-city housing, and after internal Labour dissent in 1973 the scheme was effectively put on ice awaiting the outcome of a major land use transportation survey. Lack of resources finally killed the scheme in the late 1970s, and this opened the way for a wave of subsequent conservation and environmental schemes.

At the same time as the council was moving towards some form of restraint on office development, there was an increasing concern with the decline of manufacturing jobs. The sudden jump in unemployment between 1970 and 1971 prompted an emergency Conference on Unemployment called by the Lord Mayor. It was agreed to to set up an eighteen-person committee comprised of council, business, trade union, and voluntary sector representatives to explore possible initiatives. In the event little seems to have followed except the commissioning of research by the Polytechnic into the employment impacts of the Concorde project and a delegation to Number 10 Downing Street to urge that the project be kept alive.

Following a further rise in unemployment after 1974, the Council took a major step towards the formation of an explicit economic development policy with an organizational structure to back it up. In 1976 an Economic Development Board was established for the whole Bristol area with representation from trade unions, employers, educational institutions, Avon County Council, and other district councils. This was followed by the setting up of an Economic Development Sub-committee within Bristol City Council reporting to the central Resources and Co-ordination Committee. An Industrial Development Officer was appointed the same year.

The decline of manufacturing employment was a central concern of the new committee. At its first meeting it accepted a research report prepared by a researcher at Bristol Polytechnic entitled 'The Case for the Granting of Intermediate Area Status for Greater Bristol'. The title itself gives a clue to the Committee's initial line of thought. The report placed much emphasis upon the fact that the local rate of manufacturing decline was above the national average. Between 1971 and March 1974 manufacuring employment had declined by 2.3 per cent nationally and by 5.2 per cent in Bristol (a loss of 6,546 jobs). The report also warned of the dangers of over-reliance on the two major aerospace companies, Rolls Royce and BAC. An earlier Polytechnic study had suggested that 19,720 jobs were in some way dependent on the Concorde project alone.

An important line of argument for Intermediate Area status focused on unemployment rates. These had generally been below the national average until June 1974, but by August 1976 the Bristol–Severnside rate had risen to 6.7 per cent compared with the national average of 6.3 per cent. The report noted that cities such as Manchester, Leeds, and Sheffield, which were in existing Intermediate Areas, had lower unemployment rates than Bristol. After considering the report, the Committee submitted an application for Intermediate Area status, but without much hope of getting a favourable reply. Nevertheless, an important step forward had been taken in policy development.

The economic development strategy launched in 1976 evolved rapidly over the next two years to embrace a number of major components.

1. *The protection of existing industry.* It was recognized from the beginning that the decline of manufacturing employment was largely the result of the major redundancies declared by multinational corporations located in the city, and that the industrial base would continue to be eroded in the foreseeable future by further rationalization and closure. Nevertheless, it was argued that the council must try to protect existing jobs by identifying and meeting the needs of existing employers for land, transport links, and manpower.

2. *Land assembly and estate development.* Maintaining an adequate supply of land was also a major concern from the beginning. Early reports noted the lack of inner-city sites for small businesses and the problems of assembling larger sites for major incoming firms. It was also recognized that there was an imbalance between the concentration of job losses in inner and south Bristol and the greater land availability for new development at Avonmouth and on the northern fringe of the city.

3. *Support for small firms.* Early reports noted that the demand by small firms for small sites and units exceeded the supply. In 1978 the Resources and Co-ordination Committee accepted a proposal by the other district councils in the area to appoint two Small Firms Officers under joint funding to develop policy in this direction.

4. *The attraction of outside investment in new growth sectors.* This objective was perhaps the most important component of industrial development strategy, and certainly attracted the most publicity. The reasoning behind the strategy was spelled out in a report from the Chief Executive in 1978. Given that there was a limited number of footloose industries in the current economic context, the report argued that a major effort should lie in attracting investment from overseas. (The council had also been given advice by government officials that Industrial Development Certificates would not be needed for foreign invest- ment to come to Bristol.) The Industrial Development Officer was quoted as being in favour of a selective approach, with particular emphasis on modern processing industries in the fields of electronics, pharmaceuticals, cosmetics, and plastics. The USA was identified early on as the major sources for such new investment, with West Germany offering some potential.

In summary, the economic development strategy launched in 1976 was heavily oriented towards land assembly, support for small firms, market- ing, and promotion, and was based upon close co-operation with the pri- vate sector. No alternative strategy was formulated or evaluated. Several factors explain the form the strategy took. First the elements of a radical 'alternative' Labour strategy were poorly developed, both nationally and locally at that time. The strategy adopted appeared as a bold step for- ward in the context of the time. Second, the strategy was launched 'from the top' by a moderate Labour Party leadership group working closely with the Chief Executive. It did not reflect any clearly articulated reform- ing zeal within the party 'from below'. Third, the components of the strategy were designed to secure the support of a broad alliance of inter- ests, including local employers, the Conservative opposition on Bristol Council, and the other, largely Conservative-controlled, districts. As a result, the strategy was designed to increase the overall prosperity of the city rather than transform local economic relations in the interests of workers or to concentrate aid on particular disadvantaged groups or areas.

The strategy did not, for example, address itself directly to inner-city prob- lems. However, pressure rapidly built up for an explicit inner-city dimension to local development policies. Before 1976 policies for the inner city certainly existed on paper, but they were largely focused on housing and environmen- tal problems and found expression in improvement grant policies and the designation of a limited number of General Improvement Areas (Bassett and Hauser 1976). A major step forward followed directly from shifts in central government policy which found expression in the Inner Area Studies for Lambeth, Birmingham, and Liverpool and the designation of partnership and programme authorities under the 1978 Inner Urban Areas Act. Bristol responded by launching its own inner-city study in 1977. Rates of unemploy- ment and a measure of housing quality were used to define a compact 'inner-

city' area covering approximately one-third of the urban area with a population of around 128,000 (see Figure 2.11 above).

This definition of the inner city served to focus attention on specific problems, but, as the discussion in Chapter 2 showed, the apparently precise
boundaries gave a false sense of precision to the spatial distribution of urban
problems. First, the area designated excluded some important concentrations of unemployment and social stress found in the midst of some of the
larger outlying council estates. Second, the apparent compactness of the area
designated concealed considerable internal diversity (Bassett and Short
1978).

However meaningful the definition, the identification of an 'inner-city
problem' provided the basis for a campaign to attract government aid and
also went some way towards changing the popular image of the city. The
Chief Executive's letter to the Secretary of State pointed out that the problems of the city ran counter to its image, and emphasized the acute contrasts
between the poorer and more affluent areas. The local paper heralded the
'shock report' which revealed the extent of the problems behind Bristol's
façade of affluence. In the event, Bristol's campaign to attract government
aid largely failed. Bristol was not included in any list of Urban Programme
Authorities, and the city received only £250,000 from the fund for construction work allocated by the Chancellor in July 1977. The money was used to
lay out a number of industrial sites for starter units and small firms in inner-
city areas.

The city leaders were bitterly disappointed not to receive recognition of
their newly identified problems. But did Bristol have a real case to be
included as a partnership, programme, or designated authority? Following
Peter Shore's written parliamentary answer in June 1978 on the criteria for
including local authorities, Bristol carried out its own comparison exercise.
This pointed out that the statistical criteria were based on local authority
areas as a whole. Bristol was at a disadvantage because of its overall
affluence, which concealed the marked spatial inequalities. Nevertheless, on
some demographic and social criteria, the city ranked higher than authorities
like Sheffield and Leeds which had been included in the designated lists.
With regard to unemployment, Bristol was the highest ranked non-desig-
nated district. Where the city 'lost out' by comparison was in terms of physical variables relating to housing and derelict land. Nevertheless, Bristol came
close to inclusion. Shore, in a further parliamentary reply, included Bristol in
a list of twelve 'candidates' for possible future designation.

Finally, there was another facet of economic development policy, by far
and away the most important in terms of financial commitment, and one
which did not clearly fit with the other components. In 1977 Bristol's new
dock, now named Royal Portbury, was opened. Its construction had cost the
city £37 million in capital borrowing and constituted a massive, municipal
development programme in its own right. The escalating costs during con-

struction had alarmed some of its erstwhile supporters, and it finally opened just as the recession deepened and world trade began to slump. On top of that, a row over an Industrial Development Certificate with the Department of Industry was instrumental in discouraging Toyota from locating a car import terminal on adjacent land.

In conclusion, the period 1970–9 witnessed a series of policy developments in response to changing economic and political factors. The opening of the new dock brought an earlier policy initiative to fruition just as the economic basis of that policy was being eroded. Office policies were actually aimed at trying to control the development impacts of a boom that seemed to be out of control and was partly a result of the council's own planning policies. Manu- facturing decline and inner-city decay stimulated policy packages that were not clearly integrated with each other.

Recession and crisis: 1979–1985

The deepening of the economic recession in the UK after 1978 was reflected in the further restructuring of the local economy and a rapid rise in employ- ment. A further 8,337 manufacturing jobs were lost between 1978 and 1981, and the service sector also began to decline, losing 2,813 jobs in the period. As a result, unemployment rates rose sharply, although they remained below the national average, unlike the previous period when they briefly exceeded the (much lower) national average. As the analysis in Chapter 2 showed, the great bulk of the manufacturing jobs were lost as the result of closures and redundancies by a small number of major multinational corporations with branch plants in the city. The rapid increase in overall unemployment was also associated with significant changes in its spatial distribution. Inner-city unemployment rates rose sharply, but at the same time the occurrence of high unemployment spread to the large council estates in south and north Bristol. There was some evidence also of an increasing polarization between the poorer and more affluent areas. Not only did economic problems become more acute during this period, but there was the added political pressure of the St Pauls riot in 1980 and the emergence of a massive financial crisis as the result of deficits on the operation of the docks. This was also a period of change within the parties, the rise of Liberal representation, and the emer- gence of a 'hung' council. Although Avon County Council launched its own economic development initiatives from 1983 onwards, Bristol City Council took the lead through much of the period, and its policies will be examined first.

Labour had an overall majority on Bristol City Council between 1979 and 1983, but from May 1983 onwards no party was able to obtain an overall majority. The Conservatives took control (by securing the chairmanships of committees) as the largest party in 1983, but Labour regained control as the largest party from May 1984 onwards. Its survival as the largest party depended to a great extent on the support of the six Liberals holding the balance of power.

In spite of this increasing political uncertainty, there was considerable continuity in the implementation of many economic development policies based upon a consensus between the three parties. Economic development policies also grew in complexity as more and more policy initiatives were launched. There were, however, important areas of dispute, particularly relating to the future of the docks; and towards the end of the period, in 1984, there were signs of wider disagreements as the elements of an alternative Labour Party strategy began to emerge.

The alternative strategy grew out of criticisms within the district party of elements of the strategy launched in 1976. Some felt that the latter was too preoccupied with marketing and promotion and the attraction of high-tech branch plants of multinational companies to the city, with insufficient regard for the kinds of jobs being created and the skills of the local unemployed. By 1982 the party's policy document. *A Socialist Strategy for the Labour Party in Bristol* (Bristol District Labour Party, 1983), was calling for a radically different policy based upon more direct intervention in the local economy, a greater concern with local democratic planning, the greater use of local resources, and a closer matching of new jobs to sectors and areas of high unemployment. Specifically, the party called for a full Economic Development Committee with specialist staff; a Greater Bristol Enterprise Board to be established jointly with Avon County Council to direct pension fund monies into new and existing industries through a system of Planning Agreements with priority for socially useful products; a Co-operative Development Agency to provide encouragement for co-operative and community enterprises; and the use of local authority purchasing strategies to help indigenous industry. The package of measures was based upon the increasingly publicized experiments of Labour councils such as Sheffield and the GLC. Overall, the new strategy was clearly intended to fulfil a political as well as an economic role in presenting a local version of Labour's 'Alternative Economic Strategy'.

In practice, the party's proposals had little impact on the actual direction of economic development policy until about 1984. Several of the proposals required a close working relationship with Avon County Council and the adoption of new powers. This proved difficult, given Bristol's lingering resentment at its loss of powers and tensions that arose when Avon began to launch its own economic development strategy in 1983. Furthermore, the balance of power in the Labour group did not favour serious consideration of many of the proposals. The new strategy was closely associated with the increase of left-wing influence in the party after 1979. Although the left had secured a majority of active delegates to the district party by 1982, and thus could influence the making of policy, it remained in a minority on the Labour group until 1984 and had less influence over actual policy implementation.

Economic development proposals tended to get caught up in the general atmosphere of conflict and tension between left and right that resulted in the majority of the Labour group viewing most district party proposals with suspicion. Only in 1984, when the left captured leading positions within the group, were moves initiated to implement some of the easier and more innocuous proposals, and only in 1985 did the Labour group become united behind an effort to give economic development policy a higher political profile.

It is perhaps not surprising, therefore, that the organizational structure established within the council in 1976 remained largely unchanged. Formal economic development policy remained under the control of the Economic Development Sub-committee, although there were Labour-inspired attempts to upgrade this into a fall committee in 1985. The Industrial Development Officer was renamed the Economic Development Officer in 1979 in recognition of his expanding role, and, following a proposal from the other districts, two Small Firms Officers were appointed to the Economic Development Office. The Office itself was deliberately kept separate from the other, longer established, departments and was designated as the focal point for all enquiries with investment and employment implications.

However, certain aspects of policy that were clearly related to economic development were also the responsibility of other and more powerful committees. Docks policy was largely decided by the Docks Committee, which preserved a considerable degree of autonomy within the council's structure, and the Planning Committee played a major role in research and discussions on inner-city policy. The City Valuers' Department also played a significant role when city-owned land and industrial estates were involved. This structure permitted a degree of fragmentation and overlap in policy-making and implementation. It is instructive to examine the major policy areas in turn, identifying the most significant policy shifts and their determinants, before standing back and looking at the coherence of policy as a whole.

The protection of existing industry   This was established as one of the major objectives of the strategy launched in 1976. In practice, there was little that the local authority could do to influence the restructuring decisions of the major multinationals, and the Economic Development Officer suggested that even an 'early warning' system for closures would be impractical. Nevertheless, contacts were maintained by the Economic Development Officer with most large local employers and some attempt was made to respond to emergencies. Thus the granting of concessions on rates and harbour dues had a positive, though marginal, effect on the decision of RTZ to continue its lead and zinc smelting operations at Avonmouth following European-wide rationalization. By 1985 the Resources and Co-ordination Committee had moved as far as granting an interest-free loan to help the expansion plans of a medium-sized enterprise. A wider range of companies were also helped at various times with sites and premises. On one occasion only was the council involved more overtly in a public campaign to reverse a closure decision and protect local jobs. In early 1983, British Leyland (BL) announced the closure of a local plant making bus chasses and employing 560 people. An action committee was formed at the works and the council was asked for support. A resolution was passed calling for a reversal of the decision, and the Labour leader went with a delegation to lobby the BL management. This action was not successful and the plant closed. In other cases of closure or redundancy where the decision was reluctantly accepted by the workforce and the unions, there was no organized political response.

Land assembly and estate development This continued throughout the period as a major component of policy. The Avonmouth estates were expanded to accommodate distribution and warehousing units. Sites on the north fringe (just outside the city boundary but on city-owned land) were laid out for new, 'high-tech' firms. Inner-city estates rationalized existing land uses and provided small business units. Finally, two major sites were started in south Bristol in response to the rapid increase in unemployment. One was located on the site of the board mills, closed by Imperial with the loss of 1,700 jobs. The other, next to the Knowle and Hartcliffe council estates in south Bristol, was based on a new partnership arrangement with the private sector for the development of a council-owned site.

Support for small firms Small-firm support continued but with significant developments and shifts of emphasis. In 1981 the two posts of Small Firms Officers fell vacant and were not refilled. It was argued that there was now a range of private-sector-backed agencies in the area able to offer aid and advice, and that the council should concentrate on the provision of small, low-cost units for which demand exceeded the supply. Following the St Pauls disturbances of 1980, the council established an Enterprise Workshop Centre in the area with small workshops and common equipment and facilities. Another such centre was subsequently opened in south Bristol. By 1984 policy towards a range of proposals had developed to include a number of such Enterprise Centres in a hierarchy of sites and premises in different parts of the city. The hierarchy would range upwards from simple 'business yards' in converted garage sites on council estates, through Enterprise Centres with common facilities, to intermediate sites for established businesses, and, finally, to conventional factory and warehouse estates. Only limited progress had been made towards these goals by 1985. Finally, in 1985 a further layer of policy was added with the appointment of two Co-operative Development Officers to work in conjuction with the Avon Co-operative Development Agency, on which Bristol was now granted representation. This was one of the first indications of a new, closer working relationship with Avon and reflected key aspects of the Labour District Party's policy since 1982.

The creation of new industrial sectors through the attraction of foreign investment   This remained perhaps the most salient component of economic development policy throughout the period and occupied much of the effort of the Economic Development Officer. Early attempts to attract Western European investment were not very successful, and it was argued that the most likely source of investment in Europe, the West German market, might be tapped through exploiting Bristol's close links with Hanover, built up since the end of the war. As a result, Bristol came to occupy a prominent position at the prestigious Hanover trade fairs, and some direct investment did follow.

It was the USA, however, which was quickly identified as the major source of potential investment, and from 1979 onwards the Economic Development Officer has paid regular visits, particularly to the Boston area and to 'Silicon Valley' in California. On a number of occasions 'Bristol missions' have also been sent, involving the Economic Development Officer, council leaders, and officers and representatives of the Chamber of Commerce and local industry. One of the more successful elements of such missions has been a series of 'presentations' by executives of local high-tech companies explaining the reasons for their decision to locate in the Bristol area. In 1982 Bristol consolidated its links by securing agency services through a US consultancy, enabling it to compete with other large cities and organizations such as the Scottish Development Agency, which had permanent representatives on the spot.

An important component of this strategy was the marketing of the city in a form attractive to US investors. On his visits to the USA, the Economic Development Officer deliberately 'sold' an image of the city as an aerospace centre with a skilled workforce, excellent communications, and good infrastructure. Publicity brochures produced by the city during this period reinforced this image and drew attention to the excellence of the urban environment, the quality of the surrounding countryside, and the range of educational and leisure facilities. Decisions by leading high-tech companies to locate in the area were quickly used to reinforce the image of a high-technology growth centre. In this respect, the marketing effort soon reached out to exploit Bristol's position at the western end of the M4 corridor. Articles on 'the M4 Golden Corridor' and 'Britain's Sunrise Strip' which began to appear in the press were incorporated into Bristol's publicity. In March 1982 the Chief Executive was drawing attention to the advantages of joining forces with Swindon, also an 'aggressive, dynamic, and outward-looking authority', in order to market the corridor region as a whole.

The major and most publicized achievements of these promotional activities were the attraction of the US-based companies, Hewlett Packard and Dupont, to city-owned land on the north fringe. The background to these decisions was discussed in Chapter 3. In the case of Hewlett Packard, Bristol was involved, along with other local authorities in the area, in negotiations lasting over a year. The site had a number of obvious locational advantages to the company, but the financial package on offer also had some influence. Hewlett Packard got rate concessions and the chance of purchasing up to 165 acres of city-owned land over ten years at a fixed price. Bristol would spend over £4.1 million, mainly on off-site infrastructure. In return, it would receive over £9.2 million in capital receipts, but almost £6 million of these would be received after 1993, and only if the company took up all their land options. Avon County Council and Northavon also contributed cash grants. Avon contributed £180,000, repayable if the number of jobs fell below 400 within two years of the grant being paid; Northavon contributed £20,000 on similar terms.

Hewlett Packard was not the only 'catch'. In November 1984 Dupont announced that they would build a factory to manufacture electronic connectors for the data processing and telecommunications industries on a site adjacent to the Hewlett Packard site. Again, Bristol and the other local authorities had been involved in earlier discussions with the company, but in this case there were no major financial inducements and the company's decision was based largely on the locational advantages of the site.

The overall strategy of attracting foreign investment to the area was subject to little overt criticism until 1984, when doubts were expressed by some Labour members in debate and print over the longer-term advantages. US investment, it was argued, increased the area's dependence on multinational branch plants, and the siting of these plants on the favoured northern fringe of the city actually accentuated the spatial imbalance between growth in this zone and the continuing decline of much of south Bristol. This precipitated Conservative accusations that Labour was opposed to multinational companies, and a brief debate followed in the press over the relative employment gains and losses contributed by such companies in the city. No significant changes in policy followed, however, even when Labour recaptured the committee chairs several months later. The strategy had become too entrenched to be easily revised by a party with no overall majority and more pressing problems in other policy areas.

Commercial development The economic development strategy launched in 1976 was aimed primarily at attracting industry to the area. However, commercial development has become a more and more prominent theme in economic development strategy in the 1980s. In this field Bristol has been able to rely to a great extent on its natural advantages as a commercial centre and on the marketing efforts of private sector developers and property agents. As a result, public intervention has been less direct and confined largely to information, marketing, and assistance with site selection.

In the office sector the construction boom of the mid-1970s was followed by a slump in completions between 1976 and 1980 (see Figure 2.7 above). In the early 1980s there was a revival in the market, with over 940,000 square feet under construction in buildings of over 10,000 square feet in December

1981. As a result, completions picked up rapidly from 1981 onwards, with over 1.8 million square feet being completed between 1981 and 1984. Most of this space was filled as the result of the efforts of private agents and the city's general marketing of the Bristol area. However, various council departments were involved more closely in the relocation of several major companies during this period, albeit in a largely reactive and facilitative role. The London Life Insurance Company, for example, began to move their headquarters to the city from London in 1981. The Economic Development Office had been contacted as early as May 1978 for information on sites, but at that stage the company had already decided to leave London and had put Bristol on its shortlist of alternatives. The availability of a strategically placed site was a key factor in choosing Bristol, and once the decision had been made the council was involved mainly in easing the planning process and helping the company to 'sell' the city to its staff.

In spite of this and other significant relocations, the supply of empty office space began to build up again from 1984 onwards. By November 1984 there was 1.8 million square feet of empty office space in the city, the highest ever recorded, with 158,000 square feet under construction and potential planning permission for another 1.2 million square feet. Elements within the local Labour Party and the Labour group tended to place greater emphasis on industrial than on private service development and to be critical of large-scale office redevelopment. The emergence of a large surplus of office space prompted the new left-wing chairman of the Planning Committee to propose a new policy of office constraint in November 1984, which effectively froze planning permission for new developments for twelve months except where a building was planned for a known occupier. The proposal was opposed by the Conservatives and by local property agents, who argued that an immediately available supply of large, vacant units was necessary in order to attract major companies from London. The limited restraint policy was nevertheless adopted and, given the scale of vacant space and developments in the pipeline, is unlikely significantly to reduce Bristol's continuing attractiveness as an office centre. This policy shift nevertheless appears as a policy rerun of the early 1970s and illustrates the problems of controlling unstable property booms in the long-term interests of the city.

Tourism Over the same period, the development of tourism and the conference trade has also become a more prominent policy theme. The widening of economic development policy to include tourism has reflected a growing awareness of the city's advantages in this field as an architecturally attractive city with rich historical associations, set in an area of great natural variety and beauty. In many respects this has now become a key area of policy. In 1985, for example, it was being claimed that 1 million visitors were staying in the city every year and spending over £60 million, with considerable benefit to the local economy.

The most important policy initiative in this area was the establishment of a Bristol Marketing Board in 1984. This represented a joint venture between the city council and the private sector to promote the city as a tourist destination and as a location for major conferences and exhibitions. The board has been chaired by a member of the Wills family, (the Wills company has had long associations with the city), and has included the leaders of the three political parties and chairmen or managing directors of South West Gas, DRG, and John Harvey and Sons (the last two companies also being traditional Bristol employers). The board has a small staff located in the Council House and has been jointly funded by the council and the private sector. The council included a sum of £59,000 for the board in its 1985/6 budget, with an additional sum of £73,000 reserved for the promotion of tourism and the conference trade.

Since its formation, the board has worked on partnership and sponsorship schemes with the private sector and government agencies on a scale claimed by the board to be 'unprecedented anywhere else in Great Britain'. By 1985 the board was claiming that over £3 million had been raised for projects in 'inner-city areas' with substantial employment implications. The focus of much of the board's activities has been the area of the old city docks, which has been steadily redeveloped for housing, commercial, and leisure activities since the mid-1970s. The board has worked closely with the English Tourist Board, who designated the dock area as a major pilot project leading to the establishment of the first 'maritime heritage park' in the UK. In this connection, the English Tourist Board has provided substantial grants for a Maritime Museum, improvements to the National Lifeboat Museum, and improvements to visitor facilities for the SS *Great Britain*, berthed in Brunel's original dry-dock. Tourism projects in the city docks attracted a large part of a special allocation of £2 million by the MSC fo the 'Bristol 1000' project for unemployed 18–24-year-olds in the city. Other major areas of activity by the board have centred round the rehabilitation of Brunel's engine shed and publicity campaigns associating the city with the celebrations of the 150th anniversary of the Great Western Railway.

This increasing emphasis on tourist development has not been without criticism. Some sections of the Labour group have commented on the considerable autonomy that the board seems to possess in policy making and the lack of integration between its policies and economic development policy as a whole. Questions have also been raised about the numbers and types of jobs that tourism is likely to generate. Nevertheless, this is a policy area that is likely to expand further in the future.

Inner-city policies and the emerging problems of south Bristol   The failure of the city to obtain inner-city status under the 1978 Inner Urban Areas Act has been discussed in an earlier section. In spite of repeated applications, Bristol failed to obtain any special recognition of its problems in this period either. The St

Pauls riot in 1980 brought home the problems with new force. The riot spawned a variety of initiatives, some more lasting in their effects than others. Although the government refused a public inquiry, the House of Commons Select Sub-committee on Race Relations and Immigration did visit the city to hold public hearings. These were boycotted by the Bristol Council for Racial Equality and other groups pushing for a full public inquiry, but they did elicit valuable background material on the scale of the local problems and the impact of past public policies. The council provided information on its considerable expenditure on housing and environmental improvements in the area over the previous five years (over £15 million). The area contained three of the four Housing Action Areas declared by that date. Further information, however, revealed that the unemployment situation had steadily worsened over the same period with unemployment rates approaching 40 per cent in the worst sub-areas. A subsequent public inquiry organized by the Bristol Trades Council confirmed the picture of rapid economic decline since the mid-1970s (Bristol Trades Council 1984).

The government's refusal of a full public inquiry effectively shifted the responsibility for appropriate action on to the local authorities in the area. A so-called Tripartite Committee was established with representatives from Bristol, Avon County Council, and the Bristol Council for Racial Equality (BCRE). In spite of BCRE's interest in exploring broader themes of racism, the committee quickly focused its attention on more conventional aspects of inner-city deprivation, setting up working groups on community facilities, employment, and education. The Employment Working Group proposed three lines of action, to: create new jobs in the area through the development of new sites: encourage the establishment of new small businesses: and provide additional retraining facilities for local people to enable them to compete more effectively for available jobs.

After almost a year's work, the committee presented a report and a series of proposals to the Home Office in July 1981. It became clear that no guarantee of extra resources would be made and requests for aid for specific projects would have to go through the normal Urban Aid channels. While a number of projects were funded in this way, little progress could be made in the key area of employment. By 1983 two new industrial estates had been developed near the St Pauls area, and, within St Pauls itself, an Enterprise Workshop had been established in a little used underground car park. This provided only thirteen workshops, however, and the Employment Working Group was forced to conclude in a report in the same year that, overall, 'little impact, if any, had been made on the severe problems of unemployment in the area.'

As conditions in the inner city continued to deteriorate, Bristol renewed its attempt to gain Programme Authority status. In order to build a case, researchers in the Planning Department in 1983 used the Department of the Enviroment's own criteria to show that on many comparative scales Bristol was worse off than several towns that were included in the government's list.

The research report was also able to draw upon an article in *Population Trends* which conveniently compared conditions in nineteen cities using 1981 Census data, differentiating between city-wide and inner-city averages for a range of variables (Redfern 1982). When the cities were ranked according to the number of people living in 'problem wards' (mostly inner-city wards), Bristol, with a 'problem ward' population of 62,000, came twelfth, immediately after Newcastle and above Sheffield (which, unlike Bristol, was a Programme Authority). Moreover, Bristol was the only city outside the Partnership Authorities, with the exception of Nottingham, which contained a 'Category 1' ward with the worst combinations of conditions (this was, significantly, St Pauls).

In other words, as was pointed out in Chapter 2, Bristol had inner-city conditions comparable to the worst in the country but they were concentrated in a smaller area. The Bristol research report also pointed out that the slight differences between Bristol and other authorities on various criteria had a major financial effect. Hull, for example, had a 'problem ward' population of 73,000, 17 per cent more than Bristol, but this was translated into a 730 per cent difference in urban programme funds.

Although the disturbances in St Pauls focused a great deal of attention on the inner city after 1980, the evidence of rapidly worsening employment conditions on the outer council estates meant that the inner city increasingly had to compete for limited resources with other areas. By 1983 the scale of job loss in south Bristol was causing growing concern, particularly to the large number of Labour councillors representing these traditional Labour areas. Following the 1983 election, Bristol South was to remain the only Labour-held constituency south of a line from the Wash to the Severn, excluding inner London. There were murmurings that St Pauls was absorbing a great deal of resources to the exclusion of other areas with problems almost on the same scale. As a result, the problems of south Bristol were given greater and greater prominence and a series of environmental, housing, and employment initiatives were launched from 1983 onwards. Sites for two new industrial estates were approved, and an Enterprise Workshop was established on the same lines as the one in St Pauls.

There were no major political disagreements on these initiatives. In fact, the logical step of linking the problems of inner and south Bristol to make a stronger case for government aid was taken when the Conservatives were briefly in control as the largest party between 1983 and 1984. A report was prepared requesting the government to grant Assisted Area status to a contiguous area of twelve wards covering part of the inner city and the worst affected areas of south Bristol (see Figure 2.12 above). The area defined had a population of about 200,000 and an average unemployment rate of 19.6 per cent. The accompanying report claimed that the population of the area was bigger than that of many towns in the UK, and 'if this area stood alone it would, without doubt, be one of the most depressed in the country.' Further manufacturing job losses were expected, and there was little prospect of large companies locating in an area cut off from the growth zones nearer the motorway in the north. The submission was given all-party support and a delegation visited the Department of the Environment, but, in spite of sympathetic noises, the request was turned down.

Bristol also got short shrift with a parallel request for a revision of the criteria for Urban Programme status. The burden of the complaint here was the reliance on local-authority-wide averages for key variables which worked to Bristol's disadvantage by concealing considerable local inequalities. The government's reluctance to accede to this request probably reflected the realization that, if Bristol's case was recognized, a number of other major cities would be in a strong position to demand government aid.

Although Bristol failed once again in its quest for government recognition of its problems, the evidence that had been assembled was used to secure some funding from the European Social Fund. In August 1984 it was announced that the fund had allocated £196,000 to the city for retraining women, handicapped people, and 'migrants'. Three training centres were established, one in the central area and two in south Bristol, concentrating on information technology. These and similar employment initiatives cost £472,266 in 1984/5 with a forecast of over £1.2 million for 1985/6. Bristol's applications to the Social Fund in 1985 totalled £1,079,539, and city leaders were confident, after visiting Brussels, that the city would receive a substantial allocation of funds.

Dock policies and economic development   Parallel to the above developments, there were also important changes in policies relating to the docks. These policies tended to evolve with a logic of their own, responding to a distinctive set of economic problems, but the decisions made had important implications for the other policy areas.

The financial position of the docks steadily worsened after 1979. Only two out of the seven berths could be developed, and even these were being operated at a loss. At the same time, the hoped-for development of port-related industries on surrounding land failed to materialize. Operating losses and debt charges totalled £3.4 million in 1977/8 and rose rapidly to £11.7 million in 1981/2. These deficits all fell on the city's rate fund, imposing a massive financial burden at a time of increasing government restraints on local authority expenditure. Attempts to secure government aid and 'city' finance in 1980 failed, and Bristol turned to a team of consultants, Coopers and Lybrand, to suggest ways of reconstructing the dock finances, improving the marketing of the port, and reducing the burden on the rates.

The consultants produced their final report in August 1981. It spelled out the employment consequences of the complete closure of the docks in stark terms. More than 6,500 jobs would be lost in the docks and docks-related industries, and the unemployment rate in Avonmouth would rise from 8.7 to

25 per cent. After analysing future trade prospects (gloomy), the report looked at the financial consequences of five different options. These were all based upon the common assumptions, first, that urgent action would be taken to reduce the workforce by several hundred and, second, that up to 630 acres of land for industrial and warehouse use should be disposed of by outright sale or through premium, low-rental leases. The consultants' preferred option involved the closure of the Royal Portbury dock and the retention of a modernized Avonmouth dock. The Labour and Conservative groups combined in council to reject this option and supported a different one, involving the retention of both Avonmouth and Royal Portbury in a rationalized form. The only sustained opposition came from the Liberals, who wished to see firm performance targets set which, if not met after three years, would lead to closure.

The disposal of land for industrial development, even on the new terms, proved difficult given the depressed state of the market, but in 1982 the Abbey Hill Group, a major vehicle distribution company, purchased a 35-acre site for a car import terminal. Over the same period Bristol attempted twice to obtain Enterprise Zone status for a 500-acre site next to the dock, but without success; it also failed in a subsequent bid for Freeport status. The council's sense of desperation as the financial crisis over the docks worsened led to a willingness to look seriously at proposals by the Heron Corporation in 1983 to develop land between Portbury and Portishead as an international convention and leisure centre rather than for industry.

Finally, the council's bid for Development Area status for inner and south Bristol, referred to in the previous section, was linked to a proposal for the government to create a 'Severn Estuary Port Zone' which would enable Bristol to enjoy similar access as the South Wales ports to EEC regional development funds. It was now claimed that closure of the docks would result in the loss of 15,000 jobs and unemployment rates of 40 per cent in the Avonmouth area. However, this proposal was no more successful than the request for Assisted Area status for inner and south Bristol.

By early 1984 the financial position had worsened still further, and it was forecast that the likely deficit on the docks to be covered by the general rates fund in the coming year would be of the order of £12.7 million. Even with a standstill budget for other committees, the rate increase could be as high as 105 per cent, making the city a target for future rate-capping. The Conservatives, then the largest party, proposed as a solution a complex financial deal to repay the entire docks debt, then standing at £55 million, and free the city of annual debt charges. A new loan would be raised on the money market to repay the debt, and this would be repaid over three years together with accumulated interest charges. The money to repay the loan would come from the selling of new long leases on city centre commercial sites on terms that involved large initial premiums and low rentals. The proposals were passed with Liberal support and the new loan negotiated. The deal salvaged the city's budget in the short term but did little to resolve the underlying economic problems.

It is evident that Bristol's economic development strategy developed from 1976 onwards in both scale and content. The original concern with industrial regeneration continued as an important thread throughout the period, but there were significant shifts in emphasis on industrial policy as a whole, and a tendency increasingly to broaden the scope of development to include the service sector and tourism. If for the moment we exclude expenditure on the docks, then, as Table 6.3 shows, Bristol's expenditure on economic development totalled £7.2 million between 1977/8 and 1984. This total includes those items that the council itself classified as 'economic development', but the definition is not exact in the sense that expenditure in several committee budgets on items such as 'environmental improvements' could work through to affect development projects in different areas. As far as the distribution of expenditure is concerned, the table shows that the two largest items of expenditure related to green-field development on the northern fringe (the Hewlett-Packard site) and the provision of infrastructure at the board mills site in south Bristol following the mill closure. Overall, however, approximately 67 per cent of the total capital expenditure went either on 'inner-city' (39 per cent) or 'south Bristol' (28 per cent) sites, the areas of greatest unemployment. The figures for capital expenditure in 1984/5 reveal, however, that the most recent expenditure has been directed more towards the provision of sites on the northern fringe. Finally, the table also includes the latest figures on annual revenue expenditure on 'economic development'. The most significant figure is the total for airport marketing, docks marketing, and economic development, which comes to £454,000.

The picture changes dramatically if expenditure on the docks is included. (Docks expenditure is for the most part accounted separately in the council budget.) The construction of Royal Portbury, for example, cost £37 million by the time it opened in 1977, and this capital expenditure figure and its annual debt charges ought to be included in any 'economic development' total for the longer period. By 1981/2 the city was covering a £11.7 million deficit on the docks operation as a whole, a large part of which could be counted as a subsidy for 'economic development' (however unsuccessful). Arguably, on similar criteria, part of the capital expenditure on the airport should be included in the 'economic development' total as well.

In summary, depending on what policies and expenditures are included, Bristol has had a moderate or a massive economic development programme over the past decade.

Economic development policies in Avon and inter-authority relations

Although Bristol took most of the early initiatives on economic development and incurred most of the expenditure, from 1982 onwards matters have

Table 6.3. Economic development expenditure, Bristol City Council, 1977/8–1984/5

Capital expenditure, 1977/8–1983/4	£m.
Small and starter units	1.8
Enterprise workshops	0.2
Industrial sites, acquisition and development	5.2
All	7.2
Inner-city	2.8
South Bristol	2.0
Avonmouth	0.9
Northern fringe	1.5
All	7.2

Programme, 1984/5	£m.
Capital	
Avonmouth	111,785
New sites, acquisition and development	1,643,490
Wallscourt Farm	1,037,580
Enterprise workshops	94,975
Other	93,360
All	2,984,190
Revenue	
Trading estates under development	569,125
New Enterprise Workshops (St Pauls)	23,260
South Bristol Enterprise Workshops	33,890
Urban Programme grants (council share)	131,090
Bristol Urban Aid projects	250,000
Economic development	
—Economic Development Office	80,915
—Promotional expenses	118,000
—Tourism development	65,410
Airport marketing	90,000
Docks marketing	100,000
All	1,461,690

Source: Bristol City Council.

become more complex with the emergence of Avon County Council's own economic development strategy. This strategy has differed in important respects from Bristol's, reflecting a different political context. Avon was Conservative-controlled until 1981 when Labour secured a majority for the first time. The Avon Labour Party's 1981 Policy Statement included a list of proposals for a 'new and enlarged economic policy for Avon' with different emphases from those of Bristol. The document called for closer work with trade unions to resist redundancies and investigate alternative products, full support for co-operatives and community enterprises, local planning agreements for companies receiving local authority aid, and a greatly expanded research effort.

A major step forward in the implementation of this strategy came with the decision, in May 1982, to set up an Economic Development Sub-committee of the Resources Committee. The pressure to set up a separate committee appears to have come from an enthusiastic minority of Labour councillors and followed a number of seminars and discussions with officers and a visit to the West Midlands County Council. The committee was granted £1 million as an initial budget.

A draft strategy adopted later in the year outlined an array of options, taking into account the fact that Bristol and the other districts were already active in the economic development field. Thus, the draft noted that Bristol had given priority to promotional activities to attract foreign investment in high-technology industries and proposed that Avon should concentrate more of its efforts on the support of locally established firms and the growth of small and medium-sized businesses. Support for small firms was explicitly widened to include co-operatives as a preferred form of development, and the strategy proposed establishing a separate Co-operative Development Agency to provide advice and funds. Other proposals covered support for the adoption of new technology and the development of new products by local firms; the provision of land and premises (in particular, the provision of communal workshops); the provision of finance, possibly by a local Enterprise Board, linked to planning agreements; and the development of a local authority purchasing policy to give help to local suppliers and disadvantaged groups.

A number of initiatives were subsequently launched, although on a smaller scale than Bristol's initiatives. By June 1984 £274,000 had been spent on direct expenditure, £100,700 on loans, and £414,000 on guarantees. Thirteen small industrial units were under construction, and a feasibility study had been carried out into the conversion of factory premises in Kingswood into workshops. An Industrial Directory had been published and booklets and advice made available for those starting small firms. As something of a departure from policy, a grant of £180,000 had been made available as part of a package of financial inducements offered by the local authorities in the area to Hewlett-Packard. Finally, a major step forward was taken with the setting up of the Avon Co-operative Development Agency in late 1983 with a Steering Committee drawn from the Council, Trades Council, Chamber of Commerce, and other co-operative organizations.

Avon's entry into the field of economic development policy was not viewed with immediate enthusiasm by Bristol, and disagreements rapidly emerged over responsibilities for different areas of policy. In 1982, for example, Avon refused to back Bristol's attempt to get Enterprise Zone status for the Portbury area, arguing that an Enterprise Zone would attract industry from other parts of the county, would prejudice industrial development in Portishead and Weston-super-Mare, and would have major highway expenditure implications. It was also pointed out that such a proposal was contrary to the intent of the county's Structure Plan which gave priority to port-related development in that area. Later in the year Bristol's Chief Executive submitted a detailed set of criticisms of the Avon draft Economic Development Strategy to Bristol's own Economic Development Sub-committee. Avon's strategy, he argued, duplicated the work of the districts and showed 'an alarming lack of knowledge, particularly as the County Council is represented on the Economic Development Board, about what has been going on for a number of years'. Six of the eight general objectives listed in the Avon strategy were already being pursued by Bristol, and the county should place its priorities on fulfilling its responsibilities for highway development, site infrastructure, and education and training for the job market.

These criticisms surfaced publicly in an open session of the Bristol Economic Development Board in 1983. According to press reports, Bristol and some of the other districts were 'determined to give Avon a slap on the wrist over its Draft Strategy' on the grounds that it was largely superfluous (*Bristol Trade and Industry* January 1983). The Bristol Labour leader welcomed the interest of the county 'at long last' and reminded those present of Bristol's record in spending over £6 million on sites and infrastructure since 1976. Avon Labour councillors replied that the board's attitude was 'presumptuous and insulting', and the Avon Labour leader complained at the way 'Bristol takes credit for everything that walks, breathes, and moves upon the earth'. A continuing confrontation was averted by referring the board's response to the draft to a working group of officers from both the city and other districts. Relations improved over the following year when new leaders were elected to both Bristol and Avon Labour groups, and in 1985 Bristol agreed to joint funding of the Co-operative Development Agency and participation in its management.

The other four districts in the Bristol travel-to-work area (Northavon, Kingswood, Wansdyke, and Woodspring) have generally had a more low-key involvement in economic development, and there have been few disagreements with Bristol. These other districts have been Conservative-controlled, largely 'non-interventionist', and committed to low expenditure levels. There has been little in the way of direct financial assistance, and the general promotion of the area has been largely left to Bristol. The districts contribute financially to the Bristol Economic Development office. Northavon has played an important role in 'oiling the wheels' of the development process in the north fringe area of Bristol, mainly through the planning system, although the council also made a small financial contribution by way of grant to Hewlett Packard. Kingswood, on the east fringe of the Bristol urban area, has been involved with both Bristol and Avon in limited support for the most successful small-firm project in the region, the New Work Trust Co. Ltd, located in Kingswood. This company started operations in 1981 in a disused factory and by 1984 was operating from two workshop centres, having created, it was claimed, over 300 new jobs in the area.

Economic Development Policies: Overview and Evaluation

Forms of economic development strategy

Economic development policies in Bristol and Avon have changed over time in response to a wide range of economic and political factors, becoming more and more complex in the process. Is it possible to categorize these policies in a more general way? Policy developments in the 1980s in Labour authorities such as Sheffield, the West Midlands County Council, and the GLC have led some commentators to draw a distinction between 'traditional' and 'radical' economic development strategies (e.g. Boddy 1984). Sometimes the distinction is drawn even more widely between 'restructuring for capital' and 're-structuring for labour' (Duncan and Goodwin 1985). The first type of strategy, it has been argued, has functioned mainly to underpin the private sector. It has been categorized as property-led, business and market-oriented, and concerned mainly with economic growth rather than with creating jobs for targeted groups or areas. Public activity has usually been concentrated on the provision of sites and premises, promoting the local area and limited financial aid, usually for small businesses. The second type of strategy has been categorized as public-sector-led, with greater emphasis on public intervention, local democratic planning with popular involvement, and job creation. Public activity has widened to include Enterprise Boards and Co-operative Development Agencies providing support for local small and medium enterprises, preferably those producing 'socially useful products'. There has been considerable debate over whether the second type of strategy does in fact constitute a radical alternative (Cochrane 1983). It has been suggested, for example, that the grip of multinational corporations on the local economy and the limited powers and resources of local authorities restrict them to a marginal role largely subordinate to the private sector. In this context, 'radical' strategies fulfil a more political and ideological role in posing alternatives, than in generating a significantly different pattern of local economic development.

Putting aside the complexities of this debate, how do the policies of the local authorities in the Bristol area relate to these different types of strategies? Most of Bristol's policies have until very recently fitted within the 'traditional' type of strategy, involving a heavy reliance on site assembly, support for small firms, and promotional activities. The emphasis on overseas promotions, particularly in the USA, has nevertheless been distinctive. The main thrust of policy has been aimed at generating economic growth through reducing obstacles to investment. This has been justified by the general multiplier effects of new investment in the economy as a whole. The guiding of investment to areas of high unemployment, and the targeting of job creation towards particularly vulnerable groups, has tended to be a secondary objective, although it has become more important over time. Many of the workshop and small-firm projects in inner-city areas have been small in scale and are best characterized as 'mopping-up' policies, easing the impacts of decline rather than laying the basis for economic regeneration.

The voicing of some criticisms of these policies in the recent past, particularly within the Labour Party, and the growing interest in co-operative forms of production, indicate the emergence of elements of a more 'radical' perspective, although how far this will go is not yet clear. The dock development policy does not fit easily into either category, although it is possible to see it as a spectacular example of public-sector-led investment, a monument to 'traditional municipal socialism' rather than an expression of the newer, more radical, kind of local socialism. Avon's policies, by contrast, have been a mixture of traditional and radical elements, although the radical elements are stronger on paper than in practice at the moment. Avon has also been faced with the problem that many areas of policy have already been pre-empted by Bristol, and Avon policies need to be complementary.

The determinants of local policy

It has been suggested that policies that bear directly on production and capital accumulation tend to be handled through corporatist rather than pluralist modes of decision-making, and that such policies are largely the preserve of central rather than local government. (Cawson and Saunders 1983). The emergence of local economic development strategies raises the question of whether local decision-making in this policy area may come to be dominated by corporatist modes, whereby policy emerges through high-level consultation and bargaining between leading officers and councillors and key representatives of leading industrial sectors and unions. The evidence from Bristol suggests that economic development policy has indeed hitherto been formulated at a high level within the council by a handful of leading councillors and officers, and has not emerged out of widespread debate either within or outside the parties. There is also the evidence of formal structures for consultation with business and trade unions such as the Bristol Economic Development Board. In practice, however, the board seems to function more as a talking shop and sounding board for council proposals than as a source of ideas or pressure from the private sector.

Influence can, of course, be exerted in more informal ways. Saunders (1980) has explored the ways in which policy can emerge out of a 'community of interest' formed through informal contacts between local businessmen and the council. In Bristol, Clements's study of the local élite and their relation to the council certainly suggests a convergence of viewpoint in the

1960s, but Bristol has been predominantly Labour-contolled, and there are fewer forums for informal meetings between Labour councillors and business interests than there might be for Conservatives. Also, the fact that most industrial sectors are dominated by multinational companies means that the leading executives of key firms are mostly resident elsewhere.

If there is little evidence of the direct pressure of local business interests on a large scale, this probably reflects the fact that the policies adopted through much of the 1970s and 1980s by the political parties broadly coincided with the interests of most sections of local business. Bristol's economic development strategy still bears the hallmark of a consensus between the major parties forged in the pre-Thatcher era between a moderate Labour leadership and a traditional Conservative one. Its promotional policies, designed to boost the city as a whole, benefits most sectors, and the attraction of new industrial sectors to the area does not increase the competitive pressures on existing local firms.

The reasons for limited trade union involvement are slightly different. This reflects partly the lack of a tradition of political involvement and partly the increasing dominance of service sector industries. Most Bristol workers are now white-collar workers in less unionized sectors of the local economy, which have yet to experience serious contraction and job loss. Where union links have been forged, they have been mainly in the sphere of public sector employment in response to the threat of council cutbacks in jobs and services. Recent criticisms and proposals for change which have originated within the Labour Party have been largely the result of the left 'importing' ideas from other, more radical, authorities rather than the result of emerging local pressures.

The evaluation of public policies   In many respects, market forces and government policies have worked in Bristol's favour over the last two decades, providing a firm basis for local initiatives. Government investment in transport infrastructure has increased Bristol's accessibility and linked the city to the affluent South-East through the M4 corridor. Government civil and defence contracts have been the key to the prosperity of the aerospace industry, the city's leading industrial sector, and have had important multiplier effects on the local economy as a whole. These factors, combined with an image of environmental quality and local prosperity, have helped to attract offices from London and new industrial investment from abroad. Development companies and property agencies have been very active in the area, and their extensive marketing and publicity has to some extent done the city's work for it.

In other respects, however, market forces and government policies have posed major difficulties for the local authorities in the area. Manufacturing decline has been largely the result of the decisions of multinational corporations, whose strategies are for the most part beyond local authority influence. The pattern of manufacturing growth and decline has been associated with increasing spatial inequalities within the city. The market forces and government policies referred to above have worked to accentuate the gulf between the zone of growth along the northern fringe of the city and the large area of stagnation or decline in parts of the inner city and south Bristol. At the same time, government policy has denied the Bristol area access to the powers and resources to tackle some of these problems through the urban and regional programmes.

The objectives and effectiveness of local policies need to be evaluated in the above context. It is useful to begin by looking at the way the local authorities have evaluated their own policies before standing back and attempting an objective appraisal.

The local authority evaluation   Most of the comments here relate to Bristol District Council, whose economic development policy has been running longest. Two criteria of evaluation stand out in committee and council reports: first, the number of new firms attracted to the area over the year and, second, the number of new or potential jobs. The figures given are not, however, very precise or easy to interpret. In 1982, for example, in reply to a question in council, it was claimed that, since the economic development strategy had been launched in 1976, around 300 companies had come to the area and around 30,000 new jobs had been or were being created. Under questioning, however, it was revealed that some of the names on the list were companies which had merely relocated within the area. Nor was it clear to what extent the council had been actually responsible for company location and employment growth. The Annual Report of that year subsequently contented itself with the claim that the 'Council's initiative had created the necessary stimuli and leadership' to encourage development.

More recent reports have begun to provide more detail but still do not provide a basis for any effective evaluation. The November 1984 report to the Economic Development Sub-committee, for example, records 994 enquiries over the previous nine months, 353 from the USA and 54 classified as 'high-technology'. In the same period it was reported that 80 companies had actually located in the area, generating 1,677 jobs. Current negotiations, it was estimated, might generate 'four to five thousand jobs' in the future.

It is evident that, in spite of extremely impressive claims, no detailed system of evaluating the effectiveness of policy has been developed. It is difficult to make connections between promotional activity, numbers of enquiries, the contribution of the local authority to successful relocation, and the number and type of jobs actually generated. In practice, policy is often justified by pointing to high-profile success stories, such as the attraction of Hewlett-Packard and London Life to the area. Although creating only a moderate number of jobs initially, companies such as Hewlett-Packard are regarded as occupying the growth sectors of the future.

Most of the claims to success relate to aggregate growth rather than to its distributional effect. Thus, few claims have been made about the success of policies designed to revive the inner city or combat rising unemployment in south Bristol. Indeed, Bristol has freely admitted its inability to generate significant employment growth in these areas without massive government aid. Few large firms have been attracted to these areas, in the south Bristol case partly because of its physical isolation from the major transport links which favour the northern fringe. Investment in Enterprise Workshops has been regarded at best as a way of bringing hope to deprived areas and perhaps laying a basis for a manufacturing revival when economic conditions become more favourable.

A critical view   It is useful to disaggregate economic development policy into major components and comment on aspects of them separately.

Docks development policies   Bristol's massive investment in a new dock and the subsequent volume of rate subsidy needed to keep it open constitutes a major economic development programme in its own right. We have noted that Bristol went ahead with this project in the 1970s on the grounds that a new port was essential for the survival of Avonmouth and the prosperity of the area as a whole. This decision was made in spite of outside research which suggested that the city's optimistic trade forecasts could not be achieved and that the growth of the port was not necessary anyway to the future prosperity of the area. If the actual trade outcomes in 1980 are compared with the various forecasts made in 1966 when Bristol first launched its scheme, then the gap between performance and forecast is large; the total 1980 overseas trade flows were only 59 per cent of the most pessimistic of all the estimates made back in 1966 (Bassett and Hoare 1984, p. 232). The level of national imports and exports is not to blame; in fact, the 1966 White Paper forecast these figures fairly accurately. What happened is that Bristol has suffered a loss in its *share* of this trade and has lost ground relative to other ports.

There are several ways in which this could have come about, but detailed analysis suggests that the key factor was the relative shift in UK trade towards EEC countries, a shift which has favoured east coast ports over west coast ones (Bassett and Hoare 198). The picture has improved a little since 1980, largely because Portbury has managed to capture a slice of the car import market. However, this trade is subject to considerable fluctuations and could be threatened by import quotas or the construction of car assembly plants in the UK by companies that presently import.

The success or failure of Portbury is not to be judged entirely by its trade and financial statistics. One of the major objectives behind the scheme from the beginning was to encourage the development of dock-related industries on some of the 2,000 acres of PBA land surrounding the port. In fact, apart from car storage areas, a cold store, and a molasses terminal, no significant industrial development has occurred. Discussions are under way with the

Heron Corporation on the possible development of an international convention centre, with associated light industrial and residential development, but this scheme is in no way dependent on the existence of Royal Portbury.

It has also been claimed that the survival of the port is essential for preserving jobs not only for dock workers, but also for those working in existing industries dependent on the port for essential imports. The Coopers and Lybrand report, for example, estimated that complete closure would result in the loss of 6,500 jobs in the docks and docks-related industries such as lead and zinc smelting, fertilizer production, etc. However, these industries are serviced by the old Avonmouth docks rather than Royal Portbury and are anyway losing employment through technological change. They are not the industries on which the future of the region is likely to depend.

One is forced to conclude, therefore, that, on the evidence to date, Bristol's dock development scheme was ill-judged. It is possible that a revival in international trade could enable the port to generate a small operating profit. However, one also has to ask how many new industries and jobs might have been created if the £40 million of investment had instead been used to assemble land, lay out high-quality estates, provide support for local small and medium enterprises, build research links between local industry, the Polytechnic and the University, retrain the unemployed, and launch schemes of public works to improve infrastructure and the environment.

Publicity and promotion. On the face of it, Bristol's strategy of publicity and promotion would seem to have been well judged. Both the Economic Development Office and the Bristol Marketing Board have used a variety of channels to project an image of Bristol, both at home and abroad, as a successful, environmentally attractive centre for office and high-technoloy growth. The prominently publicized arrival of key firms seems to confirm the impact of this image.

However, recent work commissioned by the Economic Development Office casts some doubt on the effectiveness of the strategy. In 1985 the Economic Development Office financed a small research project by a US public relations and advertising firm into the effectiveness of Bristol's publicity and promotional material in the USA. Extended discussions were carried out with 'site selection managers' in a number of key firms interested in European locations. The results that came back were not all what Bristol could have expected. Only half of the respondents interviewed had heard of Bristol as a potential site, and those who had heard of it tended to have 'a negative image of the locale as a heavily industrialized, smokestack area'. Site selectors for electronics and computer firms were sceptical that they would in fact be able to find the quantity and quality of highly skilled labour they required. There were also negative comments about the distance between Bristol and Heathrow and a general disinterest in the whole 'quality-of-life' image which was regarded as too general to differentiate different locations in the UK (almost every city now claimed it had a good quality of life). The only definite image of Bristol was its association with Bristol Cream Sherry.

The report went on to propose a number of changes in Bristol's promotional strategy. These included the marketing of the M4 corridor as a whole and the more precise targeting of specialist information for firms known to be looking at UK locations. It was pointed out that Bristol could do little to influence decisions over which country was selected, but it could have some impact with a more specialized information service when a company was looking specifically at UK sites. This report is likely to produce some significant changes in Bristol's approach to overseas promotion in the future.

New technology 're-industrialization'.   This has been a central component of policy since 1976. It has been based on the attraction of overseas investment, particularly from the USA. Much of the promotional work of various local authority agencies has been directed towards presenting an image of the city attractive to such investment. Not least, a large slice of capital investment on economic development has gone into the acquisition and preparation of sites suitable for high-tech companies. This policy certainly appears to have achieved some success with the attraction of such companies as Hewlett Packard and Dupont to green-field sites and the arrival of companies such as GEAC, Systime, and Digital to the nearby Aztec West business park.

There are, however, a number of broader issues to be considered in any evaluation of this strategy. First, there is the question of the actual role played by the local authorities in bringing about these developments. The Aztec West business park was already being developed when Bristol launched its economic development strategy in 1976. The high-technology companies that have located in the area since then have publicly explained their decisions in terms of factors such as local labour supplies, location of subcontractors and customers, accessibility, and amenity. Several major companies have also praised the work of local authority agencies in selling the area, providing sites, and easing the company's relocation, but these appear to have been secondary factors. In other words, if the Bristol area did not have the advantage it has, it is unlikely that the local authorities in the area could have offered sufficient inducements to attract these companies. Given that Bristol has a head-start over many of its competitors, the local authorities have been able to play an important facilitative role in marketing and site assembly.

Second, there is the question of the impact so far of this development strategy in terms of the number of jobs created. The evidence assembled in Chapters 2 and 3 indicates that the impact has not been great. In Chapter 2 it was pointed out that the bulk of employment in the high-technology sector in 1981 was in the long-established aerospace companies in the area. Non-aerospace high-tech employment in 1981 was below the national average and totalled only 2,814. Employment in this category has increased rapidly since then, but even taking into account the developments discussed in Chapter 3, we may still be talking only of 3,500–4,500 jobs at the moment. To put this figure in perspective, it must be remembered that the area lost over 23,000 manufacturing jobs between 1971 and 1981.

Third, there is the question of the longer-term growth prospects. The local authorities' strategy of attracting high-technology investment has been justified partly in terms of its immediate job impacts and partly in terms of future growth prospects. Although official reports tend to be circumspect, this has not prevented the media, urged on by some local politicians, businessmen, property developers, and estate agents, from hailing each announcement of a major new company as signalling the take-off of Bristol's very own 'Silicon Valley' (or its West Country equivalent, 'Silicon Combe').

There is, however, little evidence as yet of any pattern of local growth reminiscent of the original Californian experience. The early stages of growth in California's Silicon Valley in the 1950s were based upon massive federal funding, much of it through defence-realated contracts, and on close links between universities, research institutions, and key industries. 'By the mid-1950s the region was distinguished by a rich and supportive educational and technological milieu consisting of high-quality universities, research institutions, and older-technology-based firms . . . and had become an ideal environment for innovation and science-based industry, (Saxenian 1983, p.25). In the mid-1950s the region began a dynamic growth phase based upon the rapid development of the semiconductor industry, which grew through the spawning of small breakaway firms from a handful of original companies, mostly founded by university-trained engineers and scientists drawing upon readily available venture capital. Aerospace companies provided the main customers at first, but the newer computer industries became more important in the 1960s. This explosive pattern of agglomerative growth was generating 25,000 new jobs a year at its peak.

There is little evidence that this pattern of growth is taking place on any scale at any point on the M4 corridor, let alone at the Bristol end of it. Some of the ingredients of the Californian success *are* present, in the shape of government research establishments, universities, and aerospace firms, but many other elements are lacking. There are fewer direct links between universities, research establishments, and private firms, and little evidence of the founding of new, innovative small firms by scientists and engineers. Few of the high-technology firms already located in the M4 corridor are likely to spawn breakaway innovators on a grand scale. Many of the plants of firms with a high-technology image are regional sales and servicing centres, distributing systems and components that may be manufactured elsewhere in the country or overseas. Most of the firms at Aztec West, for example, fall into this category.

At the same time, those plants which are actually involved in production may be simply the branch plants of major multinational corporations engaged in the assembly of standardized components imported from else-

where. Such plants do not generate major multiplier effects on the local economy, and, in so far as research and development is concentrated at the company's overseas headquarters, there is less chance of spawning innovative
local firms as a spin-off effect. In the Bristol area, the Hewlett Packard development offers perhaps the best chance of generating wider impacts through
the establishment of a research laboratory as well as a production plant.
However, any significant impacts are likely to materialize only in the fairly
distant future, and only if market conditions in a volatile industry remain
favourable.

In spite of a few high-profile success stories, therefore, Bristol's high-tech
future is likely to remain tied to the success of the aerospace companies in
attracting government contracts and financial backing. There is little that
the local authorities can do to influence high-level decisions in this field.

Finally, there is the question of the distributional consequences of the
growth of high-technology industries. One aspect concerns the effects on different sectors of the labour market. Research has suggested that high-technology industries tend to create 'dual labour markets', with a substantial
number of professional and technical jobs generated at one end of the scale
and a substantial number of less skilled assembly-line jobs generated at the
other. The former jobs go mainly to male workers, the latter to lower-paid,
non-unionized female workers. In the process, relatively skilled blue-collar
jobs tend to get squeezed out (the phenomenon of the 'disappearing middle').

The growth of high-technology firms thus may benefit some sectors of the
labour market much more than others. The wages of career professionals and
technical workers may be bid up as incoming firms try to entice trained personnel away from existing firms, while the largest category of unemployed—
the less skilled, male manual workers—is comparatively untouched. There is
at least some evidence that this is happening in Bristol on a small scale,
although the labour market impacts, as previous chapters have shown, are
more complex than the picture described above. Differential impacts on the
labour market have also been reinforced by geographical factors. Most of the
new high-technology companies have located in a narrow band parallel to
the M4 along the northern fringes of the city, or in the semi-rural periphery.
However, the main concentrations of unemployment are in the inner city and
south Bristol. Even if some of the unemployed could be retrained with skills
to match the jobs being created, transport costs from south Bristol are high;
and the distribution of council housing in the city, and variations in house
prices, impose barriers to relocation.

In conclusion, although Bristol may have been astute in marketing itself
for overseas and high-tech investment, this form of development is unlikely to
go far towards solving local economic problems in the immediate future, and
the geographical pattern of development may even accentuate existing spatial inequalities.

7

Discussion

This final chapter draws out some of the main conclusions and implications of the analysis as a whole, in relation to economic and employment change, the impacts of change, and, finally, policy implications. The aim is not so much to provide a comprehensive overview of the material covered in the previous chapters as to highlight a number of points, related in particular to the issues raised in Chapter 1.

Economic and employment change

The performance of the Bristol area reflects a combination of processes operating at national and international levels and the particular character of the local economy and labour market. Economic and employment change in the locality also reflect the legacy bequeathed by the succession of previous rounds of investment, in terms of both specific 'locational factors' and the area's economic and corporate structure. Bristol is a major urban area with an urban and sub-regional environment, a 'quality of life', and a social image that is attractive to corporate decision-makers and to élite groups in the labour market, The labour market itself is diverse, including for example high-level R & D, technical and professional staff, skilled manual workers with experience of advanced manufacturing techniques, good-quality school-leavers, and basic assembly or routine clerical workers. Bristol has become a major regional service and administrative centre serving a generally prosperous wider region. Finally, it is both particularly accessible to London and yet divorced from the metropolitan labour and property markets, and also has excellent communications with the rest of the country.

Added to these specific factors, the legacy of previous rounds of investment has been relatively favourable in terms of economic structure. The area's traditional manufacturing sectors declined later and less severely than the manufacuturing core in many localities, and have been consolidated albeit on a reduced scale. Aerospace, moreover, gave the area a major stake in one of the few manufacturing sectors to survive relatively well in employment terms since the 'long boom' of the 1950s and 1960s, and a significant concentration of advanced technological activity. The inherited pattern of industrial and functional specialization has been reflected in the locality's relative resilience in economic and employment terms, particularly since the late 1970s, in the structure of the labour market already noted, and in the lack of large-scale physical dereliction associated with traditional heavy manufacturing, and the image which goes with it. The old city centre docks, the city's major 'redundant space' left by the removal downstream to Avonmouth of the docks trade, has, in the 1980s, been realized as a major asset in terms of environment, image, commercial development, and employment-generating activity.

Recession and rising unemployment have by no means bypassed the Bristol sub-region. Compared with urban areas beyond the prosperous South, however, it has survived relatively well. Manufacturing job loss has hit some sectors hard, but this has left a core of more stable employment in traditionally dominant sectors. Aerospace, in particular, shored up manufacturing employment, maintaining a dynamic core of technologically advanced activity with wider economic and employment repercussions. Particularly important here has been government defence spending and, to a much lesser extent, support for civil aerospace. Despite manufacturing job loss, moreover, Bristol has consolidated its role in terms of corporate hierarchy, retaining and extending its share of R & D and higher-order management functions. As elsewhere, service sector expansion offset manufacturing job loss in the 1970s; particularly important in the Bristol case has been the growth of financial and miscellaneous services. Also important to the stability of a large part of the local employment structure has been the maintenance of employment across a broader range of services, both public and private.

High technology

A major element in the area's 'sunbelt city' image has been high-technology industry and electronics. Technologicaly advanced activity, including electronics-based R & D and production, is however, heavily concentrated in the long-established aerospace sector, much of it specifically defence-related. High-technology growth in the sense of an influx of rapidly expanding electronics and computer companies, inward investment from the USA or Japan—the 'Hewlett Packard model' of development—or the mushrooming of new enterprises has been relatively unimportant. There are a handful of such companies of which a number are at the forefront of their particular technologies and a few have expanded rapidly. But their impact in economic and employment terms, particularly set against broader shifts in economic and employment structure, has been slight. Nationally, the electronics industry's employment prospects are only modest, and Bristol's probable share of this is unlikely to change dramatically in the future. The city's high-tech growth image and Silicon Valley comparisons are largely wishful thinking, with little immediate prospects of fulfilment.

Although the defence industries as a whole are entering a new phase of uncertainty, as described below, the continued expansion of British Aerospace Dynamics in particular is seemingly assured. The area is likely to retain its share of defence electronics. The emphasis on defence electronics R & D here contrasts with localities in South Wales and central Scotland which have attracted mainly the mass manufacture of components and business and consumer electronics; central Scotland has also acquired defence electronics but concentrates mainly on production. By the mid-1980s, with international electronics markets weakening, employment growth had tailed off in parts of the industry and there were growing signs of retrenchment— National Semiconductors, for example, laid off 400 at its Greenock, Scotland, plant in mid-1985 following a slump in demand for microchips; Inmos shelved expansion plans at its South Wales production site where employment is still well short of projected levels; and Hewlett Packard announced a series of austerity measures affecting in particular its Queensferry (Scotland) site (while pushing ahead with its expansion plans in Bristol, for which big claims were being made).

Analyses of high-technology activity in the USA in particular[1] have similarly emphasized this centrality of defence and defence-related R & D and production in High-tech employment (Saxenian 1980; Glasmeier *et al.* 1983; Malecki 1984; Markusen 1984a). This in turn, it has been suggested, has formed the basis for a specific spatial pattern of high-tech-based development and urban growth (Castells 1983; Markussen 1984b). This is seen explicitly in the case of Bristol, which emphasizes the extent to which such defence-related high technology is implicated in regional economic performance and the developmemt of specific urban areas.

Services

Service sector growth in the Bristol area, as nationally, has offset manufacturing job loss. Manufacturing will soon account for little more than a quarter of all employment in the region. The extent to which urban areas attract or generate service growth, and the structure of that activity, will be crucial determinants of economic prosperity and the scale and pattern of employment opportunities. For the USA, for example, Stanback (1979) and Noyelle (1983) have shown how metropolitan areas in regions favoured by growth and already specialized in service provision have experienced the strongest growth in business services, suggesting significant parallels with our present case. As the Bristol example demonstrates, however, it is particularly important to disaggregate overall, 'service employment' in terms of processes of change, labour market implications, and the way in which different elements of service activity articulate with economic activity in general.

Locally, while the overall shift from manufacturing to service employment reflected national trends, growth was concentrated in two areas in particular. The first was financial services. Much of this activity is essentially 'basic', exporting services beyond the immediate locality and generating local employment rather than being dependent upon local demand. The Bristol and West Building Society, as if to emphasize this, has specifically advertised itself as 'Exporting to the Rest of Britain'.[2] The growth of financial services has specifically reflected the 'relocation appeal' of the locality for such 'basic' activities, particularly insurance.

It has also reflected the city's increaing nodality as a regional financial and business centre. Scale effects, and the clustering of additional financial and business services in the urban area, seem in turn to have followed from this overlaying of major regional functions with basic activity. The growth of office-based services both stimulated and was facilitated by the boom in commercial property development, which was reflected in construction and related employment. Again, Bristol's role in terms of corporate hierarchy and function has been consolidated with the growth of headquarters functions and the centralization of regional-level activity.

The second major growth area has been 'miscellaneous services', including the 'eating, drinking, and entertainment services and also the mixed bag of 'other services', not broken down by official statistics. All of these expanded much faster in Bristol than nationally. Commonly seen as 'dependent' on demand generated elsewhere in the local economy, the strong growth of these activities reflects the strength of other sectors in the locality. More specifically it seems to indicate the relative importance of higher-income professional, technical, and white-collar staff, concentrated for example in aerospace, electronics, and financial services. Overall, the local situation supports the sense of Hall's suggestion that 'the growth of a relatively small industrial base, especially in innovative, high-technology industry and associated producer services, can create a very large income and employment multiplier effect in the form of construction, real estate, recreation, and personal service industries, (Hall 1985, p. 10). In terms of scale and detail, however, there are major contrasts with the southern Californian model on which Hall's argument is largely based.

The effects of miscellaneous service growth may go deeper than this simple model of dependence suggests. The importance of 'basic' services and the role of the local 'business service infrastructure' have increasingly been seen as a positive factor in stimulating economic activity at the urban or regional level (Marquand 1979). A range of personal and miscellaneous services would also, however, appear to be, in the Bristol case, an important component of the image and attractiveness of the locality, both to corporate decision-makers and to particular types of labour. This suggests that they are positively rather than simply passively implicated in economic and employment growth, an idea that is reinforced by the fact that an increasing share of miscellaneous service growth is specifically export-oriented, in terms of tourism, and business-related, involving for example conferences and exhibitions.

Much of the remainder of the service sector has related directly to public expenditure policy. Future employment levels in Bristol, as elsewhere, will be more dependent on public policy and expenditure decisions—potentially much more so, in the current political and economic climate—than on the impacts of new technology. In the current scenario, a shrinkage of public services employment could thus offset much of the employment gain in other sectors, as a decline in professional and scientific services (medical, dental, and education) is overlain on a contraction in local government employment and other public administration.

Service growth has therefore been strongly implicated in the better-than-average adaptation of the Bristol locality, in line with Stanback's findings for the USA. The picture in detail is, however, more complex. Although service employment as a whole, depending on the scale of public sector decline, is likely to continue to grow, the *nature* of the service sector is shifting. Public and welfare services are in decline, while financial and business services—and, to a lesser extent, private, personal service activity—continue to expand. This in turn has significant implications in terms of the structure of service sector employment as will be noted in the following section.

Overall, then, the picture of economic change, although generally favourable compared with places like Glasgow, Newcastle, and the West Midlands, has by no means been one of successful restructuring, generating significant job opportunities across the board. Growth in some sectors has been juxtaposed with decline in others, and the broad pattern of change has been determined as much by how well existing employment has stood up in the face of decline as by which sectors have been expanding. Bristol's 'success' , particularly in manufacturing, partly reflects the fact that employment locally has simply declined less than elsewhere. Growth as such, as we have seen, has been confined largely to particular components of the service sector. Much of the growth of miscellaneous services, and to some extent financial and business services, has been linked to the resilience of other basic employment sectors in a process of 'intersectoral dependent development'.

This reflects the fact that the geography of job change in manufacturing since the mid-1970s had more generally been largely a question of how employment in certain localities has fared during a period of decline; how far closure and cutbacks in surviving enterprises, coupled in some cases with reinvestment, has hit different sectors. Overlain on this has been a limited amount of relocation and new investment directed to particular localities. Differences in employment change overall, then, have reflected in particular the extent to which localities have attracted or generated financial and business services and miscellaneous service growth.

Following major restructuring and job loss, employment locally is now more stable and is likely to prove more resilient than in the late 1970s and early 1980s. Across most sectors, particularly in manufacturing but also much of the services, employment will be at best static, with gradual decline in many (Avon County Council, 1985). Aerospace is likely to remain relatively buoyant although more uncertain in the longer term, given increasing uncertainty in defence markets and a dependence on major projects including the Airbus. Employment growth in other electronics and high-technology activity is likely to be modest. Markets are characterized by increasing competition and uncertainty. Only moderate growth and inwards investment is forecast nationally, and the locality faces competition especially from the whole Cambridge/London/M4 belt.

Employment growth in the financial services is likely to continue. Further relocation of office-based employment from London remains a possibility, even though dispersal rates are well down on the early 1970s. The main growth, however, is likely to be in miscellaneous services. This will include leisure-related personal services dependent on the continued prosperity of basic employment, but also the 'export-oriented' growth of tourism and business-related activity. Continued employment shrinkage is likely in other service activities. Given current public expenditure policies, job loss in public services is likely to accelerate, offsetting gains elsewhere.

Increased productivity, related in particular to technological change, will limit employment gains in expanding sectors and permit employment cuts elsewhere. The balance of the employment structure will increasingly shift towards services, particularly miscellaneous services. Overall, then, the prospects are of 'jobless', and in many cases 'job-loss', growth, with an increasing emphasis on 'no-tech' services rather than high technology. The scale of existing unemployment and the likely balance between net new entrants to the labour market is such that job growth in the short or medium term is unlikely to take up much of the slack in the labour market overall. Any reduction in unemployment as a whole, even under optimistic forecasts, is unlikely to be rapid or far-reaching. Even in a relatively prosperous locality such as Bristol, therefore, the prospect of a return to 'full employment' and the buoyancy of the late 1960s and early 1970s, based simply on economic recovery, is not a realistic expectation.

The Good City for Everyone?

The overall picture in terms of unemployment and job loss compares favourably with cities in the Midlands and the North.[3] It is obvious, however, that the benefits of this are not evenly distributed through different groups in the labour market. This is emphasized by the scale and increase in youth and long-term unemployment. In part it reflects the pattern of sectoral change. Male manufacturing job loss has been juxtaposed with increasing female service sector employment, much of it part-time. Job opportunities beyond those created by growth, primarily in parts of the service sector, have been dependent on the replacement or turnover or existing staff. Growth has created particularly few job opportunities for the majority of less qualified school-leavers and Youth Training Scheme members, and for many of the semi-skilled and unskilled workers 'shaken out' of employment. Recruitment in the 'high-technology' sectors has emphasized skills, experience, and qualifications which exclude the majority of these groups. Recruitment to the major office employers has been carefuly targeted on selected school-leavers, with similar effects. More precisely, employers have been in a position to pick and choose between candidates, and as a result have tended to recruit people they believe to be suitable in social, as well as technical, terms. As a result, employment opportunities have been distributed extremely unevenly. In many major companies there has been little recruitment from the unemployed, the majority of vacancies being filled by those in employment, possessing skills and experience. In the context of employment shrinkage, vacancies created by such moves will often be left unfilled. The main exceptions have included miscellaneous services, retailing, typing, and junior clerical occupations.

In this sense Bristol has been at the 'forefront' of wider developments in the British economy: a small but significant number of new jobs has been created in high-technology occupations, but many more have been created at the lower end of the wage scale. To this extent the city has exemplified the 'US model' of employment growth advocated by government spokesmen (Rogers and Brummer 1984).

These processes have been reflected in an increasing polarization between core and peripheral groups in the labour market. Core groups include those relatively well paid and securely employed, possessing relevant skills, technical knowledge, or professional expertise, plus those possessing these qualifications who can successfully compete to join them. They are likely to enjoy the prospect of career or salary progression and the possibility of job mobility, either because they occupy high positions in internal labour markets, or as a result of the vigorous demand for their skills on the external market. They face little risk of unemployment, certainly for any length of time. They also include, at a less privileged level, a number of manual workers. These workers continue to enjoy the advantages of traditional forms of trade unionism, especially in the large manufacturing and public sector establishments. Other groups of production and clerical workers within this 'core' benefit from relatively benign management–labour relations designed to pre-empt unionism by the enlisting of co-operation and consent, and a non-conflictual technical and professional ethos, in return for financial and status rewards. Employment in these core groups is disproportionately white and male.

Peripheral groups include the semi-skilled and unskilled, the less well qualified school-leavers, and those whose employment or employment prospects are tied to routinized, deskilled work in manufacturing. They also include employees in the expanding service industries where growth has been based on relatively low-paid and insecure employment, often part-time and commonly non-unionized, and routinized office and clerical work with little prospect of career advancement. These groups have been termed 'service workers' as distinct from white-collar career grades and professionals. Peripheral groups are characterized by a much greater concentration of black workers and, particularly in services, women.

In part, this polarization reflects simply the pattern of job gain and loss and its impact on different groups in the labour market. Elite occupations have been maintained as a result of the resilience of certain sectors such as aerospace and finance, while the expansion of miscellaneous services has increased the number of poorly paid, insecure jobs at the other pole. Moreover, the stability and growth of élite labour in parts of manufacturing and services is structurally linked to a dependent growth of non-élite employment, much of it female and part-time, in these service sectors. Locally, miscellaneous services grew by 2,400 in just three years, 1978–81. Over 83 per cent of this was female employment growth, and, following the national average, some 66 per cent of female employment was part-time.

The changing structure of service activity noted in the last section is, then, specifically reflected in changing employment structures and opportunities. The relationship between basic and dependent activity, the process of 'intersectoral dependent development', and the operation of what has been called 'trickle-down' effects are reflected in, and effected through, structured inequalities in the labour market.

There is also evidence, both locally and nationally, of increasing differentiation within particular firms and sectors, between those in occupations where skill, specialization, and technical content are increasing, linked in some cases to new technology and with career prospects, and those performing tasks such as routine assembly, data inputting, and basic clerical work (Lloyd 1984). In a work particularly relevant to Bristol, Rajan (1984) predicts increasing differentation within the financial services between 'career' and 'non-career' clerical staff. This was supported by emerging trends in the insurance sector locally. In the UK electronics industry, Soete and Dosi (1983) see job gain in high-skill categories but a significant loss affecting operators and to some extent clerical and craft workers, with female employment most affected by the decline.

Polarization based on the continuing shift from manufacturing to service employment and the differentiation of internal labour markets is likely to become increasingly evident. The impact on individuals is increasingly emphasized by the importance of early working histories on subsequent career paths. Locally, as we have seen, the more dynamic sectors such as electronics, aerospace, and insurance are likely to be characterized by at best 'jobless growth' in output, with less than proportional employment increase. Access to employment in these sectors will be severely limited. Within services as a whole, there are strong indications, from the Bristol case study at least, of parallels with the US situation, moving, according to Stanback, 'towards a sharply dichotomized service work force offering, on the one hand, the skilled, responsible, and relatively well-paying jobs of certain professionals, trained technicians, or artisans, but on the other, the unskilled, undemanding, and poorly paid jobs of salespersons, service workers, or laborers' (Stanback 1977, p. 106).

The social impact of this polarization in the economy is evidently exacerbating existing social divisions. Polarization between occupations and individuals, reflecting both employers' recruitment practices and the structure of job opportunities thrown up by the labour market, is resulting in an increasing polarization between social groups. This in turn influences the spatial pattern of unemployment and other forms of social and economic disadvantages detailed earlier. As we have seen these divisions are being reinforced by the particular pattern of economic restructuring in the locality. If Bristol is indeed at the forefront of the transformation of the UK economy—and Stanback found that in the USA 'places in the more recently favoured sunbelt regions appear more advanced in their transformations' (Stanback 1977, p. 135)—then these tendencies do not augur at all well.

Policy Implications

The wider policy implications of the Bristol case turn both on the extent to which specific policy measures are implicated in the observed patterns of change and on the extent to which these are relevant or reproducible elsewhere. It is in fact precisely the absence of explicit central government urban and regional policy measures which characterizes the area. As suggested earlier, however, while the area has clearly lost out in straight financial terms from lack of Urban Programme status and regional assistance, this does not appear to have been a major disadvantage in overall economic and employment terms. Office dispersal policies in fact worked at Bristol's advantage— there seems to have been less concern at the time with where office development went than with squeezing it out of London.

Policy lessons?

In naive terms of direct and practicable policy lessons applicable more widely, the conclusions are limited. In part, this is simply because Bristol is no more divorced than other localities from the working-out of economic processes on a national and international scale. On the other hand, the unique and complex legacy of historical processes which constitute this particular locality cannot in any simple sense be reproduced. As we have seen, no specific urban or regional policy measures, central or local, are heavily implicated in the particular processes of economic and employment change which have been set out. There are examples of innovative and, at the local scale, effective initiatives from which lessons can be drawn. Their impact in overall economic and employment terms, however, has been essentially irrelevant.

The availability of sites and premises to suit specific users, for example, has been important in some instances, and the ability of the local authorities and other agencies to respond positively has been emphasized. Again, however, these are merely necessary factors, reproducible and indeed duplicated in many localities, and far from sufficient to attract economic growth. Location, environment, quality of life, regional centrality, labour market structure, and the legacy of past rounds of economic activity are interrelated explanatory factors—and among the least tractable in policy terms. The importance of image, urban environment, and 'milieu' and quality-of-life factors emphasizes the importance of policies and expenditure, at both national and local levels, which bear on these. It also emphasizes the limited nature of public control over many crucial economic influences.

Inner-city policy

In terms of specific inner-city policy, Bristol's problems are clearly less severe than in many localities. The absolute scale of unemployment and related adverse indicators are, however, masked by authority-wide averages and the fact that 'inner-city' indicators are not confined to inner-city locations. They display the increasingly double-sided nature of 'inner-city' problems, including both older inner areas of mixed housing tenure and peripheral council estates. On the latter, escalating housing and environmental problems, coupled with the continuing link between the poorest housing and the worst-off households, relate in particular to the financial capacity of local authorities. This has been particularly limited in the present political and economic climate, and the restrictions on both capital and revenue for housing and environmental works. Urban Programme spending, even in those areas which have benefited most in financial terms, is minimal in the face of the scale of the economic, social, and environmental problems it confronts. Such spending can have localized, small-scale but nevertheless significant effects. Moreover, Urban-Programme-funded activity has fostered policy development and innovation in many authorities. The case of Bristol emphasizes, however, that major concentrations of economic and social disadvantge can be hidden in authority-wide aggregrates. The general aura of success and attachment to the 'sunbelt' image has if anything made this harder to acknowledge. This clearly points to the need for more finely focused targeting, in terms of people, rather than places, of whatever funds are made available on a national basis.

In this situation, parts of Bristol would clearly qualify for additional spending. The argument that there is, in a generally more prosperous locality, potential for redistribution is far from convincing. As we have seen, there is evidence of persistent, structured inequality and polarization, expressed in the spatial pattern of economic and social disadvantage, which conflicts with ideas of 'trickle-down' and the spread of benefits throughout the labour market and social structure. Nor, given public expenditure constraint, is there potential for significant redistribution of resources by the local authorities.

High technology

Much more heavily implicated in the locality's relative prosperity is the spatial impact of government defence procurement and support for aerospace. Awareness of the spatial distribution of defence spending and its regional economic and employment effects has increased both in the USA, in debates about high technology (noted above), and in the UK (Short 1981; Law 1983). Some of the issues are discussed in more detail elsewhere (Lovering 1985; Boddy and Lovering 1986).

In the USA, it has been argued (Markusen 1984a) that military spending in the postwar period has increasingly served as an implicit industrial policy, spatially oriented to the least depressed, 'sunbelt' areas away from the old manufacturing core. Similarly, in Canada the federal government has played a key role in the uneven spatial development of aerospace, which has been the subject of explicit political conflict (Todd and Simpson 1985). The Bristol case emphasizes the impacts for the UK of such 'implicit spatial economic policies', which have operated particularly through defence procurement but also through other forms of sectoral assistance. As we have seen the pattern of such expenditure has run largely counter to explicit regional and urban policy, and explicitly underpins technologically advanced R & D and production.

In policy terms, the relationship between the defence sector and the national economy, and the character of defence product markets, has received considerable attention. However, in this country at least, little explicit attention has been paid to the spatial economic or employment implications of defence procurement or general sectoral assistance. There has been some concern over the employment effects of naval dockyards and shipbuilding in the Assisted Regions, and some localized lobbying activity; however, policy concern with the spatial impact of procurement as such has been insignificant.[4] The spatial economic and employment impacts, and the scope for explicit spatial policy inputs, are undoubtedly complex. There may for example be a trade-off between spatial policy concerns and questions of cost and efficiency—but not necessarily. Strategic factors may be relevant.

Clearly, it is important that these issues be explored. Such expenditures are obviously heavily implicated in the pattern of urban and regional economic performance, and their impacts must be considered explicitly in policy terms. More generally, this emphasizes the need to look closely not just at specific urban and regional policy measures but at the urban and regional impacts of the full range of state policies and expenditures if we are to understand the spatially differentiated processes of economic and employment change, and the specific role of the state in relation to particular areas. Different localities are firmly tied in various ways to different aspects of state policy and expenditure—South Wales, for example, through regional assistance, the nationalized coal and steel industries, employment in central government offices, and, more than most areas, state benefits to the unemployed; Bristol through defence procurement; the Midlands through support for the car industry; and many rural areas through national and EEC agricultural policies and expenditure. These relationships all have specific economic and employment implications going well beyond the arena of explicit urban and regional policy.

In terms of high-technology activity itself, on which the M4 image has been built, the role of explicit urban or regional policy has been very limited; more generally it is the determinants of high-technology growth that have been a key focus of analytic and policy concern—Oakey (1985), for instance, identifies the importance of specialist local input suppliers and subcontractors. It is not even clear, for example, whether local authorities themselves have the resources or leverage to exert a direct and significant influence on the location and investment decisions of major multinationals in the sector. If their goal is to promote high technology in their locality, it may be more effective for them to channel their resources into building up the infrastructure of component and service producers relevant to high-tech activity than to attempt to attract the latter directly through promotional activities. The same may apply to national programmes aiming to reinforce or stimulate high-technology growth in specific localities.

Other studies have explored the role of venture capital, university–industry links, government funding of R & D, and the pattern of science ad education expenditure. Hall (1985), for example, has suggested the need for an R & D-based regional strategy pursued in part via government research council funding to universities. Again, however, the key role of defence-related R & D, defence procurement, and aerospace more generally is only starting to be recognized. What Hall has called 'selective developments of high-technology industrial growth in older industrial regions . . . "anchor sectors" for the rejuvenation of their regions' may be more likely to succeed if built up around existing defence specialists and an explicit recognition of the spatial impacts of defence spending where regional defence activity is already of a high-technology variety, rather than by simple attempts to foster university–industry links. Linked to this might be specific strategies at local and central government levels to develop spin-offs from the defence products sector. Moreover any future policy shift in the level or composition of defence expenditure at the national level might be explicitly linked to the development of alternative products drawing on the capacity and expertise built up in the defence sector. In this agenda, the spatial distribution of such activities should be given central place.

Service-based policies

While high-technology industry has been a key policy focus in the Bristol locality and a major issue at national level, with little positive to show for it, policy development until recently has chosen largely to ignore the massive expansion of service employment. Locally, although there has been a major growth in financial and business services over the last decade, far outweighing any increase in high-technology activity, little in the way of positive action, sectoral or spatial, has been taken to reinforce or stimulate their development, This is despite the fact that financial services generally have provided relatively well paid and secure employment, in contrast to much of miscellaneous service growth—particularly important in terms of the quality of women's job opportunities.

The role of personal and business tourism and leisure and recreational activities in relation to service employment—the other major growth area— is beginning to be acknowledged nationally and locally. At the national level, support has been focused on changes in taxation and measures designed to 'price labour back into jobs' in the service sector (Kaletsky 1984). However, since this does not confront the distributional questions involved, it is likely to exacerbate, rather than moderate, the impact of 'low-tech or no-tech' service expansion on polarization in the labour market. At the local level, the attraction of grant-aid for historic conservation and tourist-related development is starting to emerge as an explicit strategy.

The importance of the personal service infrastructure is reinforced by its suggested role in attracting key labour market groups and decision-makers. Without explicit concern for the nature of employment created, however, a successful expansion of miscellaneous services threatens to exacerbate problems of polarization and the expansion of low-paid, insecure, semi-casual employment offering little if anything in terms of occupational or career advancement. This will, moreover, represent one of the few areas offering job opportunities for women, with major implications for the quality of female employment.

Bristol's experience in terms of both financial/business and miscellaneous services emphasizes the importance of developing explicit policies, at both national and local levels, relating to the service sector. Of course, service growth locally cannot be divorced from the specific character of the Bristol area and the 'raw material' that this affords including its 'relocation appeal' and to some extent the factors generating the demand for personal services. Locally specific, service-focused strategies may well be relevant elsewhere, however. They may, for example, anticipate and encourage the sort of changes in expenditure and consumption patterns which seem partly to underly the strength of miscellaneous services locally. However, the extent to which they can exert a major influence on other economic activities must naturally vary with the local 'raw material', and in many cases there must be a presumption that their impact in these terms may be mimimal (although these activities often entail benefits for local people which may be desirable in their own right).

The potential role of business services in stimulating economic activity is starting to be acknowledged more generally. However, it is important to break even more radically with the notion of manufacturing as the only source of 'real' jobs. In many respects, service-type activities are the most important components in production, especially in countries like the UK, which are increasingly unable to compete with low-cost manual labour available on the world market. Production as a whole has become increasingly 'service-intensive'. What are conventionally thought of as manufacturing and services remain interdependent. Any upturn in economic activity, however, is likely to be reflected more in the growth of white-collar occupations and the service sector. This suggests the need for a major shift in policy towards promoting the growth and development of service activities and the service infrastructure (Noyelle 1983, p. 288). Moreover, any simple translation of old policies towards manufacturing into new policies towards services is unlikely to lead to major achievements, nationally or locally, not least because it is necessary to recognize the distinctive organizational structure and economic context within which most service activities take place (Massey 1984, pp. 175–190).

Distributional issues

To the extent that Bristol has 'succeeded', in a sense it has done so partly at the expense of other localities. This emphasizes the competitive nature of the policy issues raised. In a crude sense, insurance growth for example was achieved at the expense of London; had it been possible to attract the companies involved to Wales or Glasgow, then they would obviously have been lost to Bristol, and similarly if aerospace projects had been allocated to the companies' other sites in Derby or Lancashire, or if Nottingham rather than Bristol had been selected as ITL's headquarters.

This is essentially a truism, of course, but it emphasizes the fact that, in terms of the conscious spatial allocation of investment and employment by enterprises or by the effects of spatially directed policies, Bristol's relative success does not reflect some intrinsic growth capability: it is the other side of the coin to relative failure elsewhere. There are exceptions. In the case of Hewlett Packard, for example, the choice was between Bristol and Lyons, so that Bristol was not in competition for jobs with other UK localities; other companies have expanded from local roots. The overall employment impact of such 'independent development', however, has been very limited.

Within the locality, the uneven distribution of the benefits of Bristol's economic performance, and the tendency towards increasing polarization, emphasize the fact that economic growth and policies directed to this end have specific and unequal distributional implications. Local authority policies, in Bristol as in most places, have been oriented primarily towards economic growth rather than distributional issues. Labour market training and placement agencies are similarly under increasing pressure to service the needs of private employers.

More generally, the wider national context of labour market policies, as embodied for example in the role of the MSC and national educational policies, leads in a direction which reinforces the discriminatory processes within the labour market. For example, without the positive targeting of initiatives, in terms of job entry, training and retraining, and career advancement, on less advantaged groups in the labour market, the tendency will be inevitably to deepen existing divisions and polarization. To the extent that localities elsewhere succeed in emulating Bristol's success without adopting explicitly redistributive labour market policies, this will simply tend to reproduce the sort of uneven and polarized development evident in the Bristol case. This suggests that the main concern of local economic and employment strategies should be on the quality and distribution of employment opportunities, rather than simply on attempts to generate economic growth.

Notes

1. As opposed to South-East Asia, which is predominantly specialized in the manufacture of bulk components, consumer, and some business electronics.
2. *Investor's Chronicle*, 2–8 March 1984.
3. See Chapter 4, note 1.
4. The government's Special Preference Scheme was designed to allow producers in Development Areas to re-tender for contracts. Few contracts were however ever placed under the scheme.

BIBLIOGRAPHY

Alford, B. (1973), *W. D. and H. O. Wills and the Development of the UK Tobacco Industry, 1786–1965*, Methuen, London.

—— (1976), 'The Economic Development of Bristol in the Nineteenth Century: An Enigma?' in Bristol and Gloucestershire Archeological Society, *Essays in Bristol and Gloucestershire History*.

Anderson, J., Duncan, S., and Hudson, R. (eds) (1983), *Redundant Spaces in Cities and Regions*, Academic Press, London.

Avon County Council (1984), 'The "Ethnic Minority" Population and Workforce of Avon and the Bristol Area', Report to the Employment Working Group, Planning Department.

—— (1985), *Draft Economic Review*, Planning Department.

Bacon, R. and Eltis, W. A. (1976). *Britain's Economic Problem: Too Few Producers*, Macmillan, London.

Barker, B. (1981), 'The Operation of the Bristol Labour Party', Working Paper no. 27, School for Advanced Urban Studies, University of Bristol.

Bassett, K. (1984), 'Corporate Structure and Corporate Change in a Local Economy: The Case of Bristol', *Environment and Planning A*, 16, 879–900.

—— and Hauser, D. (1976), 'Public Policy and Spatial Structure: Housing Improvement in Bristol', in R. Peel, M. Chisholm, and P. Haggett, (eds), *Processes in Physical and Human Geography: Bristol Essays*, Heinemann, London.

—— and Hoare, A. (1984), 'Bristol and the Saga of Royal Portbury: A Case Study in Local Politics and Municipal Enterprise', *Political Geography Quarterly* 3, 223–50.

—— and Short, J. (1978), 'Housing Improvement in the Inner City: A Case Study of Changes Before and After the 1974 Housing Act', *Urban Studies* 15, 333–42.

Becker, G. (1957), *The Economics of Discrimination*, University of Chicago Press.

Begg, I., Moore, B., and Rhodes, J. (1985). 'Economic and Social Change in Urban Britain and the Inner Cities', unpublished report, Economic and Social Research Council, Inner City in Context initiative.

Bishop, K. and Simpson, C. (1972), 'Components of Change Analysis: Problems and Alternative Approaches to Industrial Structure', *Regional Studies* 6, 59–68.

Blackaby, F. (ed.) (1978), *Deindustrialisation*, National Institute of Economic and Social Research, London.

Boddy, M. (1984), 'Local Economic and Employment Strategies', in M. Boddy, and C. Fudge, (eds), *Local Socialism?* Macmillan, London, pp. 160–91.

—— and Lovering, J. (1986). 'High Technology Industry in the Bristol Sub-region: The Aerospace/Defence Nexus', *Regional Studies* 20.2.

Bristol City Council (1967), 'Manufacturing Industry and Warehousing in Bristol since 1945', Research Section, City Engineer and Planning Officer's Department, Bristol.

—— (1984), 'Indicators of Deprivation in Bristol', Research Report, Planning Department, Bristol.

Bristol District Labour Party (1983), *A Socialist Strategy for the Labour Party in Bristol*.

Bristol Trades Council (1984), *Slumbering Volcano*.

British Aerospace (1985), *Prospectus*, British Aerospace Ltd., London.

—— (1984), *Annual Report 1983*, British Aerospace Ltd., London.

Britton, J. (1967). *Regional Analysis and Economic Geography: A Case Study of Manufacturing in the Bristol Region*, Bell, London.

Castells, M. (1983), 'Towards the Informational City? High Technology, Economic Change and Spatial Structure: Some Exploratory Hypotheses', Working Paper no. 430, University of California, Institute of Urban and Regional Development, Berkeley.

Cawson, A. and Saunders, P. (1983), 'Corporatism, Competitive Politics, and Class Struggle', in R. King (ed.), *Capital and Politics*, Routledge and Kegan Paul, London.

Central Unit for Environmental Planning (1971), *Severnside: A Feasibility Study*, HMSO, London.

Chiplin, B. and Sloane, P. J. (1974), 'Sexual Discrimination in the Labour Market', *British Journal of Industrial Relations* 12, 371–402.

Clements, R. (1969), *Local Notables and the City Council*, Macmillan, London.

—— (1978), 'Wally Jenkins and Gervais Walker, Political Leadership in Bristol and Avon', in G. Jones and A. Norton, (eds), *Political Leaders in Local Government*, Institute of Local Government Studies, Birmingham.

Central Statistical Office (1981), 'Output Measures', *Occasional Paper* no. 9, CSO, London.

Cochrane, A. (1983), 'Local Economic Policies', in J. Anderson, S. S. Duncan, and R. Hudson. *Redundant Spaces in Cities and Regions*, Academic Press, London.

Crompton, R. and Jones, G. (1984), *White Collar Proletariat: Deskilling and Gender in Clerical Work*, Macmillan, London.

Crossman, R. (1977), *The Diaries of a Cabinet Minister*, Vol. 3: *Secretary of State for Social Services 1966–70*, Hamish Hamilton and Jonathan Cape, London.

Daily Mirror (1967), 'A City you can Fall in Love with', supplement on Bristol, *Daily Mirror*, 20 March.

Dodd, J., Bowden, R., and Whiting, M. (1983), *Defence Spending and the Electronics Industry*, Fielding, Newson-Smith and Co. (Stockbrokers), London.

Doeringer, P. B. and Piore, M. J. (1971), *Internal Labor Markets and Manpower Analysis*, D. C. Heath, Lexington, Massachusetts.

Donnison, D. and Soto, P. (1980), *The Good City: A Study of Urban Development Policy in Britain*, Heinemann, London.

Duncan, S. S. and Goodwin, M. (1985), 'The Local State and Local Economic Policy: Why all the Fuss?', *Policy and Politics*, 13.3, 227–54.

Dunford, M. F. and Perrons, D. (1983), *The Arena of Capital*, Macmillan, London.

—— Geddes, M., and Perrons, D. (1981), 'Regional Policy and the Crisis in the UK: A Long-run Perspective', *International Journal of Urban and Regional Research* 5, 337–410.

Dunleavy, P. (1980), *Urban Political Analysis*, Macmillan, London.

Elias, P. and Keogh, G. (1982), 'Industrial Decline and Unemployment in the Inner-city Areas of Great Britain: A Review of the Evidence', *Urban Studies* 19, 1–15.

Evans, A. W. and Richardson, R. (1981), 'Urban Unemployment: Interpretation and Additional Information', *Scottish Journal of Political Economy* 28, 107–24.

Fenton, S., Davies, T., Means, R., and Burton, P. (1984), 'Ethnic Minorities and the

Youth Training Scheme', Manpower Services Commission, *Research and Development*, 20.

Fothergill, S. and Gudgin, G. (1979), 'Regional Employment Change: A Subregional Explanation', *Progress in Planning* 12.3, Pergamon Press, Oxford.

—— (1982), *Unequal Growth: Urban and Regional Employment Change in the UK*, Heinemann, London.

Fraser, D. (1979), *Power and Authority in the Victorian City*, St Martin's Press, London.

Frost, M. and Spence, N. (1984), 'The Changing Structure and Distribution of the British Workforce', *Progress in Planning*, 21.2, Pergamon Press, Oxford.

Fudge, C. (1981), 'Winning an Election and Gaining Control: The Formulation and Implementation of a "Local" Political Manifesto', in S. Barrett, and C. Fudge, (eds), *Policy and Action*, Methuen, London, pp. 133–42.

Glasmeier, A. K., Markusen, A., and Hall, P. (1983), 'Defining High Technology Industries', Working Paper no. 407, University of California, Institute of Urban and Regional Development, Berkeley.

Greenwood, D. (1984), 'Managing the Defence Programme', *Three Banks Review* 142, 26–36.

Groom, B. (1984), 'Why Pay Bargaining is Becoming a Local Matter', *Financial Times*, 3 February.

Gudgin, G., Brunskill, I., and Fothergill, S. (1979), 'New Manufacturing Firms in Regional Employment Growth', paper presented to conference on new firms in local and regional economies, Centre For Environmental Studies, October.

Hakim, C. (1979), 'Occupational Segregation', Research Paper no. 9, Department of Employment.

Hall, P. (1981) *The Inner City in Context*, Heinemann Educational, London.

—— (1985), 'The Geography of the Fifth Kondratieff', in P. Hall, and A. Markusen (eds), *Silicon Landscapes*, Allen and Unwin, London, pp. 1–19.

Hannah, L. (1976), *The Rise of the Corporate Economy*, Methuen, London.

Hartley, K. (1983), *NATO Arms Cooperation: A Study in Economics and Politics*, George Allen and Unwin, London.

HMSO (1985), *Statement on the Defence Estimates*, Cmnd 9430, HMSO, London.

Jenkins, R. (1984), 'Acceptability, Suitability, and the Search for the Habitated Worker: How Ethnic Minorities and Women Lose Out', *International Journal of Social Economics* 11, 64–76.

Jenner, M. (1984), 'Bristol Planning: The Role of Public Opinion', *University*, 8 March, University of Bristol.

Johnston, R. J. (1980), *City and Society*, Penguin, Harmondsworth.

Jones, Lang, and Wooton (Chartered Surveyors) (1983), 'The Decentralisation of Offices from Central London', Technical Paper.

Joshua, H., Wallace, T., and Booth, H. (1983), *To Ride the Storm: the 1980 Bristol 'Riot' and the State*, Heinemann, London.

Kaletsky, A. (1984), 'Think of the Wenches who Served Falstaff', *Financial Times*, 24 April.

Keeble, D. (1976), *Industrial Location and Planning in the United Kingdom*, Methuen, London.

Knight, G. (1976), *Concorde: The Inside Story*, Weidenfeld and Nicolson, London.

Knight, Frank & Rutley (1983), *Office Developments in the Western Corridor*, London.

Langridge, R. (1983), 'Defining High Technology Industry', Working Paper no. 5, Department of Economics, University of Reading.

Law, C. M. (1983), 'The Defence Sector in British Regional Development', *Geoforum* 14, 169–84.

Lawless, P. (1981), *Britain's Inner Cities: Problems and Policies*, Harper and Row, New York.

Lawrence, S. (1984), 'The Strike Barricade: It's just not Bristol', *Bristol Evening Post*, 15 August.

Levitt, M. S. (1985), 'The Economics of Defence Spending', Discussion Paper no. 92, National Institute of Economic and Social Research, London.

Lloyd, J. (1984), 'The Emergence of two new Working "Nations" ', *Financial Times*, 23 January.

Lloyd, P. E. and Dicken, P. (1983), 'The Components of Change in Metropolitan Areas: Events in their Corporate Context', in J. Goddard, and A. Champion, (eds), *The Urban and Regional Transformation of Britain*, Methuen, London, pp. 51–70.

Lovering, J. (1985), 'Regional Intervention, Defence Industries, and the Structuring of Space in Britain: The Case of Bristol and South Wales', *Environment and Planning D: Society and Space* 3, 85–107.

—— (1986), 'Defence Expenditure and the Regions—the Case of Bristol', *Built Environment*, forthcoming.

Malecki, E. J. (1984), 'Military Spending and the US Defense Industry: Regional Patterns of Military Contracts and Subcontracts', *Environment and Planning* C, 2, 31–44.

Manners, G. (1966), 'Bristol, South Wales and the Bridge', *New Society* 10, 6 June, 7–10.

—— (1972), 'The South West and South Wales', in G. Manners, D. Keeble, and K. Warren, (eds), *Regional Development in Britain*, John Wiley, Chichester, pp. 231–66.

Manwaring, T. (1984), 'The Extended Internal Labour Market', *Cambridge Journal of Economics* 8, 161–87.

Markusen, A. (1983), 'High-tech Jobs, Markets, and Economic Development Prospects: Evidence from California', *Built Environment* 9, 18–28; reprinted in P. Hall, and A. Markusen, (eds), *Silicon Landscapes*, Allen and Unwin, London, pp. 35–48.

—— (1984a), 'Defense Spending: A Successful Industrial Policy', Working Paper no. 424, University of California, Institute of Urban and Regional Development, Berkeley.

—— (1984b), 'Defense Spending and the Geography of High Tech Industries', Working Paper no. 423, University of California, Institute of Urban and Regional Development, Berkeley.

Marquand, J. (1979), 'The Service Sector and Regional Policy in the United Kingdom', *Research Series* no. 29, Centre For Environmental Studies, London.

—— (1983), 'The Changing Distribution of Service Employment', in J. Goddard, and A. Champion, (eds), *The Urban and Regional Transformation of Britain*, Methuen, London, pp. 99–134.

Martin, J. and Roberts, C. (1984), 'Women's Employment in the 1980s, Department of Employment Gazette, May, 199–204.

Martin, R. L. (1982), 'Job Loss and the Regional Incidence of Redundancies in the Current Recession', *Cambridge Journal of Economics* 6.4, 375–96.

Massey, D. (1984), *Spatial Divisions of Labour: Social Structures and the Geography of Production*, Macmillan, London.

—— and Meegan, R. A. (1982), *The Anatomy of Job Loss: The How, Why, and Where of Employment Decline*, Methuen, London.

—— and Miles, N. (1983), 'Sex, Grouse, and Happy Workers', *New Society*, 22 April, 12–13.

Ministry of Transport (1966), *Reasons for the Minister's Decision Not to Authorise the Construction of a New Dock at Portbury, Bristol*, HMSO, London.

Nichols, T. and Beynon, H. (1979), *Living with Capitalism: Class Relations and the Modern Factory*, Routledge and Kegan Paul, London.

Noyelle, T. J. (1983), The Rise of Advanced Services', *Journal of the American Planning Association*, 49.4, 280–90.

Oakey, R. (1985), 'High Technology Industry and Agglomeration Economies', in P. Hall and A. Markusen, (eds), *Silicon Landscapes*, Allen and Unwin, London, pp. 94–117.

Phelps, E. S. (1972), *Inflation Policy and Unemployment Theory*, Academic Press, New York.

Pollard, S. (1983), *The Development of the British Economy 1914–1980*, Edward Arnold, London.

Pollert, A. (1981), *Girls, Wives, Factory Lives*, Macmillan, London.

Port of Bristol Authority (PBA) (1966), 'Portbury', speech by Alderman Arthur Parrish, Chairman of the PBA.

Rajan, A. (1984), *New Technology and Employment in Insurance, Banking, and Building Societies*, Gower Press, Farnborough, Hants.

Redfern, P. (1982), 'Profile of our Cities', *Population Trends*, Winter, HMSO, London, pp. 21–32.

Robertson, J., Briggs, J., and Goodchild, A. (1982), 'Structure and Employment Prospects of the Service Industries', Research Paper no. 30, Department of Employment.

Rogers, P. and Brummer, A. (1984), 'Lawson Plots Changes in Jobs Strategy', *Guardian*, 26 September.

Rolls Royce (1983), *Annual Report 1982*, Rolls Royce Ltd., London.

Saunders, P. (1980), *Urban Politics: A Sociological Interpretation*, Penguin, Harmondsworth.

Saxenian, A. (1980), 'Silicon Chips and Spatial Structure: The Industrial Basis of Urbanisation in Santa Clara County, California', University of California, Masters Thesis, Berkeley.

—— (1983), 'The Genesis of Silicon Valley', *Built Environment* 9, 7–17; reprinted in P. Hall, and A. Markusen, (eds), *Silicon Landscapes*, Allen and Unwin, London, pp. 20–34.

Shannon, H. A. and Grebenik, B. (1944), 'The Population of Bristol', Occasional Paper no. 2, National Institute of Economic and Social Research, Cambridge.

Short, J. (1981) 'Defence Spending in the UK Regions', *Regional Studies* 15, 101–10.

Sloan, P. J. (1985), 'Discrimination in the Labour Market', in D. Carline, C. A. Passarides, W. S. Siebert, and P. J. Sloan (eds), *Labour Economics*, Longman, London, pp. 78–158.

Soete, L. and Dosi, G. (1983), *Technology and Employment in the Electronics Industry*, Francis Pinter, London.

Spence, N. A. and Frost, M. E. (1983), 'Urban Employment Change', in J. B. Goddard, and A. G. Champion, *The Urban and Regional Transformation of Britain*, Methuen, London.

Stanback, T. M. (1979), *Understanding the Service Economy*, Johns Hopkins University Press, Baltimore and London.

—— and Noyelle, T. J. (1982), *Cities in Transition*, Allenheld and Osmun, Totowa, New Jersey.

Taylor, M. and Thrift, N. (1983), 'Business Organisation, Segmentation, and Location', *Regional Studies* 17, 445–65.

Todd, D. and Simpson, J. (1985), 'Aerospace, the State and the Regions: A Canadian Perspective', *Political Geography Quarterly* 4, 111–30.

Tout, H. (1938), *The Standard of Living in Bristol: A Preliminary Report of the Work of the University of Bristol Social Survey*, Arrowsmith, Bristol.

Townsend, A. R. (1982), 'Recession and the Regions in Great Britain, 1976–1980: Analysis of Redundancy Data', *Environment and Planning* A, 14, 1389–1404.

Townsend, A. R. and Peck, M. (1985), 'The Geography of Manufacturing Redundancy' in M. Pacione (ed) *Progress in Human Geography*.

Urry, J. (1981), 'Localities, Regions and Social Class', *International Journal of Urban and Regional Research* 5(4), 455–74.

Walker, F. (1972) *The Bristol Region*, Thomas Nelson, Sunbury-on-Thames.

Warren, K. (1980), 'The South West Region', in G. Manners, D. Keeble, and K. Warren, (eds) *Regional Development in Britain*, John Wiley, Chichester.

Watts, H. (1981), *The Branch Plant Economy: A Study of External Control*, Longman, London.

Westaway, J. (1974), 'The Spatial Hierarchy of Business Organisations and its Implications for the British Urban System'. *Regional Studies*, 8, 145–55.

Wright, E. O. (1978), *Class Crisis and the State*, New Left Books, London.

INDEX